Level 1

Microsoft®

Excel®

365

2019 Edition

Nita Rutkosky | Audrey Roggenkamp | Ian Rutkosky
Pierce College Puyallup
Puyallup, Washington

Pierce College Puyallup
Puyallup, Washington

PARADIGM
EDUCATION SOLUTIONS

St. Paul

Vice President, Content and Digital Solutions: Christine Hurney
Director of Content Development, Computer Technology: Cheryl Drivdahl
Developmental Editor: Jennifer Joline Anderson
Director of Production: Timothy W. Larson
Production Editor/Project Manager: Jen Weaverling
Senior Design and Production Specialist: Jack Ross
Cover and Interior Design: Valerie King
Copy Editor: Communicáto, Ltd
Testers: Janet Blum, Traci Post
Indexer: Terry Casey
Vice President, Director of Digital Products: Chuck Bratton
Digital Projects Manager: Tom Modl
Digital Solutions Manager: Gerry Yumul
Senior Director of Digital Products and Onboarding: Christopher Johnson
Supervisor of Digital Products and Onboarding: Ryan Isdahl
Vice President, Marketing: Lara Weber McLellan
Marketing and Communications Manager: Selena Hicks

Cover Photo Credit: © lowball-jack/GettyImages
Interior Photo Credits: Follow the Index.

ISBN 978-0-76388-724-7 (print)
ISBN 978-0-76388-709-4 (digital)

© 2020 by Paradigm Publishing, LLC
875 Montreal Way
St. Paul, MN 55102
Email: CustomerService@ParadigmEducation.com
Website: ParadigmEducation.com

Brief Contents

Contents

Achieving Proficiency in Excel

The Benchmark Series, *Microsoft® Excel® 365*, 2019 Edition, is designed for students who want to learn how to use Microsoft's powerful spreadsheet program to manipulate numerical data in resolving financial and other problems requiring data management and analysis. No prior knowledge of spreadsheets is required. After successfully completing a course using this courseware, students will be able to do the following:

- Create and edit spreadsheets and worksheets of varying complexity.
- Format cells, columns, and rows as well as entire workbooks in a uniform, attractive style.
- Analyze numerical data and project outcomes to make informed decisions.
- Plan, research, create, revise, and publish worksheets and workbooks to meet specific needs.
- Given a workplace scenario requiring a numbers-based solution, assess the information requirements and then prepare the materials that achieve the goal efficiently and effectively.

Well-designed pedagogy is important, but students learn technology skills through practice and problem solving. Technology provides opportunities for interactive learning as well as excellent ways to quickly and accurately assess student performance. To this end, this course is supported with Cirrus, Paradigm's cloud-based training and assessment learning management system. Details about Cirrus as well as its integrated student courseware and instructor resources can be found on page xii.

Proven Instructional Design

The Benchmark Series has long served as a standard of excellence in software instruction. Elements of the series function individually and collectively to create an inviting, comprehensive learning environment that leads to full proficiency in computer applications. The following visual tour highlights the structure and features that comprise the highly popular Benchmark model.

Microsoft®

Excel Level 1

Unit 1
Preparing and Formatting Worksheets

Chapter 1   Preparing an Excel Workbook

Chapter 2   Inserting Formulas in a Worksheet

Chapter 3   Formatting a Worksheet

Chapter 4   Enhancing a Worksheet

Unit Openers display the unit's four chapter titles. Each level of the course contains two units with four chapters each.

Chapter Openers Present Learning Objectives

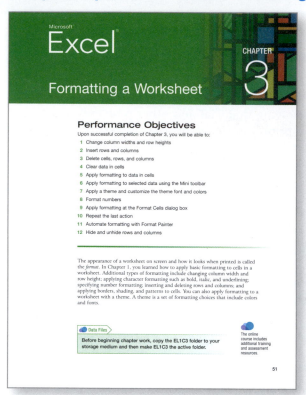

Chapter Openers present the performance objectives and an overview of the skills taught.

Data Files are provided for each chapter. A prominent note reminds students to copy the appropriate chapter data folder and make it active.

Activities Build Skill Mastery within Realistic Context

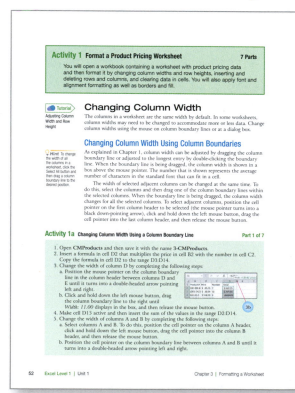

Multipart Activities provide a framework for instruction and practice on software features. An activity overview identifies tasks to accomplish and key features to use in completing the work.

Typically, a file remains open throughout all parts of the activity. Students save their work incrementally. At the end of the activity, students save, print, and then close the file.

Tutorials provide interactive, guided training and measured practice.

Hints offer useful tips on how to use features efficiently and effectively.

Step-by-Step Instructions guide students to the desired outcome for each activity part. Screen captures illustrate what the screen should look like at key points.

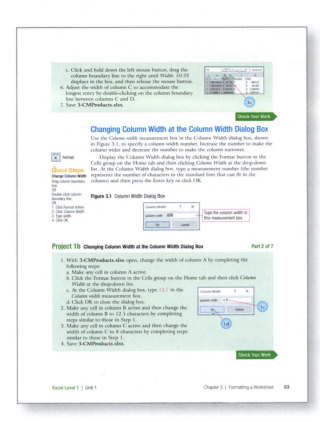

Between activity parts, the text presents instruction on the features and skills necessary to accomplish the next section of the activity.

Quick Steps in the margins allow fast reference and review of the steps needed to accomplish tasks.

Magenta Text identifies material to type.

Check Your Work model answer images are available in the online course, and students can use those images to confirm they have completed the activity correctly.

Chapter Review Tools Reinforce Learning

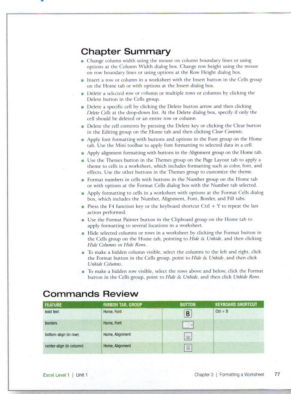

A **Chapter Summary** reviews the purpose and execution of key features.

A **Commands Review** summarizes visually the major features and alternative methods of access.

The Cirrus Solution

Elevating student success and instructor efficiency

Powered by Paradigm, Cirrus is the next-generation learning solution for developing skills in Microsoft Office. Cirrus seamlessly delivers complete course content in a cloud-based learning environment that puts students on the fast track to success. Students can access their content from any device anywhere, through a live internet connection; plus, Cirrus is platform independent, ensuring that students get the same learning experience whether they are using PCs, Macs, or Chromebook computers.

Cirrus provides Benchmark Series content in a series of scheduled assignments that report to a grade book to track student progress and achievement. Assignments are grouped in modules, providing many options for customizing instruction.

Dynamic Training

The online Benchmark Series courses include interactive resources to support learning.

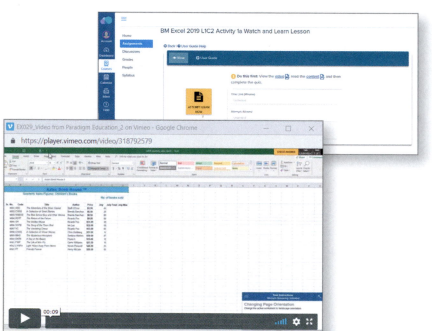

Watch and Learn Lessons include a video demonstrating how to perform the chapter activity, a reading to provide background and context, and a short quiz to check understanding of concepts and skills.

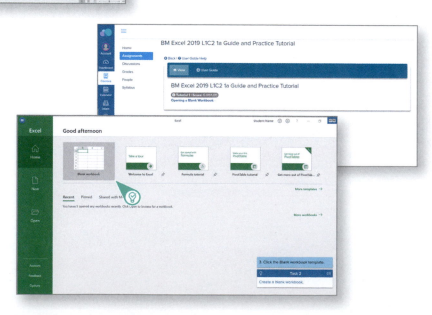

Guide and Practice Tutorials provide interactive, guided training and measured practice.

Hands On Activities enable students to complete chapter activities, compare their solutions against a Check Your Work model answer image, and submit their work for instructor review.

Chapter Review and Assessment

Review and assessment activities for each chapter are available for completion in Cirrus.

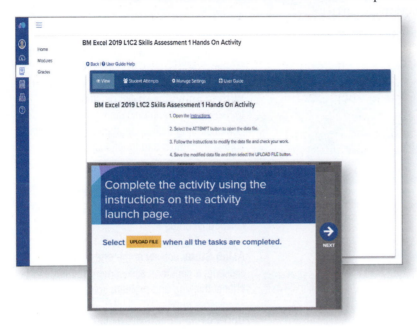

Concepts Check completion exercises assess comprehension and recall of application features and functions as well as key terminology.

Skills Assessment Hands On Activity exercises evaluate the ability to apply chapter skills and concepts in solving realistic problems. Each is completed live in Excel and is uploaded through Cirrus for instructor evaluation.

Visual Benchmark assessments test problem-solving skills and mastery of application features.

A **Case Study** requires analyzing a workplace scenario and then planning and executing a multipart project. Students search the web and/or use the program's Help feature to locate additional information required to complete the Case Study.

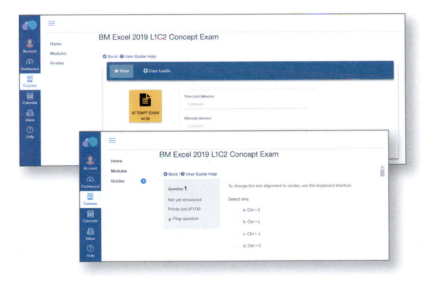

Exercises and **Projects** provide opportunities to develop and demonstrate skills learned in each chapter. Each is completed live in the Office application and is automatically scored by Cirrus. Detailed feedback and how-to videos help students evaluate and improve their performance.

Skills Check Exams evaluate students' ability to complete specific tasks. Skills Check Exams are completed live in the Office application and are scored automatically. Detailed feedback and instructor-controlled how-to videos help student evaluate and improve their performance.

Multiple-choice **Concepts Exams** assess understanding of key commands and concepts presented in each chapter.

Unit Review and Assessment

Review and assessment activities for each unit of each Benchmark course are also available for completion in Cirrus.

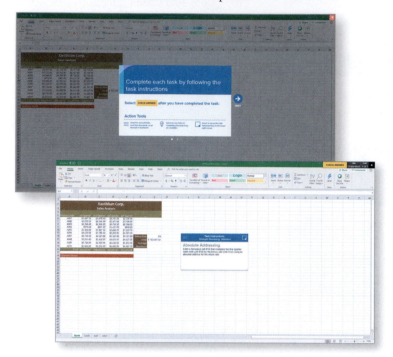

Assessing Proficiency exercises check mastery of software application functions and features.

Writing Activities challenge students to use written communication skills while demonstrating their understanding of important software features and functions.

Internet Research assignments reinforce the importance of research and information processing skills along with proficiency in the Office environment.

A **Job Study** activity at the end of Unit 2 presents a capstone assessment requiring critical thinking and problem solving.

Unit-Level Projects allow students to practice skills learned in the unit. Each is completed live in the Office application and automatically scored by Cirrus. Detailed feedback and how-to videos help students evaluate and improve their performance.

Student eBook

The Student eBook, accessed through the Cirrus online course, can be downloaded to any device (desktop, laptop, tablet, or smartphone) to make Benchmark Series content available anywhere students wish to study.

Instructor eResources

Cirrus tracks students' step-by-step interactions as they move through each activity, giving instructors visibility into their progress and missteps. With Exam Watch, instructors can observe students in a virtual, live, skills-based exam and join remotely as needed—a helpful option for struggling students who need one-to-one coaching, or for distance learners. In addition to these Cirrus-specific tools, the Instructor eResources for the Benchmark Series include the following support:

- Planning resources, such as lesson plans, teaching hints, and sample course syllabi
- Delivery resources, such as discussion questions and online images and templates
- Assessment resources, including live and annotated PDF model answers for chapter work and review and assessment activities, rubrics for evaluating student work, and chapter-based exam banks in RTF format

About the Authors

Nita Rutkosky began her career teaching business education at Pierce College in Puyallup, Washington, in 1978 and holds a master's degree in occupational education. In her years as an instructor, she taught many courses in software applications to students in postsecondary information technology certificate and degree programs. Since 1987, Nita has been a leading author of courseware for computer applications training and instruction. Her current titles include Paradigm's popular Benchmark Series, Marquee Series, and Signature Series. She is a contributor to the Cirrus online content for Office application courses and has also written textbooks for keyboarding, desktop publishing, computing in the medical office, and essential skills for digital literacy.

Audrey Roggenkamp holds a master's degree in adult education and curriculum and has been an adjunct instructor in the Business Information Technology department at Pierce College in Puyallup, Washington, since 2005. Audrey has also been a content provider for Paradigm Education Solutions since 2005. In addition to contributing to the Cirrus online content for Office application courses, Audrey co-authors Paradigm's Benchmark Series, Marquee Series, and Signature Series. Her other available titles include *Keyboarding & Applications I* and *II* and *Using Computers in the Medical Office: Word, PowerPoint, and Excel.*

Ian Rutkosky has a master's degree in business administration and has been an adjunct instructor in the Business Information Technology department at Pierce College in Puyallup, Washington, since 2010. In addition to joining the author team for the Benchmark Series and Marquee Series, he has co-authored titles on medical office computing and digital literacy and has served as a co-author and consultant for Paradigm's Cirrus training and assessment software.

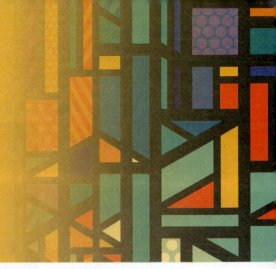

Microsoft® Office

Getting Started in Office 365

Microsoft Office is a suite of applications for personal computers and other devices. These programs, known as *software*, include Word, a word processor; Excel, a spreadsheet editor; Access, a database management system; and PowerPoint, a presentation program used to design and present slideshows. Microsoft Office 365 is a subscription service that delivers continually updated versions of those applications. Specific features and functionality of Microsoft Office vary depending on the user's account, computer setup, and other factors. The Benchmark courseware was developed using features available in Office 365. You may find that with your computer and version of Office, the appearance of the software and the steps needed to complete an activity vary slightly from what is presented in the courseware.

Identifying Computer Hardware

The Microsoft Office suite can run on several types of computer equipment, referred to as *hardware*. You will need access to a laptop or a desktop computer system that includes a PC/tower, monitor, keyboard, printer, drives, and mouse. If you are not sure what equipment you will be operating, check with your instructor. The computer system shown in Figure G.1 consists of six components. Each component is discussed separately in the material that follows.

Figure G.1 Computer System

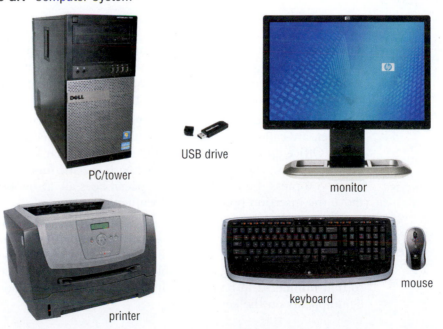

USB drive

PC/tower

monitor

printer

keyboard

mouse

Figure G.2 System Unit Ports

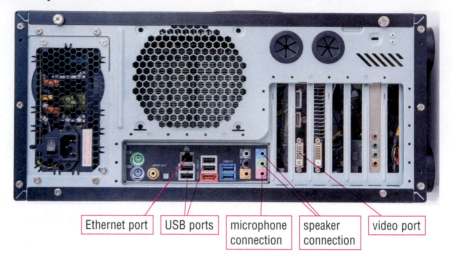

Ethernet port | USB ports | microphone connection | speaker connection | video port

System Unit (PC/Tower)

Traditional desktop computing systems include a system unit known as the *PC (personal computer)* or *tower*. This is the brain of the computer, where all processing occurs. It contains a Central Processing Unit (CPU), hard drives, and video cards plugged into a motherboard. Input and output ports are used for attaching peripheral equipment such as a keyboard, monitor, printer, and so on, as shown in Figure G.2. When a user provides input, the PC computes it and outputs the results.

Monitor

Hint Monitor size is measured diagonally and is generally the distance from the bottom left corner to the top right corner of the monitor.

A computer monitor looks like a television screen. It displays the visual information output by the computer. Monitor size can vary, and the quality of display for monitors varies depending on the type of monitor and the level of resolution.

Keyboard

The keyboard is used to input information into the computer. The number and location of the keys on a keyboard can vary. In addition to letters, numbers, and symbols, most computer keyboards contain function keys, arrow keys, and a numeric keypad. Figure G.3 shows a typical keyboard.

The 12 keys at the top of the keyboard, labeled with the letter *F* followed by a number, are called *function keys*. Use these keys to perform functions within each of the Office applications. To the right of the regular keys is a group of special or dedicated keys. These keys are labeled with specific functions that will be performed when you press the key. Below the special keys are arrow keys. Use these keys to move the insertion point in the document screen.

Some keyboards include mode indicator lights to indicate that a particular mode, such as Caps Lock or Num Lock, has been turned on. Pressing the Caps Lock key disables the lowercase alphabet so that text is typed in all caps, while pressing the Num Lock key disables the special functions on the numeric keypad so that numbers can be typed using the keypad. When you select these modes, a light appears on the keyboard.

Figure G.3 Keyboard

Drives and Ports

An internal hard drive is a disk drive that is located inside the PC and that stores data. External hard drives may be connected via USB ports for additional storage. Ports are the "plugs" on the PC, and are used to connect devices to the computer, such as the keyboard and mouse, the monitor, speakers, USB flash drives and so on. Most PCs will have a few USB ports, at least one display port, audio ports, and possibly an ethernet port (used to physically connect to the internet or a network).

Printer

An electronic version of a file is known as a *soft copy*. If you want to create a hard copy of a file, you need to print it. To print documents, you will need to access a printer, which will probably be either a laser printer or an ink-jet printer. A laser printer uses a laser beam combined with heat and pressure to print documents, while an ink-jet printer prints a document by spraying a fine mist of ink on the page.

Mouse

Most functions and commands in the Microsoft Office suite are designed to be performed using a mouse or a similar pointing device. A mouse is an input device that sits on a flat surface next to the computer. You can operate a mouse with your left or right hand. Moving the mouse on the flat surface causes a corresponding pointer to move on the screen, and clicking the left or right mouse buttons allows you to select various objects and commands.

Using the Mouse The applications in the Microsoft Office suite can be operated with the keyboard and a mouse. The mouse generally has two buttons on top, which you press to execute specific functions and commands. A mouse may also contain a wheel, which can be used to scroll in a window or as a third button. To use the mouse, rest it on a flat surface or a mouse pad. Put your hand over it with your palm resting on top of the mouse and your index finger resting on the left mouse button. As you move your hand, and thus the mouse, a corresponding pointer moves on the screen.

When using the mouse, you should understand four terms — *point, click, double-click,* and *drag*. To *point* means to position the mouse pointer on a desired item, such as an option, button, or icon. With the mouse pointer positioned on the item, *click* the left mouse button once to select the item. (In some cases you may *right-click*, which means to click the right mouse button, but generally, *click* refers to the left button.) To complete two steps at one time, such as choosing and then executing a function, *double-click* the left mouse button by tapping it twice in quick succession. The term *drag* means to click and hold down the left mouse button, move the mouse pointer to a specific location, and then release the button. Clicking and dragging is used, for instance, when moving a file from one location to another.

💡 **Hint** Instructions in this course use the verb *click* to refer to tapping the left mouse button and the verb *press* to refer to pressing a key on the keyboard.

Using the Mouse Pointer The mouse pointer will look different depending on where you have positioned it and what function you are performing. The following are some of the ways the mouse pointer can appear when you are working in the Office suite:

- The mouse pointer appears as an I-beam (called the *I-beam pointer*) when you are inserting text in a file. The I-beam pointer can be used to move the insertion point or to select text.

- The mouse pointer appears as an arrow pointing up and to the left (called the *arrow pointer*) when it is moved to the Title bar, Quick Access Toolbar, ribbon, or an option in a dialog box, among other locations.

- The mouse pointer becomes a double-headed arrow (either pointing left and right, pointing up and down, or pointing diagonally) when you perform certain functions such as changing the size of an object.

- In certain situations, such as when you move an object or image, the mouse pointer displays with a four-headed arrow attached. The four-headed arrow means that you can move the object left, right, up, or down.

- When a request is being processed or when an application is being loaded, the mouse pointer may appear as a moving circle. The moving circle means "please wait." When the process is completed, the circle is replaced with a normal mouse pointer.

- When the mouse pointer displays as a hand with a pointing index finger, it indicates that more information is available about an item. The mouse pointer also displays as a hand with a pointing index finger when you hover over a hyperlink.

Touchpad

If you are working on a laptop computer, you may be using a touchpad instead of a mouse. A *touchpad* allows you to move the mouse pointer by moving your finger across a surface at the base of the keyboard (as shown in Figure G.4). You click and right-click by using your thumb to press the buttons located at the bottom of the touchpad. Some touchpads have special features such as scrolling or clicking something by tapping the surface of the touchpad instead of pressing a button with a thumb.

Figure G.4 Touchpad

Touchscreen

Smartphones, tablets, and touch monitors all use touchscreen technology (as shown in Figure G.5), which allows users to directly interact with the objects on the screen by touching them with fingers, thumbs, or a stylus. Multiple fingers or both thumbs can be used on most touchscreens, giving users the ability to zoom, rotate, and manipulate items on the screen. While many activities in this textbook can be completed using a device with a touchscreen, a mouse or touchpad might be required to complete a few activities.

Figure G.5 Touchscreen

Choosing Commands

A *command* is an instruction that tells an application to complete a certain task. When an application such as Word or PowerPoint is open, the *ribbon* at the top of the window displays buttons and options for commands. To select a command with the mouse, point to it and then click the left mouse button.

Notice that the ribbon is organized into tabs, including File, Home, Insert, and so on. When the File tab is clicked, a *backstage area* opens with options such as opening or saving a file. Clicking any of the other tabs will display a variety of commands and options on the ribbon. Above the ribbon, buttons on the Quick Access Toolbar provide fast access to frequently used commands such as saving a file and undoing or redoing an action.

Using Keyboard Shortcuts and Accelerator Keys

As an alternative to using the mouse, keyboard shortcuts can be used for many commands. Shortcuts generally require two or more keys. For instance, in Word, press and hold down the Ctrl key while pressing P to display the Print backstage area, or press Ctrl + O to display the Open backstage area. A complete list of keyboard shortcuts can be found by searching the Help files in any Office application.

Office also provides shortcuts known as *accelerator keys* for every command or action on the ribbon. These accelerator keys are especially helpful for users with motor or visual disabilities or for power users who find it faster to use the keyboard than click with the mouse. To identify accelerator keys, press the Alt key on the keyboard. KeyTips display on the ribbon, as shown in Figure G.6. Press the keys indicated to execute the desired command. For example, to begin checking

Figure G.6 Word Home Tab KeyTips

the spelling and grammar in a document, press the Alt key, press the R key on the keyboard to display the Review tab, and then press the letter C and the number 1 on the keyboard to open the Editor task pane.

Choosing Commands from a Drop-Down List

Some buttons include arrows that can be clicked to display a drop-down list of options. Point and click with the mouse to choose an option from the list. Some options in a drop-down list may have a letter that is underlined. This indicates that typing the letter will select the option. For instance, to select the option *Insert Table*, type the letter I on the keyboard.

If an option in a drop-down list is not available to be selected, it will appear gray or dimmed. If an option is preceded by a check mark, it is currently active. If it is followed by an ellipsis (…), clicking the option will open a dialog box.

Choosing Options from a Dialog Box or Task Pane

Some buttons and options open a *dialog box* or a task pane containing options for applying formatting or otherwise modifying the data in a file. For example, the Font dialog box shown in Figure G.7 contains options for modifying the font and adding effects. The dialog box contains two tabs—the Font tab and the Advanced tab. The tab that displays in the front is the active tab. Click a tab to make it active or press Ctrl + Tab on the keyboard. Alternately, press the Alt key and then type the letter that is underlined in the tab name.

Figure G.7 Word Font Dialog Box

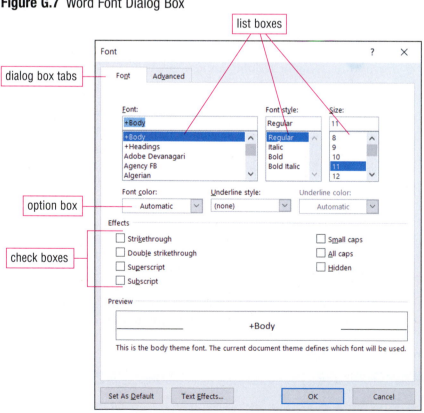

To choose an option from a dialog box using the mouse, position the arrow pointer on the option and then click the left mouse button. To move forward from option to option using the keyboard, you can press the Tab key. Press Shift + Tab to move back to a previous option. If the option displays with an underlined letter, you can choose it by pressing the Alt key and the underlined letter. When an option is selected, it is highlighted in blue or surrounded by a dotted or dashed box called a *marquee*. A dialog box contains one or more of the following elements: list boxes, option boxes, check boxes, text boxes, command buttons, radio buttons, and measurement boxes.

List Boxes and Option Boxes The fonts available in the Font dialog box, shown in Figure G.7 (on the previous page), are contained in a *list box*. Click an option in the list to select it. If the list is long, click the up or down arrows in the *scroll bar* at the right side of the box to scroll through all the options. Alternately, press the up or down arrow keys on the keyboard to move through the list, and press the Enter key when the desired option is selected.

Option boxes contain a drop-down list or gallery of options that opens when the arrow in the box is clicked. An example is the *Font color* option box in Figure G.8. To display the different color options, click the arrow at the right side of the box. If you are using the keyboard, press Alt + C.

Check Boxes Some options can be selected using a check box, such as the effect options in the dialog box in Figure G.7. If a check mark appears in the box, the option is active (turned on). If the check box does not contain a check mark, the option is inactive (turned off). Click a check box to make the option active or inactive. If you are using the keyboard, press Alt + the underlined letter of the option.

Text Boxes Some options in a dialog box require you to enter text. For example, see the Find and Replace dialog box shown in Figure G.8. In a text box, type or edit text with the keyboard, using the left and right arrow keys to move the insertion point without deleting text and use the Delete key or Backspace key to delete text.

Command Buttons The buttons at the bottom of the dialog box shown in Figure G.8 are called *command buttons*. Use a command button to execute or cancel a command. Some command buttons display with an ellipsis (...), which means another dialog box will open if you click that button. To choose a command button, click with the mouse or press the Tab key until the command button is surrounded by a marquee and then press the Enter key.

Figure G.8 Excel Find and Replace Dialog Box

Figure G.9 Word Insert Table Dialog Box

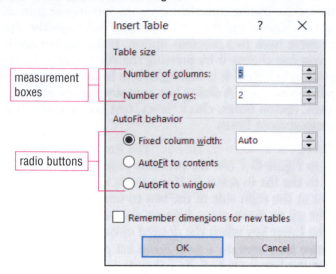

Radio Buttons The Insert Table dialog box shown in Figure G.9 contains an example of *radio buttons*. Only one radio button can be selected at any time. When the button is selected, it is filled with a dark circle. Click a button to select it, or press and hold down the Alt key, press the underlined letter of the option, and then release the Alt key.

Measurement Boxes A *measurement box* contains an amount that can be increased or decreased. An example is shown in Figure G.9. To increase or decrease the number in a measurement box, click the up or down arrow at the right side of the box. Using the keyboard, press and hold down the Alt key and then press the underlined letter for the option, press the Up Arrow key to increase the number or the Down Arrow key to decrease the number, and then release the Alt key.

Choosing Commands with Shortcut Menus

The Office applications include shortcut menus that contain commands related to different items. To display a shortcut menu, point to the item for which you want to view more options with the mouse pointer and then click the right mouse button, or press Shift + F10. The shortcut menu will appear wherever the insertion point is positioned. In some cases, the Mini toolbar will also appear with the shortcut menu. For example, if the insertion point is positioned in a paragraph of text in a Word document, clicking the right mouse button or pressing Shift + F10 will display the shortcut menu and Mini toolbar, as shown in Figure G.10.

To select an option from a shortcut menu with the mouse, click the option. If you are using the keyboard, press the Up or Down Arrow key until the option is selected and then press the Enter key. To close a shortcut menu without choosing an option, click outside the menu or press the Esc key.

Figure G.10 Shortcut Menu and Mini Toolbar

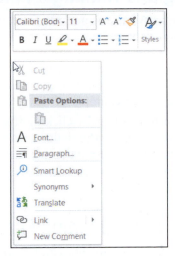

Working with Multiple Applications

As you learn the various applications in the Microsoft Office suite, you will notice many similarities between them. For example, the steps to save, close, and print are virtually the same whether you are working in Word, Excel, or PowerPoint. This consistency greatly enhances your ability to transfer knowledge learned in one application to another within the suite. Another benefit to using Microsoft Office is the ability to have more than one application open at the same time and to integrate content from one program with another. For example, you can open Word and create a document, open Excel and create a worksheet, and then copy a worksheet from the workbook into Word.

The Windows taskbar at the bottom of the screen displays buttons representing all the programs that are currently open. For example, Figure G.11 shows the taskbar with Word, Excel, Access, and PowerPoint open. To move from one program to another, click the taskbar button representing the desired application.

Maintaining Files and Folders

Windows includes a program named File Explorer that can be used to maintain files and folders. To open File Explorer, click the folder icon on the Windows taskbar. Use File Explorer to complete tasks such as copying, moving, renaming, and deleting files and folders and creating new folders. Some file management tasks can also be completed within Word, Excel, PowerPoint, or Access by clicking File and then *Open* or *Save As* and then clicking the *Browse* option to browse folders and files in a dialog box.

Directions and activities in this course assume that you are managing files and folders stored on a USB flash drive or on your computer's hard drive. If you are using your OneDrive account or another cloud-based storage service, some of the file and folder management tasks may vary.

Figure G.11 Windows Taskbar with Word, Excel, Access, and PowerPoint Open

Creating and Naming a Folder

Files (such as Word documents, Excel workbooks, PowerPoint presentations, and Access databases) are easier to find again when they are grouped logically in folders. In File Explorer and in the Open or Save As dialog box, the names of files and folders are displayed in the Content pane. Each file has an icon showing what type of file it is, while folders are identified with the icon of a folder. See Figure G.12 for an example of the File Explorer window.

Create a new folder by clicking the New folder button at the top of the File Explorer window or in the dialog box. A new folder displays with the name *New folder* highlighted. Type a name for the folder to replace the highlighted text, and then press the Enter key. Folder names can include numbers, spaces, and some symbols.

Selecting and Opening Files and Folders

Select files or folders in the window to be managed. To select one file or folder, simply click on it. To select several adjacent files or folders, click the first file or folder, hold down the Shift key, and then click the last file or folder. To select files or folders that are not adjacent, click the first file or folder, hold down the Ctrl key, click any other files or folders, and then release the Ctrl key. To deselect, click anywhere in the window or dialog box.

When a file or folder is selected, the path to the folder displays in the Address bar. If the folder is located on an external storage device, the drive letter and name may display in the path. A right-pointing arrow displays to the right of each folder name in the Address bar. Click the arrow to view a list of subfolders within a folder.

Double-click a file or folder in the Content pane to open it. You can also select one or more files or folders, right-click, and then click the *Open* option in the shortcut menu.

Figure G.12 File Explorer Window

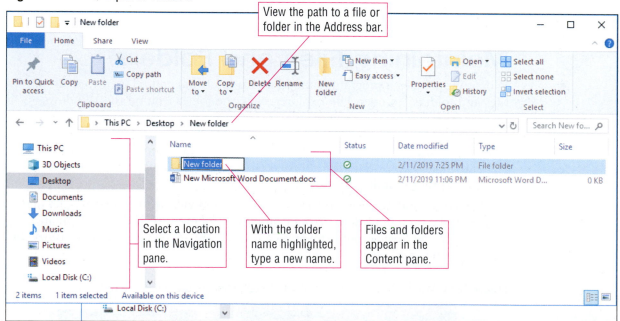

Deleting Files and Folders

Deleting files and folders is part of file maintenance. To delete a file or folder, select it and then press the Delete key. Alternatively, use the Delete button on the Home tab of the File Explorer window, or click the Organize button and then *Delete* in the dialog box. You can also right-click a file or folder and then choose the *Delete* option in the shortcut menu.

Files and folders deleted from the hard drive of the computer are automatically sent to the Recycle Bin, where they can easily be restored if necessary. If a file or folder is stored in another location, such as an external drive or online location, it may be permanently deleted. In this case, a message may appear asking for confirmation. To confirm that the file or folder should be deleted, click Yes.

To view the contents of the Recycle Bin, display the Windows desktop and then double-click the *Recycle Bin* icon. Deleted items in the Recycle Bin can be restored to their original locations, or the Recycle Bin can be emptied to free up space on the hard drive.

Moving and Copying Files and Folders

A file or folder may need to be moved or copied to another location. In File Explorer, select the file or folder and then click the Copy button at the top of the window, use the keyboard shortcut Ctrl + C, or right-click the file and select *Copy* in the shortcut menu. Navigate to the destination folder and then click the Paste button, use the keyboard shortcut Ctrl + P, or right-click and select *Paste*. If a copy is pasted to the same folder as the original, it will appear with the word *Copy* added to its name. To copy files in the Open or Save As dialog box, use the Organize button drop-down list or right-click to access the shortcut menu.

To move a file or folder, follow the same steps, but select *Cut* instead of *Copy* or press Ctrl + X instead of Ctrl + C. Files can also be dragged from one location to another. To do this, open two File Explorer windows. Click a file or folder and drag it to the other window while holding down the left mouse button.

Renaming Files and Folders

To rename a file or folder in File Explorer, click its name to highlight it and then type a new name, or right-click the file or folder and then select *Rename* at the shortcut menu. You can also select the file or folder and then click the Rename button on the Home tab of the File Explorer window or click *Rename* from the Organize button drop-down list at the Open or Save As dialog box. Type in a new name and then press the Enter key.

Viewing Files and Folders

Change how files and folders display in the Content pane in File Explorer by clicking the View tab and then clicking one of the view options in the Layout group. View files and folders as large, medium, or small icons; as tiles; in a list; or with details or information about the file or folder content. At the Open or Save As dialog box, click the Change your view button arrow and a list displays with similar options for viewing folders and files. Click to select an option in the list or click the Change your view button to see different views.

Displaying File Extensions Each file has a file extension that identifies the program and what type of file it is. Excel files have the extension *.xlsx;* Word files end with *.docx,* and so on. By default, file extensions are turned off. To view file extensions, open File Explorer, click the View tab, and then click the *File name extensions* check box to insert a check mark. Click the check box again to remove the check mark and stop viewing file extensions.

Displaying All Files The Open or Save As dialog box in an Office application may display only files specific to that application. For example, the Open or Save As dialog box in Word may only display Word documents. Viewing all files at the Open dialog box can be helpful in determining what files are available. Turn on the display of all files at the Open dialog box by clicking the file type button arrow at the right side of the *File Name* text box and then clicking *All Files* at the drop-down list.

Managing Files at the Info Backstage Area

The Info backstage area in Word, Excel, and PowerPoint provide buttons for managing files such as uploading and sharing a file, copying a path, and opening File Explorer with the current folder active. To use the buttons at the Info backstage area, open Word, Excel, or PowerPoint and then open a file. Click the File tab and then click the *Info* option. If a file is opened from the computer's hard drive or an external drive, four buttons display near the top of the Info backstage area as shown in Figure G.13.

Click the Upload button to upload the open file to a shared location such as a OneDrive account. Click the Share button and a window displays indicating that the file must be saved to OneDrive before it can be shared and provides an option that, when clicked, will save the file to OneDrive. Click the Copy Path button and a copy of the path for the current file is saved in a temporary location. This path can be pasted into another file, an email, or any other location where you want to keep track of the file's path. Click the Open file location button and File Explorer opens with the current folder active.

Figure G.13 Info Backstage Buttons

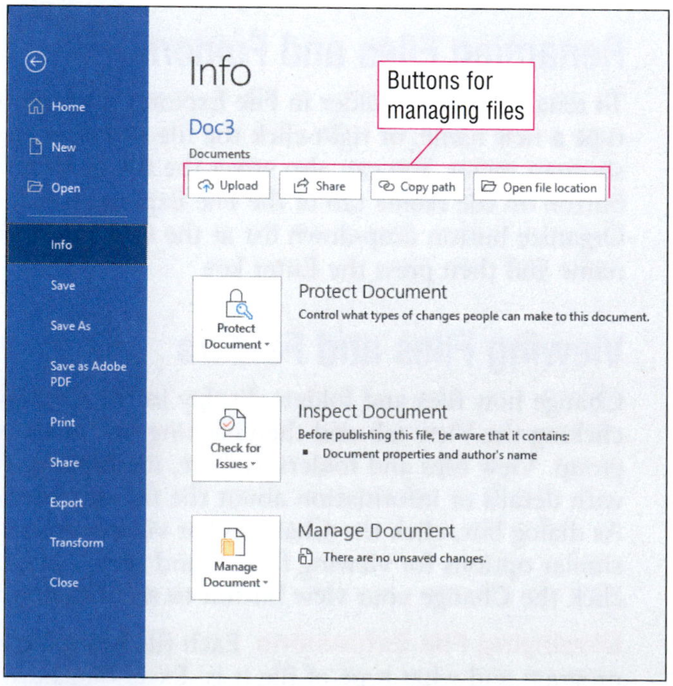

If you open Word, Excel, or PowerPoint and then open a file from OneDrive, only two buttons display—Share and Open file location. Click the Share button to display a window with options for sharing the file with others and specifying whether the file can be viewed and edited, or only viewed. Click the Open file location button to open File Explorer with the current folder active.

Customizing Settings

Before beginning computer activities in this textbook, you may need to customize your monitor's settings and change the DPI display setting. Activities in the course assume that the monitor display is set at 1920 × 1080 pixels and the DPI set at 125%. If you are unable to make changes to the monitor's resolution or the DPI settings, the activities can still be completed successfully. Some references in the text might not perfectly match what you see on your screen, so you may not be able to perform certain steps exactly as written. For example, an item in a drop-down gallery might appear in a different column or row than what is indicated in the step instructions.

Before you begin learning the applications in the Microsoft Office suite, take a moment to check the display settings on the computer you are using. Your monitor's display settings are important because the ribbon in the Microsoft Office suite adjusts to the screen resolution setting of your computer monitor. A computer monitor set at a high resolution will have the ability to show more buttons in the ribbon than will a monitor set to a low resolution. The illustrations in this textbook were created with a screen resolution display set at 1920 × 1080 pixels, as shown in Figure G.14.

Figure G.14 Word Ribbon Set at 1920 x 1080 Screen Resolution

Activity 1 Adjusting Monitor Display

Note: The resolution settings may be locked on lab computers. Also, some laptop screens and small monitors may not be able to display in a 1920 × 1080 resolution or change the DPI setting.

1. At the Windows desktop, right-click in a blank area of the screen.
2. In the shortcut menu, click the *Display settings* option.

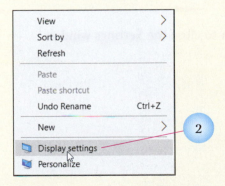

3. At the Settings window with the *Display* option selected, scroll down and look at the current setting displayed in the *Resolution* option box. If your screen is already set to 1920 × 1080, skip ahead to Step 6.

4. Click the Resolution option box and then click the *1920 × 1080* option. **Note: *Depending on the privileges you are given on a school machine, you may not be able to complete Steps 4–5. If necessary, check with your instructor for alternative instructions.***

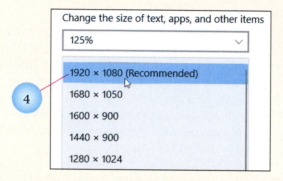

5. Click the Keep Changes button.
6. At the Settings window, take note of the current DPI percentage next to the text *Change the size of text, apps, and other items*. If the percentage is already set to 125%, skip to Step 8.
7. Click the option box below the text *Change the size of text, apps, and other items,* and then click the *125%* option in the drop-down list

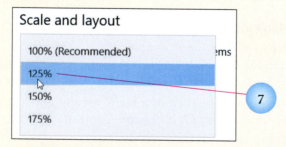

8. Click the Close button to close the Settings window.

Retrieving and Copying Data Files

While working through the activities in this course, you will often be using data files as starting points. These files are provided through your Cirrus online course, and your instructor may post them in another location such as your school's network drive. You can download all the files at once (described in the activity below), or download only the files needed for a specific chapter.

Activity 2   Downloading Files to a USB Flash Drive

Note: In this activity, you will download data files from your Cirrus online course. Make sure you have an active internet connection before starting this activity. Check with your instructor if you do not have access to your Cirrus online course.

1. Insert your USB flash drive into an available USB port.
2. Navigate to the Course Resources section of your Cirrus online course. *Note: The steps in this activity assume you are using the Chrome browser. If you are using a different browser, the following steps may vary.*
3. Click the Student Data Files link in the Course Resources section. A zip file containing the student data files will automatically begin downloading from the Cirrus website.
4. Click the button in the lower left corner of the screen once the files have finished downloading.

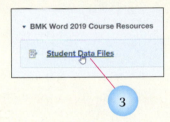

5. Right-click the *StudentDataFiles* folder in the Content pane.
6. Click the *Copy* option in the shortcut menu.
7. Click the USB flash drive that displays in the Navigation pane at the left side of the File Explorer window.
8. Click the Home tab in the File Explorer window.
9. Click the Paste button in the Clipboard group.

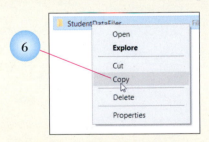

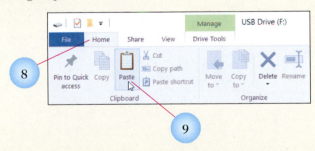

10. Close the File Explorer window by clicking the Close button in the upper right corner of the window.

Microsoft® Excel® Level 1

Unit 1

Preparing and Formatting Worksheets

1

Excel

Preparing an Excel Workbook

Performance Objectives

Upon successful completion of Chapter 1, you will be able to:

1. Identify the various elements of an Excel workbook
2. Create a worksheet
3. Enter data in a worksheet
4. Save a workbook
5. Edit data in a cell
6. Print a worksheet
7. Close a workbook and close Excel
8. Use the AutoComplete, AutoCorrect, and AutoFill features
9. Open a workbook
10. Pin and unpin a workbook and folder to and from the *Recent* option list
11. Insert a formula using the AutoSum button
12. Copy a formula using the fill handle
13. Select cells and data within cells
14. Apply basic formatting to cells in a workbook
15. Use the Tell Me feature
16. Use the Help feature

Microsoft Excel is a spreadsheet program that allows users to organize, analyze, and evaluate numerical and financial data. An Excel spreadsheet can be used for such activities as creating financial statements, preparing budgets, managing inventory, and analyzing cash flow. This chapter will introduce the basics of creating a worksheet, opening workbooks, and saving workbooks. In a worksheet, learn to enter data, as well as the use of formulas to calculate sums and averages. Learn to enter data quickly and efficiently using features such as the fill handle and to apply basic formatting to data in conventional accounting style.

 Data Files

Before beginning the chapter work, copy the EL1C1 folder to your storage medium and then make EL1C1 the active folder.

The online course includes additional training and assessment resources.

Tutorial

Opening a Blank Workbook

Creating a Worksheet

Open Excel by clicking the *Excel* tile at the Windows Start menu, or by following other steps as needed depending on the operating system. At the Excel opening screen, click the *Blank workbook* template. This displays a workbook with a blank worksheet, as shown in Figure 1.1. The elements of a blank Excel worksheet are described in Table 1.1.

A file created in Excel is referred to as a *workbook*. An Excel workbook consists of an individual worksheet (or *sheet*) by default but it can contain multiple worksheets, like the sheets of paper in a notebook. Notice the tab named *Sheet1*, at the bottom of the Excel window. The area containing the gridlines in the Excel window is called the *worksheet area*. Figure 1.2 identifies the elements of the worksheet area. Create a worksheet in the worksheet area that will be saved as part of a workbook. Columns in a worksheet are labeled with letters of the alphabet and rows are labeled with numbers. The intersection of a column and a row creates a box, which is referred to as a *cell*. A cell is where data and formulas are entered.

Figure 1.1 Blank Excel Worksheet

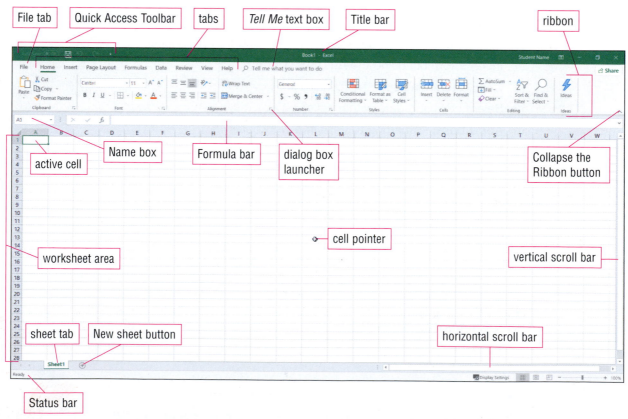

Table 1.1 Elements of an Excel Worksheet

Feature	Description
active cell	the currently selected cell, surrounded by a thick green border
cell pointer	when this icon appears, select cells by clicking or dragging the mouse
Collapse the Ribbon button	when clicked, removes the ribbon from the screen (Redisplay the ribbon by double-clicking a tab, except the File tab.)
dialog box launcher	click to open a dialog box with more options for that group
File tab	displays the backstage area that contains options for working with and managing files
Formula bar	displays the contents stored in the active cell
horizontal and vertical scroll bars	used to scroll left and right or up and down to view various parts of the worksheet
Name box	displays the active cell address or name assigned to the active cell
New sheet button	click to insert a new worksheet in the workbook
Quick Access Toolbar	contains buttons for commonly used commands that can be executed with a single mouse click
ribbon	contains the tabs with commands and buttons
sheet tab	identifies the current worksheet in the workbook
Status bar	displays the current mode, action messages, view buttons, and Zoom slider bar
tab	contains commands and buttons organized into groups
Tell Me text box	provides information and guidance on how to perform an action
Title bar	displays the workbook name followed by the application name
worksheet area	contains the cells used to create a worksheet

Figure 1.2 Elements of the Worksheet Area

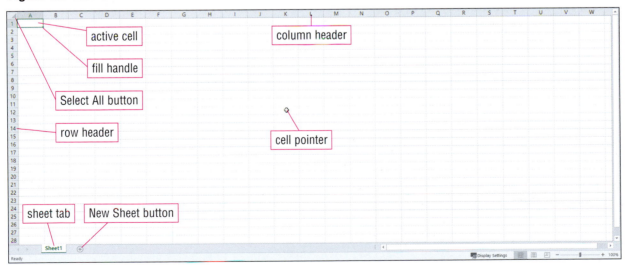

The horizontal and vertical lines that define the cells in the worksheet area are called *gridlines*. When a cell is clicked, it becomes active and a thick green border appears around it. The cell address, also called the *cell reference*, appears in the Name box. The cell reference includes the column letter and row number. For example, if the first cell of the worksheet is active, the cell reference *A1* is shown in the Name box. Any number of adjacent cells can be made active and form a range. A range is typically identified by the first cell reference and last cell reference separated by a colon. For example, the range A1:C1 contains the cells A1, B1, and C1.

Entering Data in a Worksheet

Entering Data

Navigating and Scrolling

Find & Select

💡**Hint** To make a cell active, position the cell pointer in the cell and then click the left mouse button.

💡**Hint** Ctrl + G is the keyboard shortcut to display the Go To dialog box.

Enter data such as text, a number, or a value in a cell. To enter data in a cell, make the cell active and then type the data. To make the next cell active, press the Tab key. Table 1.2 shows additional commands for making a specific cell active.

Another method for making a cell active is to use the Go To feature. To use this feature, click the Find & Select button in the Editing group on the Home tab and then click *Go To*. At the Go To dialog box, type the cell reference in the *Reference* text box and then click OK.

Before typing data into the active cell, check the Status bar. The word *Ready* should display at the left. As data is typed in a cell, the word *Ready* changes to *Enter*. Data typed in a cell is shown in the cell and in the Formula bar. If the data entered in a cell is longer than the cell can accommodate, the data overlaps the next cell to the right. (It does not become a part of the next cell—it simply overlaps it. How to change column widths to accommodate data is explained later in this chapter.)

Table 1.2 Commands for Making a Specific Cell Active

To make this cell active	Press
cell below current cell	Enter
cell above current cell	Shift + Enter
next cell	Tab
previous cell	Shift + Tab
cell at beginning of row	Home
next cell in direction of arrow	Up, Down, Left, or Right Arrow key
last cell in worksheet	Ctrl + End
first cell in worksheet	Ctrl + Home
cell in next window	Page Down
cell in previous window	Page Up
cell in window to right	Alt + Page Down
cell in window to left	Alt + Page Up

If data entered in a cell consists of text and the text does not fit in the cell, it overlaps the next cell to the right. If, however, a number is entered in a cell and the number is too long to fit in the cell, Excel changes the display of the number to number symbols *(###)*. This change is made because Excel does not want to mislead users by showing only part of a number in a cell.

Along with the keyboard, the mouse can be used to make a specific cell active. To make a specific cell active with the mouse, position the mouse pointer, which appears as a white plus symbol (⊕) (called the *cell pointer*), in the cell and then click the left mouse button. The pointer appears as a white plus sign when positioned in a cell in the worksheet and as an arrow when positioned on other elements of the Excel window, such as options and buttons on tabs and scroll bars.

Scroll through a worksheet using the horizontal and/or vertical scroll bars. Scrolling shifts the display of cells in the worksheet area but does not change the active cell. Scroll through a worksheet until the desired cell is visible and then click in the cell to make it active.

Saving a Workbook

Saving with the
Same Name

Saving with a New
Name

 Save

Quick Steps

Save Workbook
1. Click Save button on Quick Access Toolbar.
2. At Save As backstage area, click *Browse* option.
3. At Save As dialog box, navigate to folder.
4. Type workbook name.
5. Press Enter key.

💡 **Hint** Ctrl + S is the keyboard shortcut to save a workbook.

Save an Excel workbook, including all sheets within it, by clicking the Save button on the Quick Access Toolbar or by clicking the File tab and then clicking the *Save As* option at the backstage area. At the Save As backstage area, click the *Browse* option and the Save As dialog box displays. At the Save As dialog box, click the desired location in the Navigation pane, type a name for the workbook in the *File name* text box, and then press the Enter key or click the Save button. Bypass the Save As backstage area and go directly to the Save As dialog box by using the keyboard shortcut F12.

To save an Excel workbook in the EL1C1 folder, display the Save As dialog box, navigate to the correct drive in the Navigation pane, and then double-click *EL1C1* in the Content pane.

A workbook file name can contain up to 255 characters, including the drive letter and any folder names, and it can include spaces. Each file should have a distinct name. Excel will not allow two workbooks to be saved with the same file name in the same folder, even if one is in uppercase and one is lowercase. (For example, one file cannot be named *EXPENSES* and another *expenses*.) Also, some symbols cannot be used in a file name, such as the following:

forward slash (/)	question mark (?)
backslash (\)	quotation mark (")
greater-than symbol (>)	colon (:)
less-than symbol (<)	asterisk (*)
pipe symbol (|)	

If changes are made to a workbook, save the file again before closing it. It is a good practice to save periodically while working with a file to be sure no changes are lost if the application crashes or freezes or if power is interrupted.

Note: If an Excel workbook is stored in a cloud location such as Microsoft OneDrive, OneDrive for Business, or SharePoint Online, any changes to it will be saved automatically with the AutoSave feature. Multiple users can edit a file and AutoSave will save the workbook every few seconds so that changes can be seen by everyone. AutoSave can be turned on or off by clicking the toggle switch in the upper left corner of the Excel screen.

Activity 1a Creating and Saving a Workbook

Part 1 of 3

1. Open Excel by clicking the *Excel* tile at the Windows Start menu. (Depending on your operating system, the steps to open Excel may vary.)
2. At the Excel opening screen, click the *Blank workbook* template. (This opens a workbook with a blank worksheet.)
3. At the blank Excel worksheet, create the worksheet shown in Figure 1.3 by completing the following steps:
   a. Press the Enter key to make cell A2 the active cell.
   b. Type Employee in cell A2.
   c. Press the Tab key. (This makes cell B2 active.)
   d. Type Location and then press the Tab key. (This makes cell C2 active.)
   e. Type Benefits and then press the Enter key to move the insertion point to cell A3.
   f. Type Avery in cell A3.
   g. Continue typing the data shown in Figure 1.3. (For commands that make specific cells active, refer to Table 1.2.)
4. After typing the data shown in the cells in Figure 1.3, save the workbook by completing the following steps:
   a. Click the Save button on the Quick Access Toolbar.
   b. At the Save As backstage area, click the *Browse* option.
   c. At the Save As dialog box, navigate to your EL1C1 folder in the Navigation pane and then double-click the *EL1C1* folder in the Content pane.
   d. Select the text in the *File name* text box and then type 1-EmpBene.
   e. Press the Enter key or click the Save button.

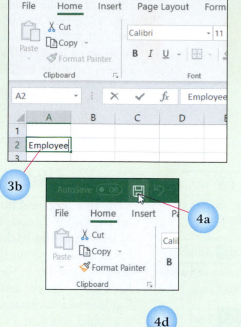

Check Your Work

Figure 1.3 Activity 1a

	A	B	C	D
1				
2	Employee	Location	Benefits	
3	Avery			
4	Connors			
5	Estrada			
6	Juergens			
7	Mikulich			
8	Talbot			
9				

8   Excel Level 1 | Unit 1   Chapter 1 | Preparing an Excel Workbook

Tutorial

Editing Data

Editing Data in a Cell

Edit data being typed in a cell by pressing the Backspace key to delete the character to the left of the insertion point or pressing the Delete key to delete the character to the right of the insertion point. To change the data in a cell, click in the cell to make it active and then type the new data. When a cell containing data is active, anything typed will take the place of the existing data.

If only a portion of the data in a cell needs to be edited, double-click in the cell. This makes the cell active, moves the insertion point inside the cell, and displays the word *Edit* at the left side of the Status bar. Move the insertion point using the arrow keys or the mouse and then make the needed corrections. Press the Home key to move the insertion point to the first character in the cell or Formula bar or press the End key to move the insertion point to the last character.

When the editing of data in a cell is complete, be sure to change out of the Edit mode. To do this, make another cell active by pressing the Enter key, the Tab key, or Shift + Tab. Two other ways to change out of the Edit mode and return to the Ready mode are to click in another cell and to click the Enter button on the Formula bar.

 Cancel

 Enter

If the active cell does not contain data, the Name box displays only the cell reference (by column letter and row number). As data is typed, two buttons become active on the Formula bar to the right of the Name box, as shown in Figure 1.4. Click the Cancel button to delete the current cell entry. (A cell entry can also be deleted by pressing the Delete key.) Click the Enter button when finished typing or editing the cell entry. Click the Enter button on the Formula bar and the word *Enter* (or *Edit*) at the left of the Status bar changes to *Ready*.

Figure 1.4 Buttons on the Formula Bar

Activity 1b Editing Data in a Cell

Part 2 of 3

1. With **1-EmpBene** open, double-click in cell A7 (contains *Mikulich*).
2. Move the insertion point immediately left of the *k* and then type c. (This changes the spelling to *Mickulich*.)
3. Click in cell A4 (contains *Connors*), type Bryant, and then press the Tab key. (Clicking only once allows you to type over the existing data.)
4. Edit cell C2 by completing the following steps:
   a. Click the Find & Select button in the Editing group on the Home tab and then click *Go To* at the drop-down list.

b. At the Go To dialog box, type c2 in the *Reference* text box and then click OK.

c. Type Classification (over *Benefits*).

5. Click in any other cell.

6. Click the Save button on the Quick Access Toolbar to save the workbook again.

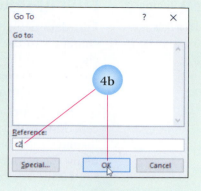

Check Your Work

Tutorial

Printing a Worksheet

💡 **Hint** Ctrl + P is the keyboard shortcut to display the Print backstage area.

Printing a Worksheet

With a workbook open, click the File tab and the Home backstage area displays, as shown in Figure 1.5. Use buttons and options at the backstage area to perform actions such as opening, closing, saving, and printing a workbook. Click the Back button (in the upper left corner of the backstage area) to exit the backstage area without completing an action or press the Esc key on the keyboard.

Print a worksheet from the Print backstage area, as shown in Figure 1.6. To display this backstage area, click the File tab and then click the *Print* option. The Print backstage area can also be displayed with the keyboard shortcut Ctrl + P.

Figure 1.5 Home Backstage Area

Figure 1.6 Print Backstage Area

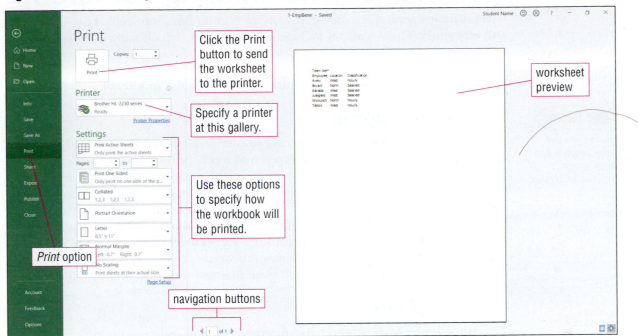

Quick Steps

Print Worksheet
1. Click File tab.
2. Click *Print* option.
3. Click Print button.

Click the Print button in the Print backstage area to send the worksheet to the printer and use the *Copies* measurement box to specify the number of copies to be printed. Below the Print button are two categories: *Printer* and *Settings*. Use the gallery in the *Printer* category to specify the printer. The *Settings* category contains a number of galleries, each with options for specifying how the workbook will be printed. Use the galleries to specify whether the pages are collated when printed; what page orientation, page size, and margins the workbook should have; and whether the worksheet will be scaled to print all rows and columns of data on one page.

Another method for printing is to click the Quick Print button on the Quick Access Toolbar to send the workbook directly to the printer. To insert this button on the Quick Access Toolbar, click the arrow button at the right of the toolbar and then click *Quick Print* at the drop-down list. To remove the button, right-click it and then click *Remove from Quick Access Toolbar* at the drop-down list.

 Tutorial

Closing a Workbook and Closing Excel

Closing a Workbook and Closing Excel

To close an Excel workbook without closing Excel, click the File tab and then click the *Close* option. Using the keyboard shortcut Ctrl + F4 will also close a workbook. To close Excel, click the Close button in the upper right corner of the screen. The Close button contains an *X*, and if the mouse pointer is positioned on the button, the button background changes from green to red and a ScreenTip displays with the name *Close*. Pressing the keyboard shortcut Alt + F4 will also close Excel.

Quick Steps

Close Workbook
1. Click File tab.
2. Click *Close* option.
OR
Press Ctrl + F4.

Close Excel
Click Close button.
OR
Press Alt + F4.

 Close

Using Automatic Entering Features

Excel contains several features that help users enter data into cells more quickly and efficiently. These features include AutoComplete, which allows users to automatically complete multiple entries of the same data; AutoCorrect, which automatically corrects many common typographical errors; and AutoFill, which automatically inserts words, numbers, or formulas in a series.

Using
AutoComplete and
AutoCorrect

Using AutoComplete

The AutoComplete feature makes it easy to complete multiple entries of the same data. As the first few characters are typed into a cell, AutoComplete predicts what will be typed next based on previous entries in the worksheet, and will automatically complete the entry based on its prediction. If the AutoComplete entry is correct, accept it by pressing the Tab key or the Enter key. If it is incorrect, simply continue typing the correct data. This feature can be very useful in a worksheet that contains repetitive data entries. For example, consider a worksheet that repeats the word *Payroll*. The second and subsequent times this word is to be inserted in a cell, simply typing the letter *P* will cause AutoComplete to insert the entire word.

Using AutoCorrect

The AutoCorrect feature automatically corrects many common typing errors. To see what symbols and words are included in AutoCorrect, click the File tab and then click *Options*. At the Excel Options dialog box, click *Proofing* in the left panel and then click the AutoCorrect Options button in the right panel. This displays the AutoCorrect dialog box with the AutoCorrect tab selected, as shown in Figure 1.7, with a list box containing the replacement data.

At the AutoCorrect dialog box, type the text shown in the first column in the list box and then press the spacebar and the text in the second column is inserted in the cell. Along with symbols, the AutoCorrect dialog box contains commonly misspelled words and common typographical errors.

Figure 1.7 AutoCorrect Dialog Box with the AutoCorrect Tab Selected

Type the text shown in the first column of this list box in a worksheet and then press the spacebar and the text is replaced by the text in the second column of this list box.

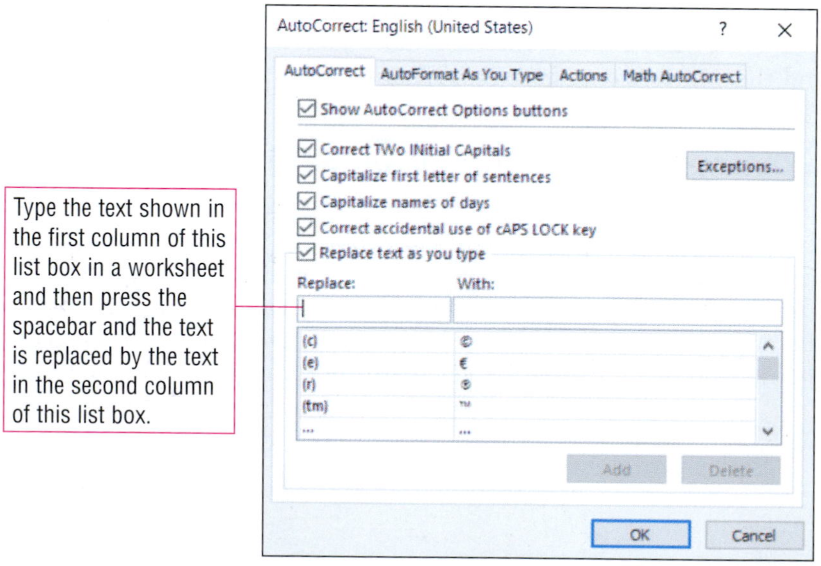

1. With **1-EmpBene** open, make cell A1 active.
2. Type text in cell A1 as shown in Figure 1.8. Insert the ® symbol by typing (r) and then pressing the Enter key. (AutoCorrect will change (r) to ®.)
3. Type the remaining text in the cells. When you type the *W* in *West* in cell B5, the AutoComplete feature will insert *West*. Accept this by pressing the Tab key. (Pressing the Tab key accepts *West* and also makes the cell to the right active.) Use the AutoComplete feature to enter *West* in cells B6 and B8 and *North* in cell B7. Use AutoComplete to enter the second and subsequent occurrences of *Salaried* and *Hourly*.
4. Click the Save button on the Quick Access Toolbar.
5. Print **1-EmpBene** by clicking the File tab, clicking the *Print* option, and then clicking the Print button at the Print backstage area. (The gridlines will not print.)

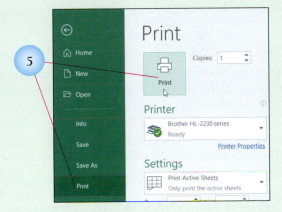

6. Close the workbook by clicking the File tab and then clicking the *Close* option at the backstage area.

 Check Your Work

Figure 1.8 Activity 1c

	A	B	C	D
1	Team Net®			
2	Employee	Location	Classification	
3	Avery	West	Hourly	
4	Bryant	North	Salaried	
5	Estrada	West	Salaried	
6	Juergens	West	Salaried	
7	Mickulich	North	Hourly	
8	Talbot	West	Hourly	
9				

Activity 2 Open and Format a Workbook and Insert Formulas   3 Parts

You will open an existing workbook and insert formulas to find the sums and averages of numbers.

Tutorial

Entering Data Using the Fill Handle

Using AutoFill

When a cell is active, a thick green border surrounds it and a small green square appears in the bottom right corner. This green square is called the AutoFill *fill handle* (see Figure 1.2 on page 5). Use the fill handle to fill a range of cells with the same data or with consecutive data. For example, suppose the year 2021 is to be inserted into a row or column of cells. To do this quickly, type *2021* in the first cell, position the mouse pointer on the fill handle, click and hold down the left mouse button, drag across or down into the cells in which the year is to be inserted, and then release the mouse button.

Hint When filling cells with the fill handle, press and hold down the Ctrl key if you want to copy the same data instead of displaying the next instance in the series.

The fill handle can also be used to insert a series in a row or column of cells. For example, suppose a worksheet is being created with data for all the months in the year. Type *January* in the first cell, position the mouse pointer on the fill handle, click and hold down the left mouse button, drag down or across into 11 more cells, and then release the mouse button. Excel automatically inserts the other 11 months of the year in the proper order. When using the fill handle, the cells must be adjacent. Table 1.3 identifies the sequences inserted in cells when specific types of data are entered.

Certain sequences—such as *2, 4* and *Jan 12, Jan 13*—require that both cells be selected before using the fill handle. If only the cell containing *2* is active, the fill handle will insert *2*s in the selected cells. The list in Table 1.3 is only a sampling of what the fill handle can do. A variety of other sequences can be inserted in a worksheet using the fill handle.

Auto Fill Options

An Auto Fill Options button appears when cells are filled with data using the fill handle. Click this button and a list of options displays for filling the cells. By default, data and formatting are filled in each cell. Use the Auto Fill Options button to choose to fill only the formatting in the cells or to fill only the data without the formatting. Other fill options include choosing to copy data into the selected cells or to fill the data as a series.

Table 1.3 AutoFill Fill Handle Series

Enter this data*	And the fill handle will insert this sequence in adjacent cells*
January	February, March, April, and so on
Jan	Feb, Mar, Apr, and so on
Jan 15, Jan 16	17-Jan, 18-Jan, 19-Jan, and so on
Monday	Tuesday, Wednesday, Thursday, and so on
Product 1	Product 2, Product 3, Product 4, and so on
Qtr 1	Qtr 2, Qtr 3, Qtr 4
2, 4	6, 8, 10, and so on

* Commas represent data in separate cells.

Tutorial

Opening a
Workbook

Opening a Workbook

Open an Excel workbook at the Open dialog box. To display this dialog box, click the File tab and then click the *Open* option. This displays the Open backstage area. Other methods of displaying the Open backstage area include using the keyboard shortcut Ctrl + O and inserting an Open button on the Quick Access Toolbar. At the Open backstage area, click the *Browse* option. At the Open dialog box, navigate to the desired folder and then double-click the workbook name in the Content pane. Bypass the Open backstage area and go directly to the Open dialog box by using the keyboard shortcut Ctrl + F12.

Tutorial

Opening from the
Recent Option List

Quick Steps

Open Workbook
1. Click File tab.
2. Click *Open* option.
3. Click *Browse* option.
4. Navigate to folder.
5. Double-click workbook name.

Pin Workbook to *Recent* Option List
1. Click File tab.
2. Click *Open* option.
3. Position mouse pointer over workbook name.
4. Click left-pointing push pin icon.

Unpin Workbook from *Recent* Option List
1. Click File tab.
2. Click *Open* option.
3. Position mouse pointer over workbook name.
4. Click down-pointing push pin icon.

Opening a Workbook from the *Recent* Option List

With the *Recent* option selected in the middle panel at the Open backstage area, a list displays with the most recently opened workbooks. Up to 50 workbook names appear in the list by default. Open a workbook from this list by clicking the workbook name.

Pinning and Unpinning Workbooks and Folders

If a workbook is opened on a regular basis, consider pinning it to the *Recent* option list so it can be found more easily. To pin a workbook, position the mouse pointer over the workbook name and then click the left-pointing push pin icon at the right of the workbook name. The left-pointing push pin icon changes to a down-pointing push pin icon and the pinned workbook appears in the *Pinned* category at the top of the *Recent* option list, where it can be easily found whenever the Open backstage area is displayed.

A workbook can also be pinned to the Recent list at the Excel opening screen and the Home backstage area. To unpin a workbook from the Recent or *Recent* option list, click the pin icon to change it from a down-pointing push pin icon to a left-pointing push pin icon. More than one workbook can be pinned to a list. Another method for pinning and unpinning documents is to use the shortcut menu. Right-click a workbook name and then click the option *Pin to list* or *Unpin from list*.

In addition to workbooks, folders can be pinned to a list at the Save As backstage area with the *Recent* option selected. The third panel in the Save As backstage area shows a list of the most recently opened folders and groups them into categories such as *Today*, *Yesterday*, and *Last Week*. Pin a folder or folders to the list to display them in the *Pinned* category at the top of the list.

Activity 2a Inserting Data in Cells with the Fill Handle

Part 1 of 3

1. Open **FillCells** by completing the following steps:
   a. Click the File tab and then click the *Open* option, if necessary.
   b. Click the *Browse* option.
   c. Navigate to the EL1C1 folder on your storage medium and then double-click *FillCells*.
2. Save the workbook with the name **1-FillCells** by completing the following steps:
   a. Press the F12 function key to display the Save As dialog box.
   b. Press the Home key on the keyboard to position the insertion point at the beginning of the name in the *File name* text box and then type 1-.
   c. Click the Save button.
3. Add data to cells as shown in Figure 1.9. Begin by making cell B1 active and then typing January.

4. Position the mouse pointer on the fill handle for cell B1, click and hold down the left mouse button, drag across into cell G1, and then release the mouse button.

5. Type a sequence and then use the fill handle to fill the remaining cells by completing the following steps:

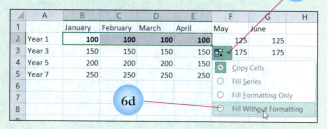

   a. Make cell A2 active and then type *Year 1*.
   b. Make cell A3 active and then type *Year 3*.
   c. Select cells A2 and A3 by clicking in cell A2 and holding down the left mouse button, dragging into cell A3, and then releasing the mouse button.
   d. Drag the fill handle for cell A3 into cell A5. (This inserts *Year 5* in cell A4 and *Year 7* in cell A5.)

6. Use the fill handle to fill adjacent cells with a number but not the formatting by completing the following steps:
   a. Make cell B2 active. (This cell contains *100* with bold formatting.)
   b. Drag the fill handle for cell B2 to the right into cell E2. (This inserts *100* in cells C2, D2, and E2.)
   c. Click the Auto Fill Options button at the bottom right of the selected cells.
   d. Click the *Fill Without Formatting* option at the drop-down list.

7. Use the fill handle to apply formatting only by completing the following steps:
   a. Make cell B2 active.
   b. Drag the fill handle into cell B5.
   c. Click the Auto Fill Options button and then click *Fill Formatting Only* at the drop-down list.

8. Make cell A10 active and then type *Qtr 1*.
9. Drag the fill handle for cell A10 into cell A13.
10. Save **1-FillCells**.

Check Your Work

Figure 1.9 Activity 2a

	A	B	C	D	E	F	G
1		January	February	March	April	May	June
2	Year 1	**100**	100	100	100	125	125
3	Year 3	**150**	150	150	150	175	175
4	Year 5	**200**	200	200	150	150	150
5	Year 7	**250**	250	250	250	250	250
6							
7							
8							
9							
10	Qtr1	$5,500	$6,250	$7,000	$8,500	$5,500	$4,500
11	Qtr2	$6,000	$7,250	$6,500	$9,000	$4,000	$5,000
12	Qtr3	$4,500	$8,000	$6,000	$7,500	$6,000	$5,000
13	Qtr4	$6,500	$8,500	$7,000	$8,000	$5,500	$6,000
14							

Entering Formulas

Quick Steps

Enter Formula Using AutoSum button
1. Click in cell.
2. Click AutoSum button.
3. Check range identified and make changes if necessary.
4. Press Enter key.

Formulas in Excel allow users to perform calculations on data and get a result in return. For example, the total cost of an item can be determined by inputting the individual costs of the item into a sum formula and the result will be the total of those costs. An active cell that contains a formula will display the results in the cell and the formula in the Formula bar. Formulas can be inserted using various methods, such as typing, using the mouse, and using buttons on the ribbon.

Formulas in Excel begin with an equals sign and may contain one or more of the following: mathematical operators (such as + or -), numerical values, references to a cell or range of cells, and/or a function (such as the SUM function, described below). For example, the formula $=A1+A2$ can be inserted in cell A3. When values are added to cells A1 and A2, their sum will automatically appear in cell A3. Formulas can be written that add, subtract, multiply, and/or divide values. Formulas can also be written that calculate averages, percentages, minimum and maximum values, and much more.

Tutorial

Entering Formulas Using the AutoSum Button

  AutoSum

💡 **Hint** You can use the keyboard shortcut Alt + = to insert the SUM function in a cell.

Using the AutoSum Button to Add Numbers

Use the AutoSum button in the Editing group on the Home tab to insert a formula for calculating the sum of numbers in a range of cells. Clicking the AutoSum button will create a formula that adds numbers automatically using the SUM function. Make active the cell in which the formula will be inserted (this cell should be empty) and then click the AutoSum button. Excel looks for a range of cells containing numbers above the active cell. If no cell above contains numbers, then Excel looks to the left of the active cell. Excel suggests the range of cells to be added. If the suggested range is not correct, drag through the range of cells with the mouse and then press the Enter key. Double-click the AutoSum button to automatically insert the SUM function with the range Excel chooses.

Activity 2b **Adding Values with the AutoSum Button**   **Part 2 of 3**

1. With **1-FillCells** open, make cell A6 active and then type Total.
2. Make cell B6 active and then calculate the sum of the cells by clicking the AutoSum button in the Editing group on the Home tab.
3. Excel inserts the formula $=SUM(B2:B5)$ in cell B6. This is the correct range of cells, so press the Enter key.

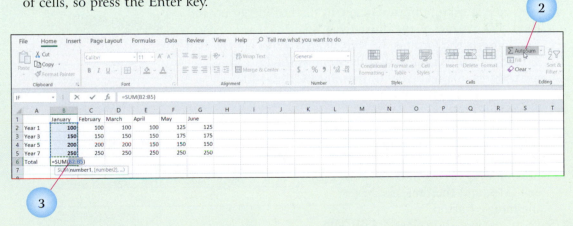

4. Make cell C6 active and then click the AutoSum button in the Editing group.

5. Excel inserts the formula *=SUM(C2:C5)* in cell C6. This is the correct range of cells, so press the Enter key.
6. Make cell D6 active.
7. Double-click the AutoSum button. This inserts the formula *=SUM(D2:D5)* in cell D6 and inserts the sums *700*.
8. Insert the sums in cells E6, F6, and G6.
9. Save **1-FillCells**.

 Check Your Work

Quick Steps

Insert Average Formula Using AutoSum Button
1. Click in cell.
2. Click AutoSum button arrow.
3. Click *Average*.
4. Specify range.
5. Press Enter key.

Using the AutoSum Button to Average Numbers

A common function in a formula is the AVERAGE function. With this function, a range of cells are added together and then the total is divided by the number of cell entries. The AVERAGE function is available on the AutoSum button. Click the AutoSum button arrow and a drop-down list displays with a number of common functions.

 Tutorial

Copying Formulas

Using the Fill Handle to Copy a Formula

Quick Steps

Copy Formula Using Fill Handle
1. Insert formula in cell.
2. Make active cell containing formula.
3. Drag fill handle across or down to fill cells.

The same basic formula can be inserted in other cells in a worksheet. When copying a formula to other locations in a worksheet, use a relative cell reference. Copy a formula containing relative cell references and the cell references change. For example, insert the formula *=SUM(A2:C2)* in cell D2 and then copy it relatively to cell D3 and the formula in cell D3 displays as *=SUM(A3:C3)*. Use the fill handle to copy a formula relatively in a worksheet. To do this, position the mouse pointer on the fill handle until the mouse pointer turns into a thin black cross, click and hold down the left mouse button, drag and select the cells, and then release the mouse button.

Activity 2c Inserting the AVERAGE Function and Copying a Formula Relatively   **Part 3 of 3**

1. With **1-FillCells** open, make cell A14 active and then type Average.
2. Insert the average of the range B10:B13 by completing the following steps:
   a. Make cell B14 active.
   b. Click the AutoSum button arrow in the Editing group and then click *Average* at the drop-down list.
   c. Excel inserts the formula *=AVERAGE(B10:B13)* in cell B14. This is the correct range of cells, so press the Enter key.
3. Copy the formula relatively to the range C14:G14 by completing the following steps:
   a. Make cell B14 active.
   b. Position the mouse pointer on the fill handle, click and hold down the left mouse button, drag across into cell G14, and then release the mouse button.
4. Save, print, and then close **1-FillCells**.

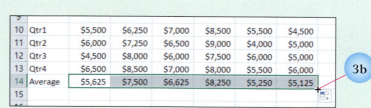

 Check Your Work

Activity 3 **Format a Monthly Expenses Worksheet** **2 Parts**

You will open a workbook containing a monthly expenses worksheet and then change the column width, merge and center cells, and apply number formatting to numbers in cells.

Tutorial

Selecting Cells

Selecting Cells

Cells in a worksheet can be formatted in a variety of ways. For example, change the alignment of data in cells or rows or add character formatting. To identify the cells that are to be affected by the formatting, select the specific cells.

Selecting Cells Using the Mouse

💡 **Hint** The first cell in a range has a white background and is the active cell.

Select specific cells, columns, or rows in a worksheet using the mouse. Table 1.4 displays the methods for selecting cells using the mouse.

Selected cells, except the active cell, display with a gray background (this may vary) rather than a white background. The active cell is the first cell in the selection block and displays in the normal manner (white background with black data). Selected cells remain selected until another cell is clicked with the mouse or an arrow key is pressed on the keyboard.

Selecting Cells Using the Keyboard

Keys on the keyboard can be used to select specific cells within a worksheet. Table 1.5 shows the commands for selecting specific cells. If a worksheet contains data, Ctrl + A selects all the cells containing data. If a worksheet contains groups of data separated by empty cells, Ctrl + A or Ctrl + Shift + spacebar selects a group of cells rather than all the cells.

Table 1.4 Selecting with the Mouse

To select this	Do this
column	Position the cell pointer on the column header (a letter) and then click the left mouse button.
row	Position the cell pointer on the row header (a number) and then click the left mouse button.
adjacent cells	Drag with the mouse into specific cells to select them.
nonadjacent cells	Press and hold down the Ctrl key while clicking the column header, row header, or specific cells.
all cells in worksheet	Click the Select All button. (Refer to Figure 1.2 on page 5.)

Table 1.5 Selecting Cells Using the Keyboard

To select	Press
cells in direction of arrow key	Shift + arrow key
from active cell to beginning of row	Shift + Home
from active cell to beginning of worksheet	Shift + Ctrl + Home
from active cell to last cell in worksheet containing data	Shift + Ctrl + End
entire column	Ctrl + spacebar
entire row	Shift + spacebar
cells containing data	Ctrl + A
groups of data separated by empty cells	Ctrl + Shift + spacebar

Selecting Data within Cells

Hint Select nonadjacent columns or rows by holding down the Ctrl key while selecting cells.

The selection commands presented in Table 1.4 and Table 1.5 select the entire cell. Specific characters within a cell can also be selected. To do this with the mouse, position the cell pointer in a cell and then double-click the left mouse button. Drag with the I-beam pointer through the data to be selected. Data selected within a cell appears with a gray background. To select data in a cell using the keyboard, press and hold down the Shift key and then press the arrow key that moves the insertion point in the desired direction. All the data the insertion point passes through will be selected. Press the F8 function key to turn on the Extend Selection mode, move the insertion point in the desired direction to select the data, and then press F8 to turn off the Extend Selection mode. When the Extend Selection mode is on, the words *Extend Selection* are shown at the left of the Status bar.

Applying Basic Formatting

Quick Steps

Change Column Width

Drag column boundary line.
OR
Double-click column boundary line.

Merge and Center Cells

1. Select cells.
2. Click Merge & Center button on Home tab.

Excel provides a wide range of formatting options that can be applied to cells in a worksheet. Some basic formatting options that are helpful when creating a worksheet include changing the column width, merging and centering cells, and formatting numbers.

Changing Column Width

If data in a cell overlaps into the next column, increase the width of the column to accommodate the data. To do this, position the mouse pointer on the gray boundary line between columns in the column header (Figure 1.2 on page 5 identifies the column header) until the pointer turns into a double-headed arrow pointing left and right and then drag the boundary to the new location. If the column contains data, double-click the column boundary line at the right to automatically adjust the width of the column to accommodate the longest entry.

A more precise way to change the width of a column is to display the Column Width dialog box, type in the desired width and then press the OK button. Open the Column Width dialog box by clicking the Format button in the Cells group and then click the *Column Width* option in the drop-down list. Alternatively, right-click the column header and then click *Column width* at the shortcut menu.

Tutorial

Merging and
Centering Cells

 Merge &
Center

Merging and Centering Cells

In some cases, as with a title or subtitle, it may look better to merge two or more cells and then center the text within the cells instead of allowing the text to overlap into the next column. To merge cells, first check to make sure that the cells to be merged do not contain any other data. (If other cells contain data, only the data in the first cell will be placed in the newly merged cell.) Select cells to be merged and then click the Merge & Center button in the Alignment group on the Home tab.

Activity 3a Changing Column Width and Merging and Centering Cells   Part 1 of 2

1. Open **MoExps** and then save it with the name **1-MoExps**.
2. Change column widths by completing the following steps:
   a. Position the mouse pointer in the column header on the boundary line between columns A and B until the pointer turns into a double-headed arrow pointing left and right.

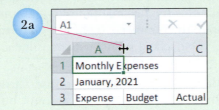

   b. Double-click the left mouse button.
   c. Position the mouse pointer in the column header on the boundary line between columns E and F and then double-click the left mouse button.
   d. Click in any cell in column F, click the Format button in the Cells group on the Home tab and then click the *Column Width* option at the drop down list.
   e. At the Column Width dialog box, type 10.25, and then click OK.
3. Merge and center cells by completing the following steps:
   a. Select the range A1:C1.
   b. Click the Merge & Center button in the Alignment group on the Home tab.

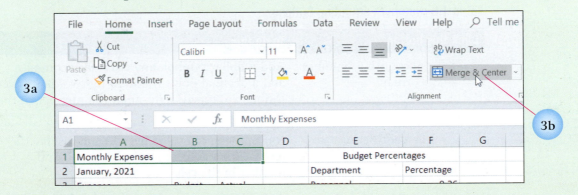

   c. Select the range A2:C2.
   d. Click the Merge & Center button.
   e. Select cells E1 and F1 and then click the Merge & Center button.
4. Save **1-MoExps**.

 Check Your Work

Tutorial

Applying Number Formatting

Formatting Numbers

Numbers in cells can be formatted to include a decimal point (45.00), comma separators (1,000,000), or symbols such as a dollar sign ($) or percentage symbol (%). As numbers are typed, Excel will recognize the formatting. For example, if *$45.50* is typed in a cell, Excel automatically applies the Currency format to the cell. If *45%* is entered in a cell, Excel automatically applies the Percentage format. Currency format, Percentage format, and other formats recognized by Excel are shown in the *Number Format* option box in the Number group on the Home tab.

Number formatting can also be applied to cells in a worksheet before or after the data is typed. To do this, select the cell or cells and then click an option in the *Number Format* option box, or click one of the buttons in the Number group on the Home tab (described in Table 1.6). For example, if the number 4500 is typed and the Accounting number formatting is applied to it, it will be formatted as $4,500.00. If the number .45 is typed and the Percentage format is applied, it will be displayed as 45%.

Use the Increase Decimal and Decrease Decimal buttons to control how many digits are displayed after the decimal point, without changing the actual value in the cell. For example, the number *1.0245* can be formatted so none or all of the digits display after the decimal point, but the value shown in the Formula bar remains the same to keep calculations accurate.

A general guideline in accounting is to insert a dollar symbol before the first amount in a column and before the total amount but not before the number amounts between them. To follow this guideline, format the first amount and total amount using the Accounting Number Format button and applying the Comma format to the number amounts between them. The Accounting number format and Comma number format are the same, except the Accounting number format includes the dollar sign. To differentiate between the two Accounting formats, steps in this textbook will use the term *Accounting format* when the Accounting Number Format button in the Number group on the Home tab is to be clicked. The term *Comma format* will be used when the Comma Style button is to be clicked.

Table 1.6 Number Formatting Buttons

Click this button		To do this
$ ⌄	Accounting Number Format	Add a dollar symbol, any necessary commas, and a decimal point followed by two digits even if none are typed; right-align the number in the cell.
%	Percent Style	Multiply the cell value by 100 and display the result with a percent symbol; right-align the number in the cell.
⟩	Comma Style	Add any necessary commas and a decimal point followed by two digits even if none are typed; right-align the number in the cell.
←.0 / .00	Increase Decimal	Increase the number of digits displayed after the decimal point in the selected cell.
.00 / →.0	Decrease Decimal	Decrease the number of digits displayed after the decimal point in the selected cell.

1. With **1-MoExps** open, make cell B13 active and then double-click the AutoSum button. (This inserts the total of the numbers in the range B4:B12.)
2. Make cell C13 active and then double-click the AutoSum button.
3. Apply the Accounting format to cells by completing the following steps:
   a. Select cells B4 and C4.
   b. Click the Accounting Number Format button in the Number group on the Home tab.
   c. Decrease the number of digits displayed after the decimal point to none by clicking the Decrease Decimal button in the Number group two times.

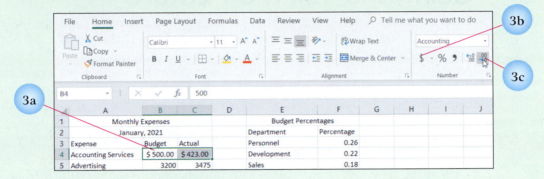

   d. Select cells B13 and C13.
   e. Click the Accounting Number Format button.
   f. Click the Decrease Decimal button two times.
4. Apply the Comma format to numbers by completing the following steps:
   a. Select the range B5:C12.
   b. Click the Comma Style button in the Number group.
   c. Click the Decrease Decimal button two times.

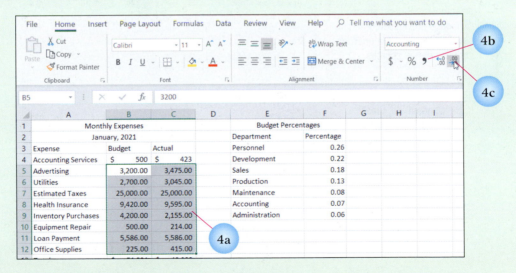

5. Apply the Percentage format to numbers by completing the following steps:
   a. Select the range F3:F9.
   b. Click the Percent Style button in the Number group on the Home tab.
6. Click in cell A1.
7. Save **1-MoExps**.

Check Your Work

You will use the Tell Me feature to learn how to change the font size of text and display the Excel Help window with information about wrapping text. You will use the Help feature to learn more about entering data in cells, changing the font color, and printing a workbook.

Tutorial

Using the Tell Me Feature

Quick Steps

Use Tell Me Feature
1. Click in *Tell Me* text box.
2. Type topic or feature.
3. Click option at drop-down list.

Using the Tell Me Feature

Excel includes a Tell Me feature that provides information and guidance on how to complete certain actions. Use the Tell Me feature by clicking in the *Tell Me* text box on the ribbon to the right of the Help tab and then typing a term, or action. As text is typed in the *Tell Me* text box, a drop-down list displays with options that are refined as more text is typed. The drop-down list contains options for completing the action, displaying information on the action from sources on the web, and displaying information on the action in the Excel Help task pane.

The Tell Me drop-down list also includes a Smart Lookup option. Clicking the Smart Lookup option opens the Smart Lookup task pane, as shown in Figure 1.10, at the right side of the screen with information on the typed text from a variety of internet sources. Smart Lookup can also be accessed using the Smart Lookup button on the Review tab or by selecting a cell, right-clicking in the selected cell, and then clicking the *Smart Lookup* option at the shortcut menu.

Figure 1.10 Smart Lookup Task Pane

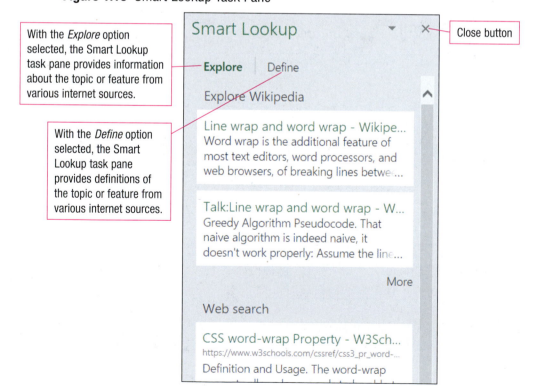

With the *Explore* option selected, the Smart Lookup task pane provides information about the topic or feature from various internet sources.

With the *Define* option selected, the Smart Lookup task pane provides definitions of the topic or feature from various internet sources.

Close button

1. With **1-MoExps** open, select the range A1:E1.
2. Click in the *Tell Me* text box and then type font size.
3. At the drop-down list, click the *Font Size* option.
4. At the side menu, click the *14* option. (This increases the font size of the text in the range A1:E1, and the height of row 1 automatically adjusts to accommodate the larger text.)

5. Use the Tell Me feature to display the Help task pane with information on wrapping text by completing the following steps:
    a. Click in the *Tell Me* text box and then type wrap text.
    b. Position the mouse pointer over the *Get Help on "wrap text"* option and then click the *Wrap text in a cell* option at the side menu.

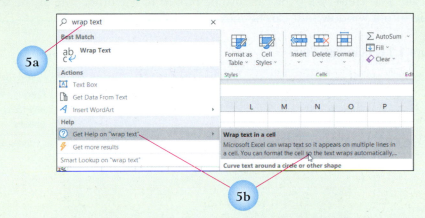

   c. At the Help task pane, read the information on wrapping text and then close the Help task pane by clicking the Close button in the upper right corner of the task pane.
6. Display information on scrolling in a workbook in the Smart Lookup task pane by completing the following steps:
    a. Click in the *Tell Me* text box and then type scrolling.
    b. Click the *Smart Lookup on "scrolling"* option. (The first time you use the Smart Lookup feature, a message may appear asking to turn on Intelligent Services. In a school setting, ask your instructor for assistance.)
    c. If two options—*Explore* and *Define*—are shown at the top of the Smart Lookup task pane, click the *Define* option. This will display a definition of the word *scrolling* in the Smart Lookup task pane.
    d. Close the Smart Lookup task pane by clicking the Close button in the upper right corner of the task pane.
7. Save, print, and then close **1-MoExps**.

Check Your Work

Quick Steps
Use Help Feature
1. Press F1.
2. Type term or action in search text box.
3. Press Enter key.
OR
1. Click in *Tell Me* text box.
2. Type term or action.
3. Click *Get Help on* option.

Using Help

Microsoft Excel includes a Help feature that contains information about Excel features and commands. This on-screen reference manual is similar to Windows Help and the Help features in Word, PowerPoint, and Access. Click the Help button in the Help group on the Help tab to display the Help task pane, as shown in Figure 1.11.

Alternatively, type a term or action in the *Tell Me* text box, position the mouse pointer over the *Get Help on* option, and then click an option at the side menu to open the Help task pane with the selected article displayed. In the Help task pane, type a topic, feature, or question in the search text box and then press the Enter key or click the Search help button. Articles related to the search text display in the Help task pane. Click an article and the article information displays in the Help task pane.

The Help task pane contains buttons at the top, as identified in Figure 1.11. Use the Back button to navigate to the previous page in the task pane. Click the three dots button to display more options, such as *Home*, *Office help center*, and *Contact us*. Resize or move the task pane by clicking the down arrow left of the Close button. The Help task pane can be made larger so it is easier to read the articles. The Help task pane can also be moved to the other side of the screen or made into a window that can be moved anywhere on the screen.

Figure 1.11 Help Task Pane

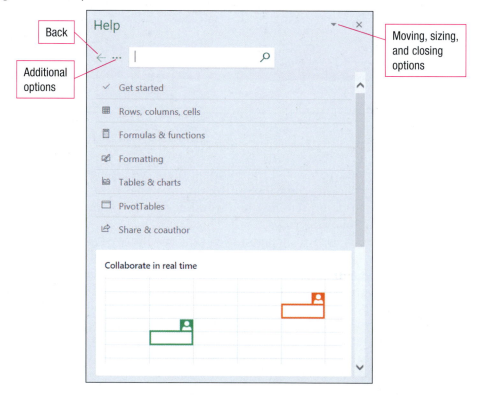

Getting Help from a ScreenTip

Hover the mouse pointer over a button and a ScreenTip displays with information about the button. Some button ScreenTips display with a Help icon and the <u>Tell me more</u> hyperlink. Click the <u>Tell me more</u> hyperlink text or press the F1 function key and the Help task pane opens with information about the button feature.

Activity 4b Using the Help Feature   **Part 2 of 3**

1. At a blank screen, press Ctrl + N to display a blank workbook. (Ctrl + N is the keyboard shortcut to open a blank workbook.)
2. Click the Help tab and then click the Help button.

3. With the insertion point in the search text box in the Help task pane, type enter data and then press the Enter key.
4. When the Help task pane displays with a list of articles, click the article <u>Enter data manually in worksheet cells</u> hyperlink.
5. In the displayed article, expand some of the topics in the article and then read the information about entering data in cells.
6. Click the down arrow button in the Help task pane and then click the *Size* option at the drop-down list.

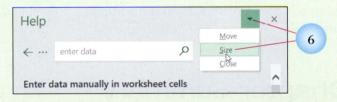

7. Resize the Help task pane to make the information in the article easier to read by moving the mouse pointer to a desired point (approximately one inch wider than it was previously) and then clicking the left mouse button.
8. Click the Back button to return to the previous page.
9. Click another article hyperlink in the Help task pane and then read in the information in the article.
10. Click the three dots button and then click the *Home* option at the drop-down list.
11. Click the Close button to close the Help task pane.
12. Click the Home tab, hover the mouse pointer over the Font Color button in the Font group until the ScreenTip displays, and then click the <u>Tell me more</u> hyperlink at the bottom of the ScreenTip.
13. Read the information that displays in the Help task pane, and then close the task pane.

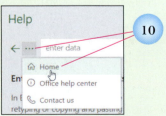

Getting Help in a Dialog Box or at the Backstage Area

Some dialog boxes and the backstage area contain a Help button, labeled with a question mark (?). Click this button and the Microsoft Office support website opens in a browser window with specific information about the dialog box or backstage area. After reading the information, close the browser window and return to Excel. If a dialog box is open in Excel, close it by clicking the Close button in the upper right corner. Exit the backstage area by clicking the Back button or pressing the Esc key.

Activity 4c Getting Help in a Dialog Box and Backstage Area   Part 3 of 3

1. At the blank workbook, click the File tab and then click the *Print* option.
2. At the Print backstage area, click the Microsoft Excel Help button in the upper right corner of the backstage area.
3. At the Microsoft Office support website, click the hyperlink to an article on printing that interests you. Read the article and then close the window.
4. Click the Back button to return to the blank workbook.
5. At the blank workbook, click the Home tab and then click the Number group dialog box launcher.
6. At the Format Cells dialog box with the Number tab selected, click the Help button in the upper right corner of the dialog box.

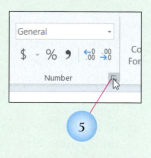

7. Read the information at the Microsoft Office support website and then close the browser window to return to Excel. In Excel, close the Format Cells dialog box.
8. Close the blank workbook.

Chapter Summary

- A file created in Excel is called a *workbook* and consists of one or more individual worksheets.

- The intersection of a column and a row in a worksheet is referred to as a *cell*. Gridlines are the horizontal and vertical lines that define cells.

- When the insertion point is positioned in a cell, the cell name (also called the *cell reference*) displays in the Name box at the left of the Formula bar. The cell name includes the column letter and row number.

- If the data entered in a cell consists of text (letters) and does not fit into the cell, it overlaps the cell to the right. If the data consists of numbers and does not fit into the cell, the numbers change to number symbols (###).

- Save a workbook by clicking the Save button on the Quick Access Toolbar or by clicking the File tab and then clicking the *Save As* option. At the Save As backstage area, click the *Browse* option. At the Save As dialog box, navigate to the desired folder, type the workbook name in the *File name* text box, and then press the Enter key.

- To replace data in a cell, click in the cell and then type the new data. To edit data within a cell, double-click in the cell and then make the necessary changes.

- Print a worksheet by clicking the File tab, clicking the *Print* option, and then clicking the Print button.

- Close a workbook by clicking the File tab and then clicking the *Close* option or by using the keyboard shortcut Ctrl + F4.

- Close Excel by clicking the Close button in the upper right corner of the screen or by using the keyboard shortcut Alt + F4.

- The AutoComplete feature automatically inserts a previous entry if the character or characters being typed in a cell match a previous entry. The AutoCorrect feature corrects many common typing errors. The AutoFill fill handle adds the same or consecutive data into a range of cells.

- Open a workbook by clicking the File tab and then clicking the *Open* option. At the Open backstage area, click the *Browse* option. At the Open dialog box, double-click the workbook name.

- Workbooks can be pinned to the *Recent* option list at the Open backstage area or the Recent list at the Home backstage area so that they can be easily accessed in the future.

- Use the AutoSum button in the Editing group on the Home tab to find the total or average of data in columns or rows.

- Use the fill handle to copy a formula in a cell to adjacent cells. The fill handle is the solid box in the bottom right of an active cell.

- Select all the cells in a column by clicking the column header. Select all the cells in a row by clicking the row header. Select all the cells in a worksheet by clicking the Select All button immediately to the left of the column headers.

- Change the column width by dragging or double-clicking the column boundary line.

- Merge and center adjacent cells by selecting them and then clicking the Merge & Center button in the Alignment group on the Home tab.

- Format numbers in cells with buttons in the Number group on the Home tab.

- The Tell Me feature provides information and guidance on how to complete certain actions. The *Tell Me* text box is located on the ribbon to the right of the Help tab.

- Use the Tell Me feature, click a hyperlink in a button ScreenTip, or press F1 to display the Help task pane. At this task pane, type a topic in the search text box and then press the Enter key.

- Some dialog boxes and the backstage area contain a Help button that, when clicked, displays the Microsoft Office support website with information specific to the dialog box or backstage area.

Commands Review

FEATURE	RIBBON TAB, GROUP/OPTION	BUTTON	KEYBOARD SHORTCUT
Accounting format	Home, Number	$ ˅	
AutoSum	Home, Editing	Σ	Alt + =
close Excel		✕	Alt + F4
close workbook	File, *Close*		Ctrl + F4
Comma format	Home, Number	﹐	
decrease decimal place	Home, Number	.00 →.0	
Go To dialog box	Home, Editing	🔍	Ctrl + G
Help task pane	Help, Help	⍰	F1
increase decimal place	Home, Number	←.0 .00	
merge and center cells	Home, Alignment	⊞	
Open backstage area	File, *Open*		Ctrl + O
Percentage format	Home, Number	%	Ctrl + Shift + %
Print backstage area	File, *Print*		Ctrl + P
Save As backstage area	File, *Save As*	💾	Ctrl + S

Microsoft® Excel®

Inserting Formulas in a Worksheet

Performance Objectives

Upon successful completion of Chapter 2, you will be able to:

1. Write formulas with mathematical operators
2. Type a formula in the Formula bar
3. Copy a formula
4. Determine the order of operations
5. Identify common formula and function errors
6. Use the Insert Function dialog box to insert a function in a cell
7. Write formulas with the AVERAGE, MAX, MIN, COUNT, COUNTA, NOW, and TODAY functions
8. Display formulas
9. Use absolute and mixed cell references in formulas

Excel is a powerful decision-making tool that contains data that can be manipulated in "What if?" situations. Insert a formula in a worksheet and then manipulate the data to make projections, answer specific questions, and plan for the future. For example, the owner of a company might prepare a worksheet on production costs and then determine the impact on company revenues if production is increased or decreased.

As explained in Chapter 1, formulas can be inserted into Excel worksheets to add, subtract, multiply, and/or divide values as well as calculate averages, percentages, and much more. Chapter 1 described how to use the AutoSum button to insert formulas for calculating totals and averages. In Chapter 2, you will learn to use the Formulas tab to create formulas with a variety of different functions.

 Data Files

Before beginning chapter work, copy the EL1C2 folder to your storage medium and then make EL1C2 the active folder.

 The online course includes additional training and assessment resources.

Activity 1 Insert Formulas in a Worksheet

4 Parts

You will open a worksheet containing data and then insert formulas to calculate differences, salaries, and percentages of budgets and equipment usage down time.

Tutorial

Entering Formulas
Using the Keyboard

💡 **Hint** After typing a formula in a cell, press the Enter key, the Tab key, or Shift + Tab.

Writing Formulas with Mathematical Operators

As explained in Chapter 1, the AutoSum button in the Editing group on the Home tab creates a formula for calculating the sum or average of values. A formula can also be written using mathematical operators. Commonly used mathematical operators and their purposes are shown in Table 2.1. When writing a formula, begin it with the equals sign (=). For example, to create a formula that divides the contents of cell B2 by the contents of cell C2 and inserts the result in cell D2, make D2 the active cell and then type *=b2/c2*. The column reference letters used in formulas can be entered as either lowercase or uppercase letters. If the column reference letters are entered in a formula in lowercase, Excel will automatically convert the column reference letters to uppercase. Formulas entered in a cell will also display in the Formula bar, where the formula can be modified.

Tutorial

Copying Formulas

Copying a Formula with Relative Cell References

In many worksheets, the same basic formula is used repetitively. In a situation where a formula is copied to other locations in a worksheet, use a relative cell reference. Copy a formula containing relative cell references and the cell references change. For example, if the formula *=SUM(A2:C2)* is entered in cell D2 and then copied relatively into cell D3, the formula in cell D3 appears as *=SUM(A3:C3)*. (Additional information on cell references is provided later in this chapter in the section "Using an Absolute Cell Reference in a Formula.")

To copy a formula with a relative cell reference, use the Fill button or the fill handle. (You used the fill handle to copy a formula in Chapter 1.) To use the Fill button, select the cell containing the formula and all the cells to which the formula is to be copied and then click the Fill button in the Editing group on the Home tab. At the Fill button drop-down list, click the direction. For example, click the *Down* option if the formula is being copied down the worksheet.

 Fill

⚡ **Quick Steps**

Copy Formulas with Relative Cell References

1. Insert formula in cell.
2. Select cell containing formula and all cells to which formula is to be copied.
3. Click Fill button.
4. Click direction option.

Table 2.1 Mathematical Operators

Operator	Purpose	Operator	Purpose
+	addition	/	division
-	subtraction	%	percentage
*	multiplication	^	exponentiation

1. Open **HCReports** and then save it with the name **2-HCReports**.
2. Insert a formula by completing the following steps:
   a. Make cell D3 active.
   b. Type the formula =c3-b3.
   c. Press the Enter key.
3. Copy the formula to the range D4:D10 by completing the following steps:
   a. Select the range D3:D10.
   b. Click the Fill button in the Editing group on the Home tab and then click *Down* at the drop-down list.

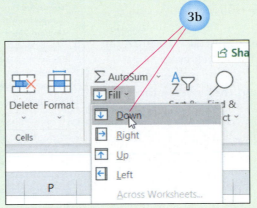

4. Save **2-HCReports**.
5. With the worksheet open, make the following changes to cell contents:
   - B4: Change *48,290* to *46425*
   - C6: Change *61,220* to *60000*
   - B8: Change *55,309* to *57415*
   - B9: Change *12,398* to *14115*
6. Make cell D3 active, apply the Accounting format by clicking the Accounting Number Format button in the Number group on the Home tab, and then click the Decrease Decimal button two times to decrease the digits displayed past the decimal point to none.
7. Save **2-HCReports**.

Hint Use the fill handle to copy a relative version of a formula.

As explained in Chapter 1, the fill handle can be used to copy a formula up, down, left, or right within a worksheet. To use the fill handle, insert the data in the cell (text, value, formula, etc.). With the cell active, position the mouse pointer on the fill handle until the mouse pointer turns into a thin black cross. Click and hold down the left mouse button, drag and select the cells, and then release the mouse button. When dragging a cell containing a formula, a relative version of the formula is copied to the selected cells.

Checking Cell References in a Formula

To verify if a formula is using the correct cell references, double-click in a cell containing the formula and the cells referenced in the formula display with a colored border and shading in the worksheet. This feature makes it easy to identify which cells are being referenced in a formula and is helpful when trying to identify errors that may occur in a formula.

1. With **2-HCReports** open, insert a
   formula by completing the following steps:
   a. Make cell D15 active.
   b. Click in the Formula bar text box and then
      type =c15*b15.
   c. Click the Enter button on the Formula bar.
2. Copy the formula to the range D16:D20 by
   completing the following steps:
   a. Make sure cell D15 is still the active cell.
   b. Position the mouse pointer on the fill handle
      at the lower right corner of cell D15 until the
      pointer turns into a thin black cross.
   c. Click and hold down the left mouse button,
      drag into cell D20, and then release the
      mouse button.
3. Save **2-HCReports**.
4. Double-click in cell D20 to display the formula
   with cell references color coded to ensure the
   formula was copied relatively and then press the
   Enter key to exit the Edit mode.
5. Make the following changes to cell contents in
   the worksheet:
   B16: Change *20* to *28*
   C17: Change *18.75* to *19.10*
   B19: Change *15* to *24*
6. Select the range D16:D20 and then apply the
   Comma format by clicking the Comma Style
   button in the Number group on the Home tab.
7. Save **2-HCReports**.

1c   1b

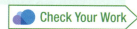

| PMT | ▾ | : | ✕ | ✓ | *fx* | =c15*b15 |

	A	B	C	D
1	**Highland Construction**			
2	**Customer**	**Actual**	**Planned**	**Difference**
3	Sellar Corporation	$ 30,349	$ 34,109	$ 3,760
4	Main Street Photos	46,425	48,100	1,675
5	Sunset Automotive	34,192	32,885	(1,307)
6	Linstrom Enterprises	63,293	60,000	(3,293)
7	Morcos Media	29,400	30,500	1,100
8	Green Valley Optics	57,415	58,394	979
9	Detailed Designs	14,115	13,100	(1,015)
10	Arrowstar Company	87,534	86,905	(629)
11				
12				
13				
14	**Name**	**Hours**	**Rate**	**Salary**
15	Carolyn Bentley	35	$ 23.15	=c15*b15

	A	B	C	D
13				
14	**Name**	**Hours**	**Rate**	**Salary**
15	Carolyn Bentley	35	$ 23.15	$ 810.25
16	Lindon Cassini	20	19.00	$ 380.00
17	Michelle DeFord	40	18.75	$ 750.00
18	Javier Farias	24	16.45	$ 394.80
19	Deborah Gould	15	11.50	$ 172.50
20	William Jarman	15	11.50	$ 172.50
21				

2c

Check Your Work ›

 Tutorial ›

Entering Formulas
Using the Mouse

Quick Steps

**Write Formula
by Pointing**
1. Click in cell that will
   contain formula.
2. Type equals sign.
3. Click in cell to
   be referenced in
   formula.
4. Type mathematical
   operator.
5. Click in next cell
   reference.
6. Press Enter key.

Writing a Formula by Pointing

The formulas written in Activity 1a and Activity 1b used cell references such as
=*c3-b3*. Another method for writing a formula is to "point" to the specific cells that
are to be part of the formula. Creating a formula by pointing is more accurate than
typing the cell reference because a mistake can be made when the cell reference is
typed.

To write a formula by pointing, click in the cell that will contain the
formula, type the equals sign to begin the formula, and then click in the cell to
be referenced in the formula. This inserts a moving border around the cell and
changes the mode from Enter to Point. (The word *Point* displays at the left side
of the Status bar.) Type the mathematical operator and then click in the next
cell reference. Continue in this manner until all the cell references are specified
and then press the Enter key. This ends the formula and inserts the result of the
calculation in the active cell. When a formula is written by pointing, the range of
cells to be included in the formula can be selected.

1. With **2-HCReports** open, enter a formula by pointing that calculates the percentage of actual budget by completing the following steps:
   a. Make cell D25 active.
   b. Type an equals sign (=).
   c. Click in cell B25. (This inserts a moving border around the cell and changes the mode from Enter to Point.)
   d. Type a forward slash symbol (/).
   e. Click in cell C25.
   f. Make sure the formula in D25 is *=B25/C25* and then press the Enter key.
2. Make cell D25 active, click the fill handle and hold down the left mouse button, drag into cell D31, and then release the mouse button.

	Expense	Actual	Budget	% of Actual
23				
24	**Expense**	**Actual**	**Budget**	**% of Actual**
25	Salaries	$126,000	$124,000	=B25/C25
26	Commissions	58,000	54,500	
27	Media space	8,250	10,100	
28	Travel expenses	6,350	6,000	
29	Dealer display	4,140	4,500	
30	Payroll taxes	2,430	2,200	
31	Telephone	1,450	1,500	
32				

Budget	**% of Actual**
$124,000	102%
54,500	106%
10,100	82%
6,000	106%
4,500	92%
2,200	110%
1,500	97%

3. Save **2-HCReports**.

> Check Your Work

> Tutorial

Determining the
Order of Operations

Determining the Order of Operations

If a formula contains two or more operators, Excel uses the same order of operations used in algebra. From left to right in a formula, this order is negations (negative number—a number preceded by -) first, then percentages (%), then exponentiations (^), followed by multiplications (*), divisions (/), additions (+), and subtractions (-). To change the order of operations, put parentheses around the part of the formula that is to be calculated first. For example, if cells A1, B1, and C1 all contain the value *5*, the result of the formula *=a1+b1*c1* will be 30 (because 5*5=25 and 5+25=30). However, if parentheses are placed around the first two cell references so the formula appears as *=(a1+b1)*c1*, the result will be 50 (because 5+5=10 and 10*5=50).

Excel requires each left parenthesis to be paired with a right parenthesis. If a formula is missing a left or right parenthesis, a message box will display explaining that an error exists in the formula and providing a possible correction, which can be accepted or declined. This feature is useful when creating a formula that contains multiple layers of parentheses (called *nested parentheses*) because it will identify any missing left or right parentheses in the formula. Parentheses can also be used in various functions to further determine the order of operations.

Tutorial

Using the Trace
Error Button

 Trace Error

Using the Trace Error Button

When typing or editing data in a worksheet, a button may display near the active cell. The general term for this button is a *smart tag*. The display of the smart tag button varies depending on the action performed. In Activity 1d, you will insert a formula that causes a smart tag button named the Trace Error button to appear. When the Trace Error button appears, a small dark-green triangle also appears in the upper left corner of the cell. Click the Trace Error button and a drop-down list displays with options for updating the formula to include specific cells, getting help with the error, ignoring the error, editing the error in the Formula bar, and completing an error check. In Activity 1d, two of the formulas you insert return the correct results. You will click the Trace Error button, read about what Excel perceives to be the error, and then tell Excel to ignore the error.

Identifying Common Formula Errors

Excel is a sophisticated program that requires data input and formula creation to follow strict guidelines in order to function properly. When guidelines that specify how data or formulas are entered are not followed, Excel will display one of many error codes. When an error is identified with a code, determining and then fixing the problem is easier than if no information is provided. Table 2.2 lists some common error codes.

Most errors in Excel result from the user incorrectly inputting data into a worksheet. However, most error messages will not display until the data is used in a formula or function. Common mistakes made while inputting data include placing text in a cell that requires a number, entering data in the wrong location, and entering numbers in an incorrect format. Other errors result from entering a formula or function improperly. A formula will often produce an error message if it is trying to divide a number by 0 or contains a circular reference (that is, when a formula within a cell uses the results of that formula in the same cell).

Table 2.2 Common Error Codes

Error Code	Meaning
#DIV/O	A formula is attempting to divide a number by 0.
#N/A	An argument parameter has been left out of a function.
#NAME?	A function name is not entered correctly.
#NUM!	An argument parameter does not meet a function's requirements.
#REF!	A referenced cell no longer exists within a worksheet.
#VALUE	The data entered is the wrong type (for example, text instead of numbers).

Activity 1d Writing a Formula by Pointing That Calculates the Percentage of Down Time

1. With **2-HCReports** open, enter a formula by pointing that calculates the percentage of equipment down time by completing the following steps:
   a. Make cell B45 active.
   b. Type an equals sign followed by a left parenthesis (=().
   c. Click in cell B37. (This inserts a moving border around the cell and changes the mode from Enter to Point.)
   d. Type a minus symbol (-).
   e. Click in cell B43.
   f. Type a right parenthesis followed by a forward slash ()/).
   g. Click in cell B37.
   h. Make sure the formula in cell B45 is *=(B37-B43)/B37* and then press the Enter key.

2. Make cell B45 active, click the fill handle and press and hold down the left mouse button, drag into cell G45, and then release the mouse button.

3. Enter a formula by dragging to a range of cells by completing the following steps:
   a. Click in cell B46 and then click the AutoSum button in the Editing group on the Home tab.
   b. Select the range B37:D37.
   c. Click the Enter button on the Formula bar. (This inserts *7,260* in cell B46.)

4. Click in cell B47 and then complete steps similar to those in Step 3 to create a formula that totals hours available from April through June (the range E37:G37). (This inserts *7,080* in cell B47.)

5. Click in cell B46 and notice the Trace Error button. Complete the following steps to read about the error and then tell Excel to ignore it:
   a. Click the Trace Error button.
   b. At the drop-down list, click the *Help on this Error* option.
   c. Read the information in the Excel Help window and then close the window.
   d. Click the Trace Error button again and then click *Ignore Error* at the drop-down list.

6. Remove the dark-green triangle from cell B47 by completing the following steps:
   a. Click in cell B47.
   b. Click the Trace Error button and then click *Ignore Error* at the drop-down list.

7. Save, print, and then close **2-HCReports**.

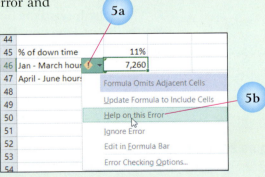

Check Your Work

Activity 2 **Insert Formulas with Statistical Functions** **4 Parts**

You will use the AVERAGE function to determine average test scores, use the MINIMUM and MAXIMUM functions to determine lowest and highest averages, use the COUNT function to count the number of students taking a test, and use the COUNTA function to determine the number of tests administered. You will also use date and time functions and display a formula in a cell rather than the result of a formula.

Inserting Formulas with Functions

In Activity 2b in Chapter 1, the AutoSum button was used to insert the formula *=SUM(b2:b5)* in a cell. The beginning section of the formula, *=SUM*, is called a *function*. Functions are built-in formulas. Inserting a formula takes fewer keystrokes than creating one from scratch. For example, using the *=SUM* function made it unnecessary to type a string of cell references with the plus symbol (+) between each one.

Excel provides other functions for writing formulas. A function operates on what is referred to as an *argument*. An argument may consist of a constant, a cell reference, or another function. In the formula *=SUM(b2:b5)*, the cell range *(b2:b5)* is an example of a cell reference argument. An argument may also contain a *constant*. A constant is a value entered directly into the formula. For example, in the formula *=SUM(b3:b9,100)*, the cell range *b3:b9* is a cell reference argument and *100* is a constant. In this formula, 100 is always added to the sum of the cells.

The phrase *returning the result* is used to describe when a value calculated by the formula is inserted in a cell. The term *returning* refers to the process of calculating the formula and the term *result* refers to the value inserted in the cell.

fx Insert Function

Type a function in a cell in a worksheet or use the Insert Function button on the Formula bar or the Formulas tab to write the formula. Figure 2.1 shows the Formulas tab, which provides the Insert Function button and other buttons for inserting functions in a worksheet. The Function Library group on the Formulas tab contains a number of buttons for inserting functions from a variety of categories, such as *Financial*, *Logical*, *Text*, and *Date & Time*.

Click the Insert Function button on the Formula bar or the Formulas tab and the Insert Function dialog box displays, as shown in Figure 2.2. The Insert Function dialog box can also be accessed using the keyboard shortcut Shift + F3. At the Insert Function dialog box, the most recently used functions display in the *Select a function* list box. Choose a function category by clicking the *Or select a category* option box arrow and then clicking the category at the drop-down list. Use the *Search for a function* search box to locate a specific function.

Figure 2.1 Formulas Tab

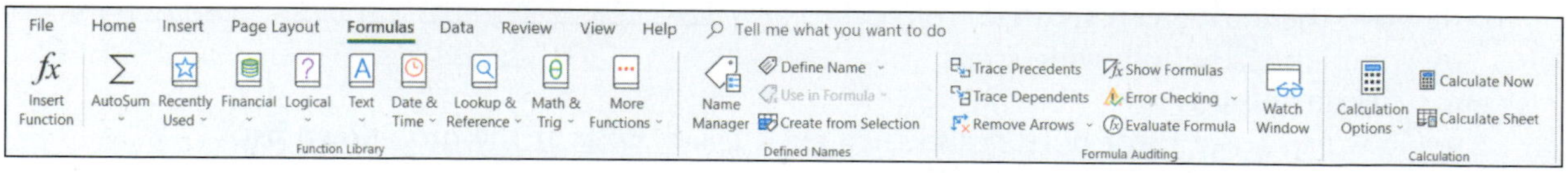

Figure 2.2 Insert Function Dialog Box

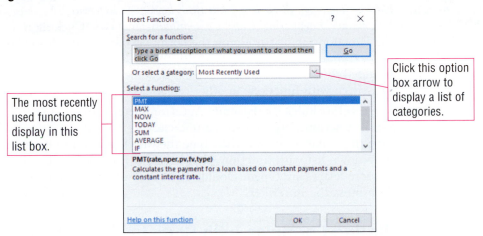

The most recently used functions display in this list box.

Click this option box arrow to display a list of categories.

With the function category selected, choose a function in the *Select a function* list box and then click OK. This displays a Function Arguments dialog box, like the one shown in Figure 2.3. At this dialog box, enter in the *Number1* text box the range of cells to be included in the formula, any constants to be included as part of the formula, or another function.

Type a cell reference or a range of cells in an argument text box or point to a cell or select a range of cells with the mouse pointer. Pointing to cells or selecting a range of cells using the mouse pointer is the preferred method of entering data into an argument text box because there is less chance of making errors. After entering a range of cells, a constant, or another function, click OK.

More than one argument can be included in a function. If the function contains more than one argument, click in the *Number2* text box or press the Tab key to move the insertion point to the *Number2* text box and then enter the second argument. If the function dialog box covers a specific cell or cells, move the dialog box by positioning the mouse pointer on the dialog box title bar, clicking and holding down the left mouse button, dragging the dialog box to a different location, and then releasing the mouse button.

Figure 2.3 Example of a Function Arguments Dialog Box

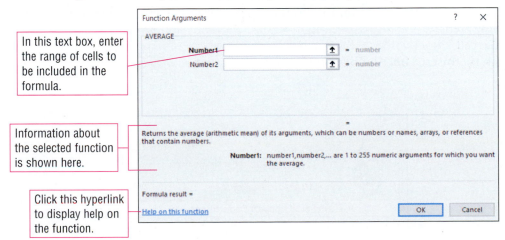

In this text box, enter the range of cells to be included in the formula.

Information about the selected function is shown here.

Click this hyperlink to display help on the function.

Excel performs over 300 functions that are divided into 13 categories: *Financial, Date & Time, Math & Trig, Statistical, Lookup & Reference, Database, Text, Logical, Information, Engineering, Cube, Compatibility,* and *Web.* Clicking the AutoSum button in the Function Library group on the Formulas tab or the Editing group on the Home tab automatically adds numbers with the SUM function. The SUM function is included in the *Math & Trig* category. In some activities in this chapter, formulas will be written with functions in other categories, including *Statistical* and *Date & Time.*

Excel includes the Formula AutoComplete feature, which displays a drop-down list of functions. To use this feature, click in the cell or in the Formula bar text box, type the equals sign, and then type the first letter of the function. This displays a drop-down list with functions that begin with the letter. The list is further refined as more letters are typed. Double-click the function, enter the cell references, and then press the Enter key.

Tutorial

Using Statistical Functions

Writing Formulas with Statistical Functions

Write formulas with statistical functions such as AVERAGE, MAX, MIN, and COUNT. The AVERAGE function returns the average (arithmetic mean) of the arguments. The MAX function returns the largest value in a set of values and the MIN function returns the smallest value in a set of values. Use the COUNT or COUNTA functions to count the number of cells that contain numbers or letters within the specified range.

Finding Averages A common function in a formula is the AVERAGE function. With this function, the values in a range of cells are added together and then divided by the number of cells. In Activity 2a, you will use the AVERAGE function to add all the test scores for a student and then divide that number by the total number of scores. You will use the Insert Function button to simplify the creation of the formula containing an AVERAGE function.

One of the advantages to using formulas in a worksheet is that the data can be easily manipulated to answer certain questions. In Activity 2a, you will learn how retaking certain tests affects the final average score.

Activity 2a Averaging Test Scores in a Worksheet   Part 1 of 4

1. Open **DWTests** and then save it with the name **2-DWTests**.
2. Use the Insert Function button to find the average of test scores by completing the following steps:
   a. Make cell E4 active.
   b. Click the Insert Function button on the Formula bar.

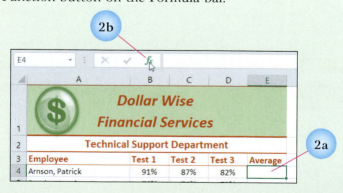

c. At the Insert Function dialog box, click the *Or select a category* option box arrow and then click *Statistical* at the drop-down list.

d. Click *AVERAGE* in the *Select a function* list box.

e. Click OK.

f. At the Function Arguments dialog box, make sure *B4:D4* displays in the *Number1* text box. (If not, type b4:d4 in the *Number1* text box.)

g. Click OK.

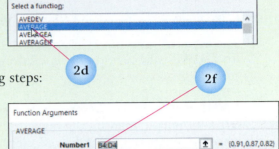

3. Copy the formula by completing the following steps:
   a. Make sure cell E4 is still active.
   b. Position the mouse pointer on the fill handle until the pointer turns into a thin black cross.
   c. Click and hold down the left mouse button, drag into cell E16, and then release the mouse button.

4. Save and then print **2-DWTests**.

5. After viewing the averages of test scores, you notice that a couple of students have low averages. You decide to see what happens to these average scores if students retake the tests on which they scored the lowest. You decide that a student can score a maximum of 70% on a retake of the test. Make the following changes to test scores to see how the changes affect the test averages:

   B9: Change *50* to *70*
   C9: Change *52* to *70*
   D9: Change *60* to *70*
   B10: Change *62* to *70*
   B14: Change *0* to *70*
   D14: Change *0* to *70*
   D16: Change *0* to *70*

6. Save and then print **2-DWTests**. (Compare the test averages of Teri Fisher-Edwards, Stephanie Flanery, Claude Markovits, and Douglas Pherson to see how retaking the tests affects their final test averages.)

When a function such as the AVERAGE function calculates cell entries, it ignores certain cell entries. The AVERAGE function will ignore text in cells and blank cells (not zeros). For example, in the worksheet containing test scores, a couple of cells contained *0%*. These entries were included in the averaging of the test scores. To exclude a particular test from the average, enter text in the cell such as *N/A* (for *not applicable*) or leave the cell blank.

Finding Maximum and Minimum Values The MAX function in a formula returns the maximum value in a cell range and the MIN function returns the minimum value in a cell range. For example, the MAX and MIN functions in a worksheet containing employee hours can be used to determine which employee worked the most hours and which worked the least. In a worksheet containing sales commissions, the MAX and MIN functions can be used to identify the salesperson who earned the highest commission and the one who earned the lowest.

Insert a MAX or a MIN function into a formula in the same manner as an AVERAGE function. In Activity 2b, you will use the Formula AutoComplete feature to insert the MAX function in cells to determine the highest test score average and the Insert Function button to insert the MIN function to determine the lowest test score average.

Activity 2b Finding Maximum and Minimum Values in a Worksheet

Part 2 of 4

1. With **2-DWTests** open, type the following in the specified cells:
   A19: Highest Test Average
   A20: Lowest Test Average
   A21: Average of Completed Tests
2. Insert a formula to identify the highest test score average by completing the following steps:
   a. Make cell B19 active.
   b. Type =m. (This displays the Formula AutoComplete list.)
   c. Double-click *MAX* in the Formula AutoComplete list.
   d. Type e4:e16) and then press the Enter key.
3. Insert a formula to identify the lowest test score average by completing the following steps:
   a. Make sure cell B20 is active.
   b. Click the Insert Function button on the Formula bar.
   c. At the Insert Function dialog box, make sure *Statistical* is selected in the *Or select a category* option box and then click *MIN* in the *Select a function* list box. (You will need to scroll down the list to locate *MIN*.)
   d. Click OK.
   e. At the Function Arguments dialog box, type e4:e16 in the *Number1* text box.
   f. Click OK.
4. Insert a formula to determine the average of the completed test scores by completing the following steps:
   a. Make cell B21 active.
   b. Click the Formulas tab.
   c. Click the Insert Function button in the Function Library group.
   d. At the Insert Function dialog box, make sure *Statistical* is selected in the *Or select a category* option box and then click *AVERAGE* in the *Select a function* list box.
   e. Click OK.
   f. At the Function Arguments dialog box, make sure the insertion point is positioned in the *Number1* text box with existing text selected, use the mouse pointer to select the range E4:E16 in the worksheet (you may need to move the dialog box to display the cells), and then click OK.

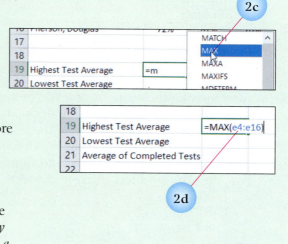

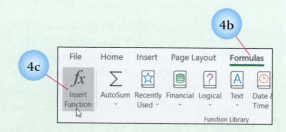

5. Save and then print **2-DWTests**.
6. Change the *70%* values (which were previously *0%*) in cells B14, D14, and D16 to *N/A*. (This will cause the average test scores for Claude Markovits and Douglas Pherson to increase and will change the average of completed tests.)
7. Save and then print **2-DWTests**.

Check Your Work

Counting Numbers in a Range   Use the COUNT function to count the numeric values in a range and use the COUNTA function to count the cells in a range containing any characters. In Activity 2c, you will use the COUNT function to specify the number of students who have completed Test 3. In the worksheet, the cells containing the text *N/A* are not counted by the COUNT function. Additionally, you will use the COUNTA function to determine how many students should have completed Test 3 by counting the cells that contain test scores and the text N/A.

Activity 2c   Counting the Number of Students Taking Tests

Part 3 of 4

1. With **2-DWTests** open, make cell A22 active.
2. Type Test 3 Completed.
3. Make cell B22 active.
4. Insert a formula counting the number of students who have completed Test 3 by completing the following steps:
   a. With cell B22 active, click in the Formula bar text box.
   b. Type =c.
   c. At the Formula AutoComplete list, scroll down the list until *COUNT* displays and then double-click *COUNT*.
   d. Type d4:d16) and then press the Enter key.

5. Count the number of students who have been given Test 3 by completing the following steps:
   a. Make cell A23 active.
   b. Type Test 3 Administered.
   c. Make cell B23 active.
   d. Click the Insert Function button on the Formula bar.
   e. At the Insert Function dialog box, make sure *Statistical* is selected in the *Or select a category* option box.
   f. Scroll down the list of functions in the *Select a function* list box until *COUNTA* is visible and then double-click *COUNTA*.
   g. At the Function Arguments dialog box, type d4:d16 in the *Value1* text box and then click OK.
6. Save and then print **2-DWTests**.

Check Your Work

Tutorial

Using Date and
Time Functions

Writing Formulas with the NOW and TODAY Functions

The NOW and TODAY functions are part of the *Date & Time* category of functions. The NOW function returns the current date and time in a date-and-time format. The TODAY function returns the current date in a date format. Both the NOW and TODAY functions automatically update when a workbook is opened. To access the NOW and TODAY functions, click the Date & Time button in the Function Library group on the Formulas tab. The formulas can also be accessed at the Insert Function dialog box.

Date & Time

The NOW and TODAY functions can also be updated without closing and then reopening the workbook. To update a workbook that contains a NOW or TODAY function, click the Calculate Now button in the Calculation group on the Formulas tab or press the F9 function key.

Calculate Now

Tutorial

Displaying
Formulas

Displaying Formulas

In some situations, displaying the formulas in a worksheet, rather than the results, may be useful—for example, to display formulas for auditing purposes or to check formulas for accuracy. Display all the formulas in a worksheet, rather than the results, by clicking the Formulas tab and then clicking the Show Formulas button in the Formula Auditing group. The display of formulas can also be turned on with the keyboard shortcut Ctrl + `. (This symbol is the grave accent, generally to the left of the 1 key on the keyboard.) To turn off the display of formulas, press Ctrl + ` or click the Show Formulas button on the Formulas tab.

Show
Formulas

💡 **Hint** Press Ctrl + ` to display the formulas in a worksheet rather than the results.

Activity 2d Using the NOW Function and Displaying Formulas

Part 4 of 4

1. With **2-DWTests** open, make cell A26 active and then type Prepared by:.
2. Make cell A27 active and then type your first and last names.
3. Insert the current date and time by completing the following steps:
   a. Make cell A28 active.
   b. Click the Date & Time button in the Function Library group on the Formulas tab and then click *NOW* at the drop-down list.
   c. At the Function Arguments dialog box stating that the function takes no argument, click OK.
4. Update the time in cell A28 by completing the following steps:
   a. Wait for 1 minute.
   b. Click the Calculate Now button in the Calculation group on the Formulas tab.
5. Click the Show Formulas button in the Formula Auditing group to turn on the display of formulas.
6. Print the worksheet with the formulas. (The worksheet will print on two pages.)
7. Press Ctrl + ` to turn off the display of formulas.
8. Save, print, and then close **2-DWTests**.

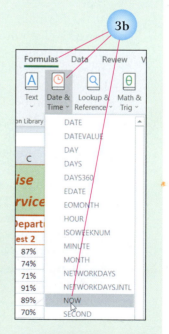

Check Your Work

Activity 3   Insert Formulas Using Absolute and Mixed Cell References   4 Parts

You will insert a formula containing an absolute cell reference that determines the effect on earnings with specific increases, insert a formula with multiple absolute cell references that determines the weighted average of scores, and use mixed cell references to determine simple interest.

Using Absolute and Mixed Cell References in Formulas

A reference identifies a cell or range of cells in a worksheet and can be relative, absolute, or mixed. A relative cell reference refers to a cell relative to a position in a formula. An absolute cell reference refers to a cell in a specific location. When a formula is copied, a relative cell reference adjusts whereas an absolute cell reference remains constant. A mixed cell reference does both: either the column remains absolute and the row is relative or the column is relative and the row remains absolute. Distinguish among relative, absolute, and mixed cell references using the dollar symbol ($). Type a dollar symbol before the column and/or row cell reference in a formula to specify that the column or row is an absolute cell reference.

Tutorial

Absolute Addressing

Using an Absolute Cell Reference in a Formula

In this chapter, you have learned to copy a relative formula. For example, if the formula *=SUM(A2:C2)* in cell D2 is copied relatively into cell D3, it changes to *=SUM(A3:C3)*. In some situations, a formula may contain an absolute cell reference, which always refers to a cell in a specific location. In Activity 3a, you will add a column for projected job earnings and then consider "What if?" situations using a formula with an absolute cell reference. To identify an absolute cell reference, insert a dollar symbol before the row and the column. For example, the absolute cell reference *C12* is typed as *c12* in a formula.

Activity 3a   Inserting and Copying a Formula with an Absolute Cell Reference   Part 1 of 4

1. Open **CCReports** and then save it with the name **2-CCReports**.
2. Determine the effect of a 10% pay increase on actual job earnings by completing the following steps:
   a. Make cell C3 active, type the formula *=b3*b12*, and then press the Enter key.
   b. Make cell C3 active and then use the fill handle to copy the formula to the range C4:C10.
   c. Make cell C3 active, click the Accounting Number Format button on the Home tab, and then click the Decrease Decimal button two times.

	A	B	C
		Cedarview	
	Customer	Planned	Actual
	ar Corporation	$ 34,109	=b3*b12
	n Street Photos	48,100	
	set Automotive	32,885	
	trom Enterprises	61,220	
	cos Media	30,500	
	en Valley Optics	58,394	
	iled Designs	13,100	
	wstar Company	86,905	
	crease/Decrease	1.1	

2a

Cedarview

Planned	Actual
$ 34,109	37,520
48,100	52,910
32,885	36,174
61,220	67,342
30,500	33,550
58,394	64,233
13,100	14,410
86,905	95,596

2b

3. Save and then print **2-CCReports**.
4. With the worksheet still open, determine the effect of a 10% pay decrease on actual job earnings by completing the following steps:
   a. Make cell B12 active.
   b. Type 0.9 and then press the Enter key.
5. Save and then print the **2-CCReports**.
6. Determine the effect of a 20% pay increase on actual job earnings. (To do this, type 1.2 in cell B12 and then press the Enter key.)
7. Save and then print **2-CCReports**.

	B	C
	Cedarview	
	Planned	**Actual**
	$ 34,109	$ 30,698
	48,100	43,290
	32,885	29,597
	61,220	55,098
	30,500	27,450
	58,394	52,555
4b	13,100	11,790
	86,905	78,215
	0.9	

Check Your Work

In Activity 3a, you created a formula with one absolute cell reference. A formula can also be created with multiple absolute cell references. For example, in Activity 3b, you will create a formula that contains both relative and absolute cell references to determine the average of training scores based on specific weight percentages. In a weighted average, some scores have more value (weight) than others. For example, in Activity 3b, you will create a formula that determines the weighted average of training scores that gives more weight to the *Carpentry* percentages than the *Plumbing* or *Electrical* percentages.

Activity 3b Inserting and Copying a Formula with Multiple Absolute Cell References

Part 2 of 4

1. With **2-CCReports** open, insert the following formulas:
   a. Insert a formula in cell B23 that averages the percentages in the range B17:B22.
   b. Copy the formula in cell B23 to cells C23 and D23.
2. Insert a formula that determines the weighted average of training scores by completing the following steps:
   a. Make cell E17 active.
   b. Type the following formula:
      =b24*b17+c24*c17+d24*d17
   c. Press the Enter key.
   d. Copy the formula in cell E17 to the range E18:E22.
   e. With the range E17:E22 selected, click the Decrease Decimal button three times.
3. Save and then print **2-CCReports**.
4. With the worksheet still open, determine the effect on weighted training scores if the weighted values change by completing the following steps:
   a. Make cell B24 active, type 30, and then press the Enter key.
   b. Make cell D24 active, type 40, and then press the Enter key.
5. Save and then print **2-CCReports**.

15		Employee Training			
16	**Name**	**Plumbing**	**Electrical**	**Carpentry**	**Weighted Average**
17	Allesandro	76%	80%	84%	80%
18	Ellington	66%	72%	64%	67%
19	Goodman	90%	88%	94%	91%
20	Huntington	76%	82%	88%	83%
21	Kaplan-Downing	90%	84%	92%	89%
22	Larimore	58%	62%	60%	60%
23	Training Averages	76%	78%	80%	
24	Training Weights	30%	30%	40%	
25					

4a   4b

Check Your Work

Using a Mixed Cell Reference in a Formula

The formula you created in Step 2a in Activity 3a contained a relative cell reference (b3) and an absolute cell reference (b12). A formula can also contain a mixed cell reference. As stated earlier, in a mixed cell reference, either the column remains absolute and the row is relative or the column is relative and the row remains absolute. In Activity 3c, you will insert a number of formulas—two of which will contain mixed cell references. You will insert the formula *=e29*e$26* to calculate withholding tax and *=e29*h$36* to calculate social security tax. The dollar symbol before each row number indicates that the row is an absolute reference.

Activity 3c Determining Payroll Using Formulas with Absolute and Mixed Cell References

Part 3 of 4

1. With **2-CCReports** open, make cell E29 active and then type the following formula that calculates the gross pay, including overtime (press the Enter key after typing each formula):
    =(b29*c29+(b29*b36*d29))
2. Copy the formula in cell E29 to the range E30:E34.
3. Make cell F29 active and then type the following formula that calculates the amount of withholding tax:
    =e29*e$36
4. Copy the formula in cell F29 to the range F30:F34.
5. Make cell G29 active and then type the following formula that calculates the amount of social security tax:
    =e29*h$36
6. Copy the formula in cell G29 to the range G30:G34.
7. Make cell H29 active and then type the following formula that calculates net pay:
    =e29-(f29+g29)
8. Copy the formula in cell H29 to the range H30:H34.
9. Select the range E29:H29 and then click the Accounting Number Format button.
10. Save **2-CCReports**.

 Check Your Work

As you learned in Activity 3c, a formula can contain a mixed cell reference. In Activity 3d, you will create the formula *=$a41*b$40*. In the first cell reference in the formula, *$a41*, the column is absolute and the row is relative. In the second cell reference, *b$40*, the column is relative and the row is absolute. The formula containing the mixed cell reference allows you to fill in the column and row data using only one formula.

Identify an absolute or mixed cell reference by typing a dollar symbol before the column and/or row reference or press the F4 function key to cycle through the various cell references. For example, type *=a41* in a cell, press the F4 function key, and the cell reference changes to *=a41*. Press F4 again and the cell reference changes to *=a$41*. Press F4 a third time and the cell reference changes to *=$a41* and press F4 a fourth time and the cell reference changes back to *=a41*.

1. With **2-CCReports** open, make cell B41 the active cell and then insert a formula
   containing mixed cell references by completing the following steps:
   a. Type =a41 and then press the F4 function key three
      times. (This changes the cell reference to *$A41*.)
   b. Type *b40 and then press the F4 function key
      two times. (This changes the cell reference to
      B$40.)
   c. Make sure the formula displays as =*$A41*B$40*
      and then press the Enter key.

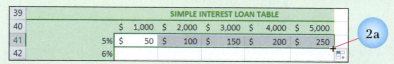

		SIMP
39		
40	$ 1,000	$ 2,0
41	5% =$A41*B$40	
42	6%	

1c

2. Copy the formula to the right by completing the
   following steps:
   a. Make cell B41 active and then use the fill handle to copy the formula to cell F41.

39	SIMPLE INTEREST LOAN TABLE				
40		$ 1,000	$ 2,000	$ 3,000	$ 4,000	$ 5,000
41	5%	$ 50	$ 100	$ 150	$ 200	$ 250
42	6%					

2a

b. With the range B41:F41 selected, use the fill handle to copy the formula to cell F51.

39	SIMPLE INTEREST LOAN TABLE					
40		$ 1,000	$ 2,000	$ 3,000	$ 4,000	$ 5,000
41	5%	$ 50	$ 100	$ 150	$ 200	$ 250
42	6%	$ 60	$ 120	$ 180	$ 240	$ 300
43	7%	$ 70	$ 140	$ 210	$ 280	$ 350
44	8%	$ 80	$ 160	$ 240	$ 320	$ 400
45	9%	$ 90	$ 180	$ 270	$ 360	$ 450
46	10%	$ 100	$ 200	$ 300	$ 400	$ 500
47	11%	$ 110	$ 220	$ 330	$ 440	$ 550
48	12%	$ 120	$ 240	$ 360	$ 480	$ 600
49	13%	$ 130	$ 260	$ 390	$ 520	$ 650
50	14%	$ 140	$ 280	$ 420	$ 560	$ 700
51	15%	$ 150	$ 300	$ 450	$ 600	$ 750

2b

3. Save, print, and then close **2-CCReports**.

 Check Your Work

Chapter Summary

- Type a formula in a cell and the formula displays in the cell and in the Formula
  bar. If cell entries are changed, a formula automatically recalculates the values
  and inserts the result in the cell.

- Write a formula using commonly used operators, such as addition (+),
  subtraction (-), multiplication (*), division (/), percentage (%), and
  exponentiation (^). When writing a formula, begin with the equals sign (=).

- Copy a formula to other cells in a row or column with the Fill button in the
  Editing group on the Home tab or with the fill handle in the bottom right
  corner of the active cell.

- Double-click in a cell containing a formula and the cell references display with a
  colored border and cell shading.

- Another method for writing a formula is to point to specific cells that are part of the formula as the formula is being built.

- Excel uses the same order of operations as algebra and that order can be modified by adding parentheses around certain parts of a formula.

- If Excel detects an error in a formula, a Trace Error button appears and a small dark-green triangle displays in the upper left corner of the cell containing the formula.

- Excel provides different error codes for different formula errors. An error code helps identify an error in a formula by providing information on the specific issue.

- A function operates on an argument, which may consist of a cell reference, a constant, or another function. When a value calculated by a formula is inserted in a cell, this is referred to as *returning the result*.

- Excel performs over 300 functions that are divided into 13 categories.

- The AVERAGE function returns the average (arithmetic mean) of the arguments. The MAX function returns the largest value in a set of values and the MIN function returns the smallest value in a set of values. The COUNT function counts the number of cells containing numbers within the list of arguments. The COUNTA function counts the number of cells containing any data, numerical or alphabetical.

- The NOW function returns the current date and time and the TODAY function returns the current date.

- Turn on the display of formulas in a worksheet with the Show Formulas button in the Formula Auditing group on the Formulas tab or with the keyboard shortcut Ctrl + ` (grave accent).

- A reference identifies a cell or a range of cells in a worksheet and can be relative, absolute, or mixed. Identify an absolute cell reference by inserting a dollar symbol ($) before the column and row. Cycle through the various cell reference options by typing the cell reference and then pressing the F4 function key.

Commands Review

FEATURE	RIBBON TAB, GROUP	BUTTON	KEYBOARD SHORTCUT
cycle through cell references			F4
display formulas	Formulas, Formula Auditing		Ctrl + `
Insert Function dialog box	Formulas, Function Library		Shift + F3
SUM function	Home, Editing OR Formulas, Function Library		Alt + =
update formulas	Formulas, Calculation		F9

Microsoft® Excel®

Formatting a Worksheet

Performance Objectives

Upon successful completion of Chapter 3, you will be able to:

1 Change column widths and row heights

2 Insert rows and columns

3 Delete cells, rows, and columns

4 Clear data in cells

5 Apply formatting to data in cells

6 Apply formatting to selected data using the Mini toolbar

7 Apply a theme and customize the theme font and colors

8 Format numbers

9 Apply formatting at the Format Cells dialog box

10 Repeat the last action

11 Automate formatting with Format Painter

12 Hide and unhide rows and columns

The appearance of a worksheet on screen and how it looks when printed is called the *format*. In Chapter 1, you learned how to apply basic formatting to cells in a worksheet. Additional types of formatting include changing column width and row height; applying character formatting such as bold, italic, and underlining; specifying number formatting; inserting and deleting rows and columns; and applying borders, shading, and patterns to cells. You can also apply formatting to a worksheet with a theme. A theme is a set of formatting choices that include colors and fonts.

 Data Files

Before beginning chapter work, copy the EL1C3 folder to your storage medium and then make EL1C3 the active folder.

 The online course includes additional training and assessment resources.

Tutorial

Adjusting Column Width and Row Height

Changing Column Width

The columns in a worksheet are the same width by default. In some worksheets, column widths may need to be changed to accommodate more or less data. Change column widths using the mouse on column boundary lines or at a dialog box.

Changing Column Width Using Column Boundaries

💡 *Hint* To change the width of all the columns in a worksheet, click the Select All button and then drag a column boundary line to the desired position.

As explained in Chapter 1, column width can be adjusted by dragging the column boundary line or adjusted to the longest entry by double-clicking the boundary line. When the boundary line is being dragged, the column width is shown in a box above the mouse pointer. The number that is shown represents the average number of characters in the standard font that can fit in a cell.

The width of selected adjacent columns can be changed at the same time. To do this, select the columns and then drag one of the column boundary lines within the selected columns. When the boundary line is being dragged, the column width changes for all the selected columns. To select adjacent columns, position the cell pointer on the first column header to be selected (the mouse pointer turns into a black down-pointing arrow), click and hold down the left mouse button, drag the cell pointer into the last column header, and then release the mouse button.

Activity 1a **Changing Column Width Using a Column Boundary Line** **Part 1 of 7**

1. Open **CMProducts** and then save it with the name **3-CMProducts**.
2. Insert a formula in cell D2 that multiplies the price in cell B2 with the number in cell C2. Copy the formula in cell D2 to the range D3:D14.
3. Change the width of column D by completing the following steps:
   a. Position the mouse pointer on the column boundary line in the column header between columns D and E until it turns into a double-headed arrow pointing left and right.
   b. Click and hold down the left mouse button, drag the column boundary line to the right until *Width: 11.00* displays in the box, and then release the mouse button.
4. Make cell D15 active and then insert the sum of the values in the range D2:D14.
5. Change the width of columns A and B by completing the following steps:
   a. Select columns A and B. To do this, position the cell pointer on the column A header, click and hold down the left mouse button, drag the cell pointer into the column B header, and then release the mouse button.
   b. Position the cell pointer on the column boundary line between columns A and B until it turns into a double-headed arrow pointing left and right.

c. Click and hold down the left mouse button, drag the column boundary line to the right until *Width: 10.43* displays in the box, and then release the mouse button.

6. Adjust the width of column C to accommodate the longest entry by double-clicking on the column boundary line between columns C and D.

7. Save **3-CMProducts**.

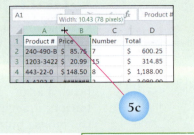

Check Your Work

Changing Column Width at the Column Width Dialog Box

Use the *Column width* measurement box in the Column Width dialog box, shown in Figure 3.1, to specify a column width number. Increase the number to make the column wider and decrease the number to make the column narrower.

Display the Column Width dialog box by clicking the Format button in the Cells group on the Home tab and then clicking *Column Width* at the drop-down list. At the Column Width dialog box, type a measurement number (the number represents the number of characters in the standard font that can fit in the column) and then press the Enter key or click OK.

Format

Quick Steps

Change Column Width

Drag column boundary line.
OR
Double-click column boundary line.
OR
1. Click Format button.
2. Click *Column Width*.
3. Type width.
4. Click OK.

Figure 3.1 Column Width Dialog Box

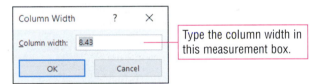

Type the column width in this measurement box.

Activity 1b Changing Column Width at the Column Width Dialog Box .... **Part 2 of 7**

1. With **3-CMProducts** open, change the width of column A by completing the following steps:
   a. Make any cell in column A active.
   b. Click the Format button in the Cells group on the Home tab and then click *Column Width* at the drop-down list.
   c. At the Column Width dialog box, type 12.7 in the *Column width* measurement box.
   d. Click OK to close the dialog box.
2. Make any cell in column B active and then change the width of column B to 12.5 characters by completing steps similar to those in Step 1.
3. Make any cell in column C active and then change the width of column C to 8 characters by completing steps similar to those in Step 1.
4. Save **3-CMProducts**.

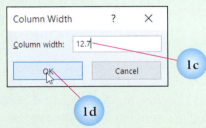

Check Your Work

Changing Row Height

Quick Steps

Change Row Height
Drag row boundary line.
OR
1. Click Format button.
2. Click *Row Height*.
3. Type height.
4. Click OK.

💡 **Hint** To change the height of all the rows in a worksheet, click the Select All button and then drag a row boundary line to the desired position.

💡 **Hint** Excel measures row height in points and column width in characters.

Change row height in much the same manner as column width. Change row height using the mouse on a row boundary line or at the Row Height dialog box. Change row height using a row boundary line by positioning the cell pointer on the boundary line between rows in the row header until it turns into a double-headed arrow pointing up and down, clicking and holding down the left mouse button, dragging up or down until the row is the desired height, and then releasing the mouse button.

Change the height of adjacent rows by selecting the rows and then dragging one of the row boundary lines within the selected rows. As the boundary line is being dragged, the row height changes for all the selected rows.

As a row boundary line is being dragged, the row height displays in a box above the mouse pointer. The number that is shown represents a point measurement. Increase the point size to increase the row height; decrease the point size to decrease the row height.

Another method for changing row height is to use the *Row height* measurement box at the Row Height dialog box, shown in Figure 3.2. Display this dialog box by clicking the Format button in the Cells group on the Home tab and then clicking *Row Height* at the drop-down list.

Figure 3.2 Row Height Dialog Box

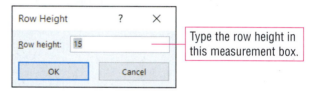

Type the row height in this measurement box.

Activity 1c Changing Row Height

Part 3 of 7

1. With **3-CMProducts** open, change the height of row 1 by completing the following steps:
   a. Position the cell pointer in the row header on the row boundary line between rows 1 and 2 until it turns into a double-headed arrow pointing up and down.
   b. Click and hold down the left mouse button, drag the row boundary line down until *Height: 19.50* displays in the box, and then release the mouse button.

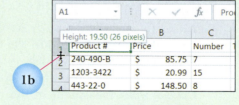

2. Change the height of rows 2 through 14 by completing the following steps:
   a. Select rows 2 through 14. To do this, position the cell pointer on the number *2* in the row header, click and hold down the left mouse button, drag the cell pointer to the number *14* in the row header, and then release the mouse button.
   b. Position the cell pointer on the row boundary line between rows 2 and 3 until it turns into a double-headed arrow pointing up and down.

c. Click and hold down the left mouse button, drag the row boundary line down until *Height: 16.50* displays in the box, and then release the mouse button.

3. Change the height of row 15 by completing the following steps:

   a. Make cell A15 active.

   b. Click the Format button in the Cells group on the Home tab and then click *Row Height* at the drop-down list.

   c. At the Row Height dialog box, type 20 in the *Row height* measurement box and then click OK.

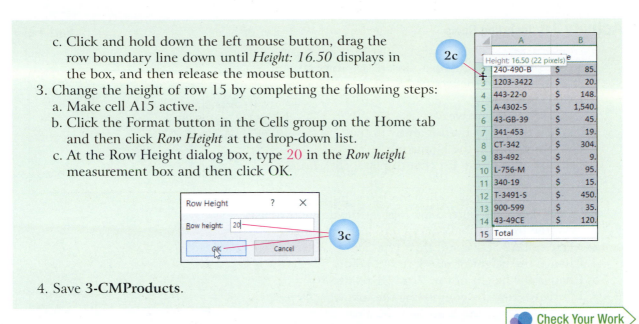

4. Save **3-CMProducts**.

Check Your Work >

Tutorial >
Inserting Columns and Rows

Inserting and Deleting Cells, Rows, and Columns

New data may need to be included in an existing worksheet. For example, a row or several rows of new data may need to be inserted into a worksheet or data may need to be removed from a worksheet.

Inserting Rows

Hint When you insert cells, rows, or columns in a worksheet, all the references affected by the insertion automatically adjust.

 Insert

A row or rows can be inserted in an existing worksheet. Insert a row with the Insert button in the Cells group on the Home tab or with options at the Insert dialog box. By default, a row is inserted above the row containing the active cell. To insert a row in a worksheet, select the row below where the row is to be inserted and then click the Insert button. To insert more than one row, select the number of rows to be inserted in the worksheet and then click the Insert button.

Another method for inserting a row is to make a cell active in the row below where the row is to be inserted, click the Insert button arrow, and then click *Insert Sheet Rows*. A row can also be inserted by clicking the Insert button arrow and then clicking *Insert Cells*. This displays the Insert dialog box, as shown in Figure 3.3. At the Insert dialog box, click *Entire row* and then click OK. This inserts a row above the active cell.

Quick Steps

Insert Row
Click Insert button.
OR
1. Click Insert button arrow.
2. Click *Insert Sheet Rows*.
OR
1. Click Insert button arrow.
2. Click *Insert Cells*.
3. Click *Entire row*.
4. Click OK.

Figure 3.3 Insert Dialog Box

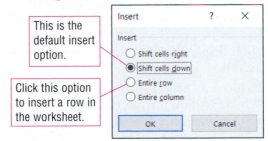

This is the default insert option.

Click this option to insert a row in the worksheet.

1. With **3-CMProducts** open, insert two rows at the beginning of the worksheet by completing the following steps:
    a. Make cell A1 active.
    b. Click the Insert button arrow in the Cells group on the Home tab.
    c. At the drop-down list that displays, click *Insert Sheet Rows*.
    d. With cell A1 active, click the Insert button arrow and then click *Insert Sheet Rows* at the drop-down list.

2. Type the text Capstan Marine Products in cell A1.
3. Make cell A2 active and then type Purchasing Department.
4. Change the height of row 1 to 42 points.
5. Change the height of row 2 to 21 points.
6. Insert two rows by completing the following steps:
    a. Select rows 7 and 8 in the worksheet.
    b. Click the Insert button in the Cells group on the Home tab.

7. Type the following data in the specified cells. For the cells that contain money amounts, you do not need to type the dollar symbols:
    A7: 855-495
    B7: 42.75
    C7: 5
    A8: ST039
    B8: 12.99
    C8: 25
8. Make cell D6 active and then use the fill handle to copy the formula into cells D7 and D8.
9. Save **3-CMProducts**.

> **Check Your Work**

Inserting Columns

Quick Steps
Insert Column
Click Insert button.
OR
1. Click Insert button arrow.
2. Click *Insert Sheet Columns*.
OR
1. Click Insert button arrow.
2. Click *Insert Cells*.
3. Click *Entire column*.
4. Click OK.

Insert columns in a worksheet in much the same way as rows. Insert a column with options from the Insert button drop-down list or with options at the Insert dialog box. By default, a column is inserted immediately to the left of the column containing the active cell. To insert a column in a worksheet, make a cell active in the column immediately to the right of where the new column is to be inserted, click the Insert button arrow, and then click *Insert Sheet Columns* at the drop-down list. To insert more than one column, select the number of columns to be inserted in the worksheet, click the Insert button arrow, and then click *Insert Sheet Columns*.

Another method for inserting a column is to make a cell active in the column immediately to the right of where the new column is to be inserted, click the Insert button arrow, and then click *Insert Cells* at the drop-down list. At the Insert dialog box that displays, click *Entire column*. This inserts a column immediately left of the active cell.

Excel includes an especially helpful and time-saving feature related to inserting columns. When columns are inserted in a worksheet, all the references affected by the insertion automatically adjust.

1. With **3-CMProducts** open, insert a column to the left of column A by completing the following steps:
   a. Click in any cell in column A.
   b. Click the Insert button arrow in the Cells group on the Home tab and then click *Insert Sheet Columns* at the drop-down list.
2. Type the following data in each specified cell:
   A3: Company
   A4: RD Manufacturing
   A8: Smithco, Inc.
   A11: Sunrise Corporation
   A15: Geneva Systems
3. Make cell A1 active and then adjust the width of column A to accommodate the longest entry.
4. Insert another column to the left of column B by completing the following steps:
   a. Make cell B1 active.
   b. Click the Insert button arrow and then click *Insert Cells* at the drop-down list.
   c. At the Insert dialog box, click *Entire column*.
   d. Click OK.
5. Type Date in cell B3 and then press the Enter key.
6. Save **3-CMProducts**.

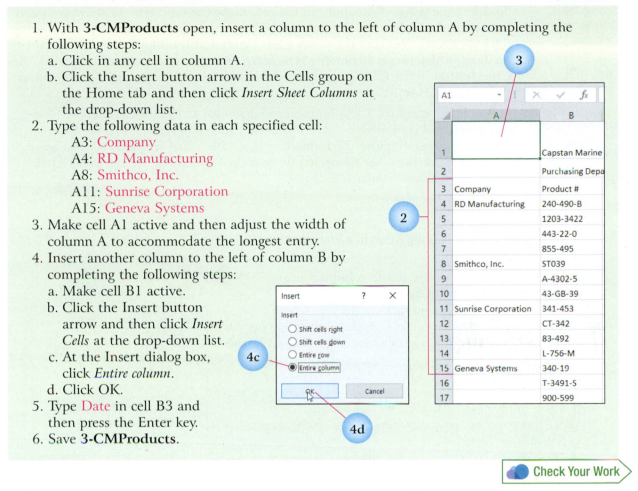

Check Your Work

Tutorial

Deleting Columns
and Rows

 Delete

💡 **Hint** Display the Delete dialog box by positioning the cell pointer in the worksheet, clicking the right mouse button, and then clicking *Delete* at the shortcut menu.

Deleting Cells, Rows, or Columns

Specific cells in a worksheet or rows or columns in a worksheet can be deleted. To delete a row, select it and then click the Delete button in the Cells group on the Home tab. To delete a column, select it and then click the Delete button. Delete a specific cell by making it active, clicking the Delete button arrow, and then clicking *Delete Cells* at the drop-down list. This displays the Delete dialog box, shown in Figure 3.4. At the Delete dialog box, specify what is to be deleted and then click OK. Delete adjacent cells by selecting them and then displaying the Delete dialog box.

Figure 3.4 Delete Dialog Box

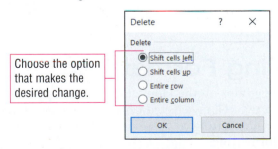

Tutorial

Clearing Cell
Contents and
Formatting

 Clear

Clearing Data in Cells

To delete the cell contents but not the cell, make the cell active or select cells and then press the Delete key. A quick method for clearing the contents of a cell is to right-click in the cell and then click *Clear Contents* at the shortcut menu. Another method for deleting cell contents is to make the cell active or select cells, click the Clear button in the Editing group on the Home tab, and then click *Clear Contents* at the drop-down list.

Use options at the Clear button drop-down list to clear the contents of the cell or selected cells as well as the formatting and comments. Click the *Clear Formats* option to remove the formatting from the cell or selected cells but leave the data. Click the *Clear All* option to clear the contents of the cell or selected cells as well as the formatting.

Quick Steps

Clear Data in Cells
1. Select cells.
2. Press Delete key.
OR
1. Select cells.
2. Click Clear button.
3. Click *Clear Contents*.

Activity 1f Deleting and Clearing Rows in a Worksheet

Part 6 of 7

1. With **3-CMProducts** open, delete column B in the worksheet by completing the following steps:
   a. Click in any cell in column B.
   b. Click the Delete button arrow in the Cells group on the Home tab and then click *Delete Sheet Columns* at the drop-down list.
2. Delete row 5 by completing the following steps:
   a. Select row 5.
   b. Click the Delete button in the Cells group.
3. Clear row contents by completing the following steps:
   a. Select rows 7 and 8.
   b. Click the Clear button in the Editing group on the Home tab and then click *Clear Contents* at the drop-down list.
4. Type the following data in each specified cell:
   A7: Ray Enterprises
   B7: S894-T
   C7: 4.99
   D7: 30
   B8: B-3448
   C8: 25.50
   D8: 12
5. Make cell E6 active and then copy the formula into cells E7 and E8.
6. Save **3-CMProducts**.

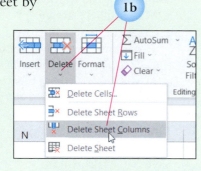

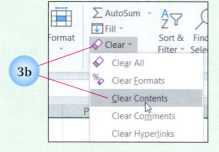

6			855-495	$	42.75	5	$	213.75
7	Ray Enterprises	S894-T		$	4.99	30	
8			B-3448	$	25.50	12	
9			43-GB-39	$	45.00	20	$	900.00

 Check Your Work

Applying Formatting

Many of the groups on the Home tab contain options for applying formatting to text in the active cell or selected cells. Use buttons and options in the Font group to apply font formatting to text and use buttons in the Alignment group to apply alignment formatting.

Figure 3.5 Font Group

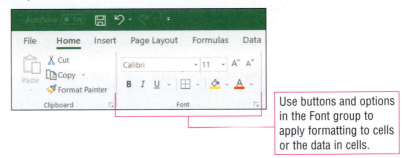

Use buttons and options in the Font group to apply formatting to cells or the data in cells.

☁ Tutorial

Applying Font Formatting

Applying Font Formatting

Apply a variety of formatting to cells in a worksheet with buttons and options in the Font group on the Home tab. Use buttons and options in the Font group, shown in Figure 3.5, to change the font, font size, and font color; to bold, italicize, and underline data in cells; to change the text color; and to apply a border or add fill to cells.

 Bold

 Italic

 Underline

 Increase Font Size

 Decrease Font Size

 Borders

 Fill Color

 Font Color

Use the *Font* option box in the Font group to change the font of the text in a cell and use the *Font Size* option box to specify the size of the text. Apply bold formatting to text in a cell with the Bold button, italic formatting with the Italic button, and underlining with the Underline button, or use the keyboard shortcuts Ctrl + B, Ctrl + I, and Ctrl + U.

Click the Increase Font Size button and the text in the active cell or selected cells increases to the next font size in the *Font Size* option box drop-down gallery. Click the Decrease Font Size button and the text in the active cell or selected cells decreases to the next point size.

Use the Borders button in the Font group to insert a border on any or all sides of the active cell or any or all sides of selected cells. The name of the button changes depending on the most recent border applied to a cell or selected cells. Use the Fill Color button to insert color in the active cell or in selected cells. Change the color of the text within a cell with the Font Color button.

Formatting with the Mini Toolbar

Double-click in a cell and then select the data within it and the Mini toolbar displays above the selected data. The Mini toolbar also displays when right-clicking in a cell. The Mini toolbar contains buttons and options for applying font formatting, such as font, font size, and font color, as well as bold and italic formatting. Click a button or option on the Mini toolbar to apply formatting to selected text.

☁ Tutorial

Applying Alignment Formatting

Applying Alignment Formatting

The alignment of data in cells depends on the type of data entered. Enter words or text combined with numbers in a cell and the text aligns at the left edge of the cell. Enter numbers in a cell and the numbers align at the right of the cell. Use buttons in the Alignment group to align data at the left, center, or right of the cell; align data at the top, center, or bottom of the cell; increase and/or decrease the indent of data in a cell; and change the orientation of data in a cell.

 Merge & Center

As explained in Chapter 1, selected cells can be merged by clicking the Merge & Center button. If cells are merged, the merged cell can be split into the original cells by selecting the cell and then clicking the Merge & Center button. Click the

Merge & Center button arrow and a drop-down list of options displays. Click the *Merge & Center* option to merge all the selected cells and to apply center cell alignment. Click the *Merge Across* option to merge each row of selected cells. For example, if three cells and two rows are selected, clicking the *Merge Across* option will merge the three cells in the first row and merge the three cells in the second row, resulting in two cells. Click the *Merge Cells* option to merge all the selected cells but not apply center cell alignment. Use the last option, *Unmerge Cells*, to split cells that were previously merged. If cells that are selected and then merged contain data, only the data in the upper left cell remains. Data in the other merged cells is deleted.

 Orientation

 Wrap Text

Click the Orientation button in the Alignment group and a drop-down list displays with options for rotating data in a cell. If the data typed in a cell is longer than the cell, it overlaps the next cell to the right. To wrap the data to the next line within the cell, click the Wrap Text button in the Alignment group.

Activity 1g Applying Font and Alignment Formatting

1. With **3-CMProducts** open, make cell B1 active and then click the Wrap Text button in the Alignment group on the Home tab. (This wraps the company name within the cell.)
2. Select the range B1:C2, click the Merge & Center button arrow in the Alignment group on the Home tab, and then click *Merge Across* at the drop-down list.
3. After looking at the merged cells, you decide to merge additional cells and horizontally and vertically center the text in the cells by completing the following steps:
   a. With the range B1:C2 selected, click the Merge & Center button arrow and then click *Unmerge Cells* at the drop-down list.
   b. Select the range A1:E2.
   c. Click the Merge & Center button arrow and then click the *Merge Across* option at the drop-down list.
   d. Click the Middle Align button in the Alignment group and then click the Center button.

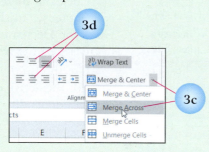

4. Rotate the text in the third row by completing the following steps:
   a. Select the range A3:E3.
   b. Click the Orientation button in the Alignment group and then click *Angle Counterclockwise* at the drop-down list.
   c. After looking at the rotated text, you decide to return the orientation to horizontal by clicking the Undo button on the Quick Access Toolbar.

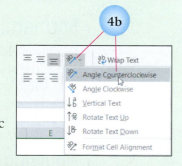

5. Change the font, font size, and font color for the text in specific cells by completing the following steps:
   a. Make cell A1 active.
   b. Click the *Font* option box arrow in the Font group, scroll down the drop-down gallery, and then click *Bookman Old Style*.
   c. Click the *Font Size* option box arrow in the Font group and then click *22* at the drop-down gallery.

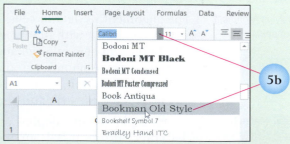

d. Click the Font Color button arrow and then click the *Dark Blue* option (ninth option in the *Standard Colors* section).

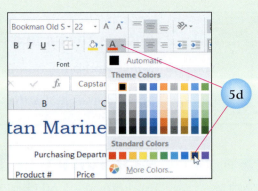

6. Make cell A2 active and then complete steps similar to those in Step 5 to change the font to Bookman Old Style, the font size to 16 points, and the font color to Dark Blue.

7. Select the range A3:E3 and then click the Center button in the Alignment group.

8. With the range A3:E3 still selected, click the Bold button in the Font group and then click the Italic button.

9. Select the range A3:E18 and then change the font to Bookman Old Style.

10. Use the Mini toolbar to apply formatting to selected data by completing the following steps:
    a. Double-click in cell A4.
    b. Select the letters *RD*. (This displays the Mini toolbar above the selected word.)

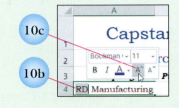

    c. Click the Increase Font Size button on the Mini toolbar.
    d. Double-click in cell A14.
    e. Select the word *Geneva* and then click the Italic button on the Mini toolbar.

11. Adjust columns A through E to accommodate the longest entry in each column. To do this, select columns A through E and then double-click any selected column boundary line.

12. Select the range D4:D17 and then click the Center button in the Alignment group.

13. Add a double-line bottom border to cell A2 by completing the following steps:
    a. Make cell A2 active.
    b. Click the Borders button arrow in the Font group. (The name of this button varies depending on the last option selected.)
    c. Click the *Bottom Double Border* option at the drop-down list.

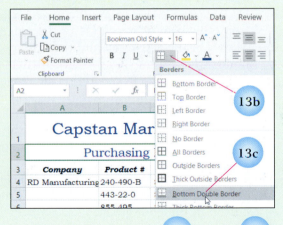

14. Add a single-line bottom border to the range A3:E3 by completing the following steps:
    a. Select the range A3:E3.
    b. Click the Borders button arrow and then click the *Bottom Border* option.

15. Apply a fill color to specific cells by completing the following steps:
    a. Select the range A1:E3.
    b. Click the Fill Color button arrow in the Font group.
    c. Click the *Blue, Accent 5, Lighter 80%* color option (ninth column, second row in the *Theme Colors* section).

16. Select the range C5:C17 and then click the Comma Style button.

17. Select the range E5:E17 and then click the Comma Style button.

18. Save, print, and then close **3-CMProducts**.

Check Your Work

You will open a workbook containing a worksheet with payroll information and then insert text in cells, apply formatting to the cells and cell contents, apply a theme, and then change the theme font and colors.

 Tutorial

Applying and
Modifying Themes

 Themes

💡 **Hint** Apply
a theme to give
your worksheet a
professional look.

Applying a Theme

Excel provides a number of themes that can be used to format text and cells in a worksheet. A theme is a set of formatting choices that includes a color theme (a set of colors), a font theme (a set of heading and body text fonts), and an effects theme (a set of lines and fill effects). To apply a theme, click the Page Layout tab and then click the Themes button in the Themes group. At the drop-down gallery that displays, click the desired theme. Position the mouse pointer over a theme and the live preview feature displays the worksheet with the theme formatting applied.

Activity 2 Applying a Theme   **Part 1 of 1**

1. Open **SBAPayroll** and then save it with the name **3-SBAPayroll**.
2. Make cell G4 active and then insert a formula that calculates the amount of social security tax. (Multiply the gross pay amount in cell E4 with the social security rate in cell H11; you will need to use the mixed cell reference H$11 when writing the formula.)
3. Copy the formula in cell G4 to the range G5:G9.
4. Make H4 the active cell and then insert a formula that calculates the net pay (gross pay minus withholding and social security tax).
5. Copy the formula in cell H4 to the range H5:H9.
6. Increase the height of row 1 to 36.00 points.
7. Make cell A1 active, click the Middle Align button in the Alignment group, click the *Font Size* option box arrow, click *18* at the drop-down gallery, and then click the Bold button.
8. Type Stanton & Barnett Associates in cell A1.
9. Select the range A2:H3 and then click the Bold button in the Font group.
10. Apply a theme and customize the font and colors by completing the following steps:
    a. Make cell A1 active.
    b. Click the Page Layout tab.
    c. Click the Themes button in the Themes group, hover the mouse pointer over individual themes at the drop-down gallery to see how they affect the formatting of the worksheet, and then click *Wisp*.

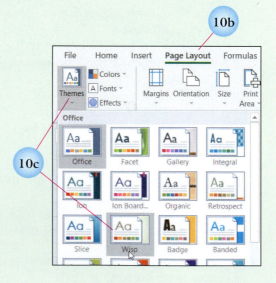

d. Click the Colors button in the Themes group and
then click *Red Orange* at the drop-down gallery.

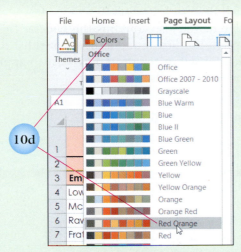

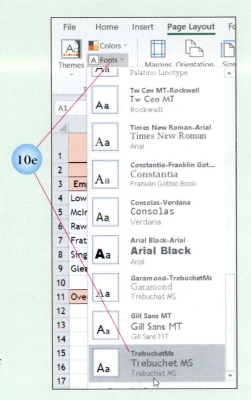

e. Click the Fonts button in the Themes group,
scroll down the drop-down gallery, and then
click *Trebuchet MS*.

11. Select columns A through H and adjust the width of
the columns to accommodate the longest entries.

12. Save, print, and then close **3-SBAPayroll**.

 **Check Your Work**

Activity 3 Format an Invoices Worksheet   2 Parts

You will open a workbook containing an invoice worksheet and apply number
formatting to the numbers in the cells.

Applying Number
Formatting

Formatting Numbers

By default, the numbers in a cell align at the right and decimals and commas do
not appear unless they are typed in the cell. Change the format of numbers with
buttons in the Number group on the Home tab or with options at the Format
Cells dialog box with the Number tab selected.

Formatting Numbers Using Number Group Buttons

The format symbols available for formatting numbers include a percent symbol
(%), comma (,), and dollar symbol ($). For example, type *$45.50* in a cell and
Excel automatically applies the Currency format to the number. Type *45%* in a
cell and Excel automatically applies the Percentage format to the number. The
Number group on the Home tab contains five buttons for formatting numbers in
cells. (These buttons were explained in Chapter 1.)

Specify the formatting for numbers in cells in a worksheet before typing the numbers or format existing numbers in a worksheet. Use the Increase Decimal and Decrease Decimal buttons in the Number group on the Home tab to change the number of digits after the decimal point for existing numbers only.

The Number group on the Home tab also contains the *Number Format* option box. Click the *Number Format* option box arrow and a drop-down list displays common number formats. Click a format at the drop-down list to apply the number formatting to the cell or selected cells.

Activity 3a Formatting Numbers with Buttons in the Number Group   Part 1 of 2

1. Open **RPInvoices** and then save it with the name **3-RPInvoices**.
2. Make the following changes to column widths:
   a. Change the width of column C to 17.00 characters.
   b. Change the width of column D to 10.00 characters.
   c. Change the width of column E to 7.00 characters.
   d. Change the width of column F to 12.00 characters.
3. Select row 1 and then click the Insert button in the Cells group on the Home tab.
4. Change the height of row 1 to 42.00 points.
5. Select the range A1:F1 and then make the following changes:
   a. Click the Merge & Center button in the Alignment group on the Home tab.
   b. With cell A1 active, change the font size to 24 points and the font color to Green, Accent 6, Darker 50% (last column, sixth row in the *Theme Colors* section).

   c. Click the Fill Color button arrow in the Font group and then click *Gray, Accent 3, Lighter 60%* (seventh column, third row in the *Theme Colors* section).
   d. Click the Borders button arrow in the Font group and then click the *Top and Thick Bottom Border* option.
   e. With cell A1 active, type REAL PHOTOGRAPHY and then press the Enter key.
6. Change the height of row 2 to 24.00 points.
7. Select the range A2:F2 and then make the following changes:
   a. Click the Merge & Center button in the Alignment group.
   b. With cell A2 active, change the font size to 18 points.

   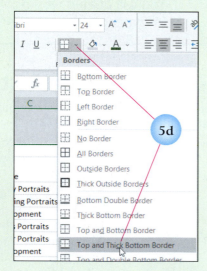

   c. Click the Fill Color button in the Font group. (This will fill the cell with the gray color applied in Step 5c.)
   d. Click the Borders button arrow in the Font group and then click the *Bottom Border* option.
8. Make the following changes to row 3:
   a. Change the height of row 3 to 18.00 points.
   b. Select the range A3:F3, click the Bold button in the Font group, and then click the Center button in the Alignment group.
   c. With the cells still selected, click the Borders button.

9. Make the following number formatting changes:
   a. Select the range E4:E16 and then click the Percent Style button in the Number group on the Home tab.
   b. With the cells still selected, click the Increase Decimal button in the Number group. (The percentages should include one digit after the decimal point.)

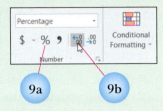

9a   9b

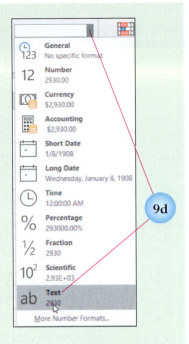

9d

   c. Select the range A4:B16.
   d. Click the *Number Format* option box arrow, scroll down the drop-down list, and then click *Text*.
   e. With the range A4:B16 still selected, click the Center button in the Alignment group.
10. Save **3-RPInvoices**.

Check Your Work

Applying Number Formatting at the Format Cells Dialog Box

In addition to using buttons in the Number group, numbers can be formatted with options at the Format Cells dialog box with the Number tab selected, as shown in Figure 3.6. Display this dialog box by clicking the Number group dialog box launcher or by clicking the *Number Format* option box arrow and then clicking *More Number Formats* at the drop-down list. The left side of the dialog box shows number categories; the default category is *General*. At this setting, no specific formatting is applied to numbers except right alignment in cells. The other number categories are described in Table 3.1.

Figure 3.6 Format Cells Dialog Box with the Number Tab Selected

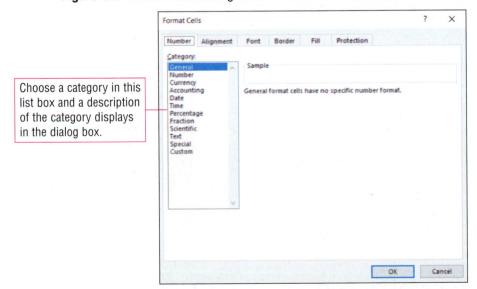

Choose a category in this list box and a description of the category displays in the dialog box.

Table 3.1 Number Formatting Options at the Format Cells Dialog Box

Category	Formatting
Number	Specify the number of digits after the decimal point and whether a "thousand" separator should be used; choose the appearance of negative numbers; right-align numbers in the cell.
Currency	Apply general monetary values; add a dollar symbol as well as commas and decimal points, if needed; right-align numbers in the cell.
Accounting	Line up the currency symbols and decimal points in a column; add a dollar symbol and two digits after the decimal point; right-align numbers in the cell.
Date	Show the date as a date value; specify the type of formatting desired by clicking an option in the *Type* list box; right-align the date in the cell.
Time	Show the time as a time value; specify the type of formatting desired by clicking an option in the *Type* list box; right-align the time in the cell.
Percentage	Multiply the cell value by 100 and show the result with a percent symbol; add a decimal point followed by two digits by default; change the number of digits with the *Decimal places* option; right-align numbers in the cell.
Fraction	Specify how a fraction appears in the cell by clicking an option in the *Type* list box; right-align a fraction in the cell.
Scientific	Use for very large or very small numbers; use the letter *E* to have Excel move the decimal point a specified number of digits.
Text	Treat a number in the cell as text; the number is shown in the cell exactly as typed.
Special	Choose a number type, such as *Zip Code*, *Phone Number*, or *Social Security Number*, in the *Type* option list box; useful for tracking list and database values.
Custom	Specify a numbering type by choosing an option in the *Type* list box.

Activity 3b Formatting Numbers at the Format Cells Dialog Box

Part 2 of 2

1. With **3-RPInvoices** open, make cell F4 active, type the formula =(d4*e4)+d4, and then press the Enter key.
2. Make cell F4 active and then copy the formula to the range F5:F16.
3. Apply the Accounting format by completing the following steps:
   a. Select the range D4:D16.
   b. Click the Number group dialog box launcher.

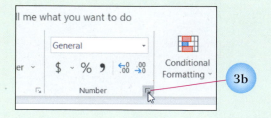

c. At the Format Cells dialog box with the Number tab selected, click *Accounting* in the *Category* list box.

d. Make sure a *2* appears in the *Decimal places* option box and a *$* (dollar symbol) appears in the *Symbol* option box.

e. Click OK.

4. Apply the Accounting format to the range F4:F16 by completing actions similar to those in Step 3.

5. Save, print, and then close **3-RPInvoices**.

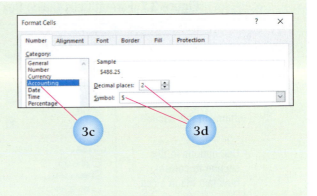

 Check Your Work

---

Activity 4 Format a Company Budget Worksheet   6 Parts

You will open a workbook containing a company budget worksheet and then apply formatting to cells with options at the Format Cells dialog box, use Format Painter to apply formatting, and hide and unhide rows and columns.

 Tutorial

Applying Formatting Using the Format Cells Dialog Box

Applying Formatting Using the Format Cells Dialog Box

As explained earlier in this chapter, the Format Cells dialog box with the Number tab selected provides options for formatting numbers. This dialog box also contains other tabs with options for formatting cells.

Aligning and Indenting Data

Align and indent data in cells using buttons in the Alignment group on the Home tab or using options at the Format Cells dialog box with the Alignment tab selected, as shown in Figure 3.7. Display this dialog box by clicking the Alignment group dialog box launcher.

Use options in the *Orientation* section to rotate data. A portion of the *Orientation* section shows points on an arc. Click a point on the arc to rotate the text along that point. Or type a rotation degree in the *Degrees* measurement box. Type a positive number to rotate selected text from the lower left to the upper right side of the cell. Type a negative number to rotate selected text from the upper left to the lower right side of the cell.

If the data typed in a cell is longer than the cell, it overlaps the next cell to the right. To wrap text to the next line within a cell, insert a check mark in the *Wrap text* check box in the *Text control* section of the dialog box. Insert a check mark in the *Shrink to fit* check box to reduce the size of the text font so all the data fits within the cell. Insert a check mark in the *Merge cells* check box to combine two or more selected cells into a single cell. To enter data on more than one line within a cell, enter the data on the first line and then press Alt + Enter. Pressing Alt + Enter moves the insertion point to the next line within the same cell.

Figure 3.7 Format Cells Dialog Box with the Alignment Tab Selected

Specify horizontal and vertical alignment with options in this section.

Use options in this section to control how text fits in a cell.

Rotate text in a cell by clicking a point on the arc or by entering a number in the *Degrees* measurement box.

Activity 4a **Aligning and Rotating Data in Cells at the Format Cells Dialog Box** Part 1 of 6

1. Open **HBCJobs** and then save it with the name **3-HBCJobs**.
2. Make the following changes to the worksheet:
   a. Insert a new row at the beginning of the worksheet.
   b. Change the height of row 1 to 66.00 points.
   c. Merge and center the range A1:E1.
   d. Type Harris & Briggs in cell A1 and then press Alt + Enter. (This moves the insertion point down to the next line in the same cell.)
   e. Type Construction and then press the Enter key.
   f. With cell A2 active, type Preferred, press Alt + Enter, type Customer, and then press the Enter key.
   g. Change the width of column A to 22.00 characters.
   h. Change the width of column B to 7.00 characters.
   i. Change the widths of columns C, D, and E to 10.00 characters.
3. Make cell E3 active and then type the formula =d3-c3. Copy this formula to the range E4:E11.
4. Change the number formatting for specific cells by completing the following steps:
   a. Select the range C3:E3.
   b. Click the Number group dialog box launcher.
   c. At the Format Cells dialog box with the Number tab selected, click *Accounting* in the *Category* list box.
   d. Click the *Decimal places* measurement box down arrow until *0* displays.
   e. Make sure a *$* (dollar symbol) appears in the *Symbol* option box.
   f. Click OK.

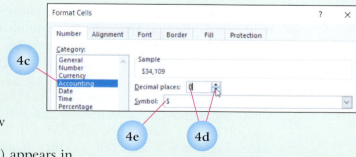

5. Select the range C4:E11, click the Comma Style button in the Number group on the Home tab, and then decrease the number of digits after the decimal point to 0.

6. Change the orientation of data in cells by completing the following steps:
   a. Select the range B2:E2.
   b. Click the Alignment group dialog box launcher.
   c. At the Format Cells dialog box with the Alignment tab selected, select *0* in the *Degrees* measurement box and then type 45.
   d. Click OK.

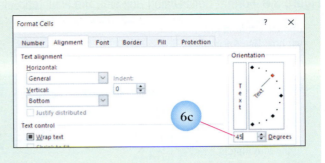

7. Change the vertical alignment of text in cells by completing the following steps:
   a. Select the range A1:E2.
   b. Click the Alignment group dialog box launcher.
   c. At the Format Cells dialog box with the Alignment tab selected, click the *Vertical* option box arrow.
   d. Click *Center* at the drop-down list.
   e. Click OK.

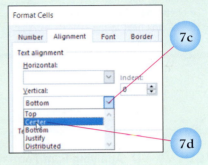

8. Change the horizontal alignment of text in cells by completing the following steps:
   a. Select the range A2:E2.
   b. Click the Alignment group dialog box launcher.
   c. At the Format Cells dialog box with the Alignment tab selected, click the *Horizontal* option box arrow.
   d. Click *Center* at the drop-down list.
   e. Click OK.

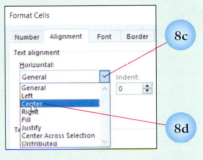

9. Change the horizontal alignment and indent of text in cells by completing the following steps:
   a. Select the range B3:B11.
   b. Click the Alignment group dialog box launcher.
   c. At the Format Cells dialog box with the Alignment tab selected, click the *Horizontal* option box arrow and then click *Right (Indent)* at the drop-down list.
   d. Click the *Indent* measurement box up arrow. (This displays *1*.)
   e. Click OK.

10. Save **3-HBCJobs**.

Changing the Font

As explained earlier in this chapter, the Font group on the Home tab contains buttons and options for applying font formatting to data in cells. The font for data in cells can also be changed with options at the Format Cells dialog box with the Font tab selected, as shown in Figure 3.8. Use options at the Format Cells dialog box with the Font tab selected to change the font, font style, font size, and font color; to change the underlining method; and to add effects such as superscript and subscript. Click the Font group dialog box launcher to display this dialog box.

Figure 3.8 Format Cells Dialog Box with the Font Tab Selected

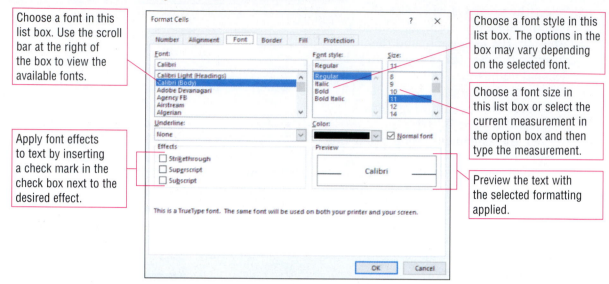

Choose a font in this list box. Use the scroll bar at the right of the box to view the available fonts.

Choose a font style in this list box. The options in the box may vary depending on the selected font.

Choose a font size in this list box or select the current measurement in the option box and then type the measurement.

Apply font effects to text by inserting a check mark in the check box next to the desired effect.

Preview the text with the selected formatting applied.

Activity 4b Applying Font Formatting at the Format Cells Dialog Box

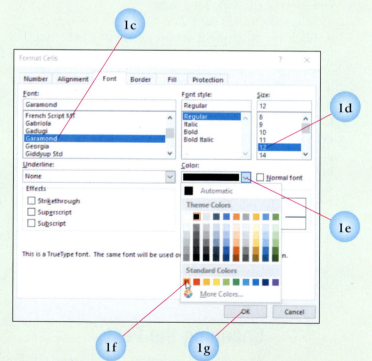

1. With **3-HBCJobs** open, change the font and font color by completing the following steps:
   a. Select the range A1:E11.
   b. Click the Font group dialog box launcher.
   c. At the Format Cells dialog box with the Font tab selected, scroll down the *Font* option list box and then click *Garamond*.
   d. Click *12* in the *Size* list box.
   e. Click the *Color* option box arrow.
   f. At the color palette, click the *Dark Red* color (first option in the *Standard Colors* section).
   g. Click OK to close the dialog box.
2. Make cell A1 active and then change the font size to 24 points and apply bold formatting.
3. Select the range A2:E2 and then apply bold formatting.
4. Save and then print **3-HBCJobs**.

Check Your Work

Tutorial

Adding Borders to Cells

Adding Borders to Cells

The gridlines in a worksheet do not print. As explained earlier in this chapter, use the Borders button in the Font group to add borders to cells that will print. Borders can also be added to cells with options at the Format Cells dialog box with the Border tab selected, as shown in Figure 3.9. Display this dialog box by clicking the Borders button arrow in the Font group and then clicking *More Borders* at the drop-down list.

Quick Steps

Add Borders to Cells
1. Select cells.
2. Click Borders button arrow.
3. Click border.
OR
1. Select cells.
2. Click Borders button arrow.
3. Click *More Borders*.
4. Use options in dialog box to apply border.
5. Click OK.

With options in the *Presets* section, remove borders with the *None* option, add only outside borders with the *Outline* option, and add borders to the insides of selected cells with the *Inside* option. In the *Border* section of the dialog box, specify the side of the cell or selected cells to which the border is to be applied. Choose the line style for the border with options in the *Style* list box. Add color to border lines by clicking the *Color* option box arrow and then clicking a color at the color palette that displays.

Figure 3.9 Format Cells Dialog Box with the Border Tab Selected

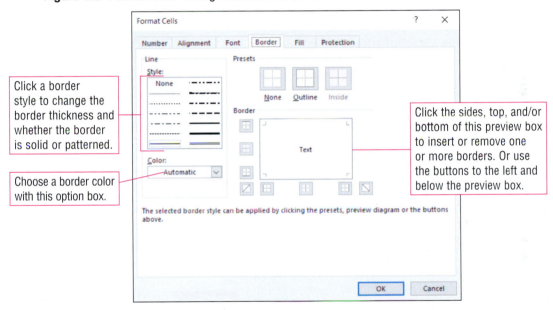

Click a border style to change the border thickness and whether the border is solid or patterned.

Choose a border color with this option box.

Click the sides, top, and/or bottom of this preview box to insert or remove one or more borders. Or use the buttons to the left and below the preview box.

Activity 4c **Adding Borders to Cells at the Format Cells Dialog Box**   **Part 3 of 6**

1. With **3-HBCJobs** open, remove the 45-degree orientation you applied in Activity 4a by completing the following steps:
    a. Select the range B2:E2.
    b. Click the Alignment group dialog box launcher.
    c. At the Format Cells dialog box with the Alignment tab selected, select *45* in the *Degrees* measurement box and then type 0.
    d. Click OK.
2. Change the height of row 2 to 33.00 points.

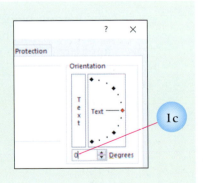

3. Add a thick, dark red border line to cells by completing the following steps:
   a. Select the range A1:E11.
   b. Click the Borders button arrow and then click the *More Borders* option at the drop-down list.
   c. At the Format Cells dialog box with the Border tab selected, click the *Color* option box arrow and then click the *Dark Red* color (first option in the *Standard Colors* section).
   d. Click the thick single-line option in the *Style* list box in the *Line* section (sixth option in the second column).
   e. Click the *Outline* option in the *Presets* section.
   f. Click OK.

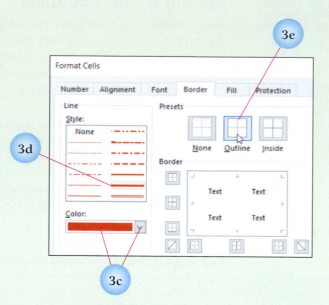

4. Add borders above and below cells by completing the following steps:
   a. Select the range A2:E2.
   b. Click the Borders button arrow and then click *More Borders* at the drop-down list.
   c. At the Format Cells dialog box with the Border tab selected, make sure the color is still Dark Red.
   d. Make sure the thick single-line option is still selected in the *Style* list box in the *Line* section.
   e. Click the top border of the sample cell in the *Border* section of the dialog box.
   f. Click the double-line option in the *Style* list box (last option in the second column).
   g. Click the bottom border of the sample cell in the *Border* section of the dialog box.
   h. Click OK.
5. Save **3-HBCJobs**.

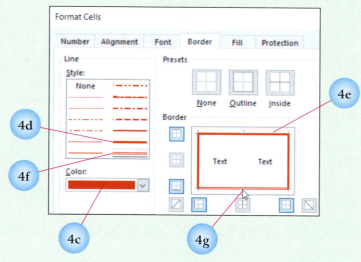

Check Your Work

Adding Fill and Shading to Cells

Adding Fill Color to Cells

To enhance the appearance of cells and data within cells, consider adding fill color. As explained earlier in this chapter, fill color can be added to cells with the Fill Color button in the Font group. Fill color can also be added to cells in a worksheet with options at the Format Cells dialog box with the Fill tab selected, as shown in Figure 3.10. Display the Format Cells dialog box by clicking the Format button in the Cells group and then clicking *Format Cells* at the drop-down list. The dialog box can also be displayed by clicking the Font group, Alignment group, or Number group dialog box launcher. At the Format Cells dialog box, click the Fill tab or right-click in a cell and then click *Format Cells* at the shortcut menu. Choose a fill color for a cell or selected cells by clicking a color choice in the *Background Color* section. To add gradient fill to a cell or selected cells, click the Fill Effects button and then click a style at the Fill Effects dialog box.

Quick Steps

Add Fill and Shading
1. Select cells.
2. Click Fill Color button arrow.
3. Click color.
OR
1. Select cells.
2. Click Format button.
3. Click *Format Cells*.
4. Click Fill tab.
5. Use options in dialog box to apply shading.
6. Click OK.

Repeating the Last Action

To apply the same formatting to other cells in a worksheet, use the Repeat command by pressing the F4 function key or the keyboard shortcut Ctrl + Y. The Repeat command repeats the last action performed.

Using Format Painter and the Repeat Command

Quick Steps

Repeat Last Action
1. Apply formatting.
2. Move to location.
3. Press F4 or Ctrl + Y.

Figure 3.10 Format Cells Dialog Box with the Fill Tab Selected

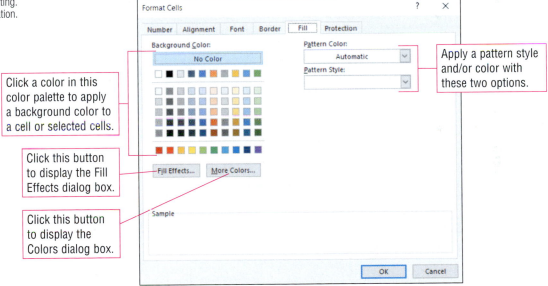

Click a color in this color palette to apply a background color to a cell or selected cells.

Click this button to display the Fill Effects dialog box.

Click this button to display the Colors dialog box.

Apply a pattern style and/or color with these two options.

1. With **3-HBCJobs** open, add a fill color to cell A1 and repeat the formatting by completing the following steps:
   a. Make cell A1 active.
   b. Click the Format button in the Cells group and then click *Format Cells* at the drop-down list.
   c. At the Format Cells dialog box, click the Fill tab.
   d. Click the light gold color in the *Background Color* section (eighth column, second row).

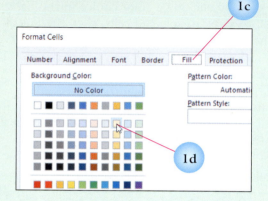

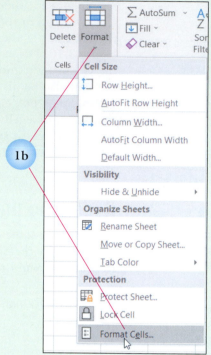

   e. Click OK.
   f. Select the range A2:E2 and then press the F4 function key. (This repeats the application of the light gold fill.)
2. Select row 2, insert a new row, and then change the height of the new row to 12.00 points.
3. Add gradient fill to cells by completing the following steps:
   a. Select the range A2:E2.
   b. Click the Format button in the Cells group and then click *Format Cells* at the drop-down list.
   c. At the Format Cells dialog box, click the Fill tab, if necessary.
   d. Click the Fill Effects button.
   e. At the Fill Effects dialog box, click the *Color 2* option box arrow and then click the *Gold, Accent 4* option (eighth column, first row in the *Theme Colors* section).
   f. Click OK to close the Fill Effects dialog box.
   g. Click OK to close the Format Cells dialog box.
4. Save **3-HBCJobs**.

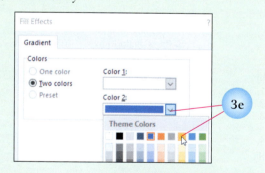

 **Check Your Work**

Formatting with Format Painter

Use the Format Painter button in the Clipboard group on the Home tab to copy formatting to different locations in the worksheet. To use the Format Painter button, make active a cell or selected cells that contain the desired formatting, click the Format Painter button, and then click in the cell or selected cells to which the formatting is to be applied.

Format Painter

Click the Format Painter button and the mouse pointer displays with a paintbrush attached. To apply formatting in a single location, click the Format Painter button. To apply formatting in more than one location, double-click the Format Painter button, select the desired cells, and then click the Format Painter button to turn off the feature.

Activity 4e **Formatting with Format Painter**   Part 5 of 6

1. With **3-HBCJobs** open, select the range A5:E5.
2. Click the Font group dialog box launcher.
3. At the Format Cells dialog box, click the Fill tab.
4. Click the light green color in the *Background Color* section (last column, second row).
5. Click OK to close the dialog box.
6. Use Format Painter to apply the light green color to rows by completing the following steps:
   a. With the range A5:E5 selected, double-click the Format Painter button in the Clipboard group.
   b. Select the range A7:E7.
   c. Select the range A9:E9.
   d. Select the range A11:E11.
   e. Turn off Format Painter by clicking the Format Painter button.
7. Save and then print **3-HBCJobs**.

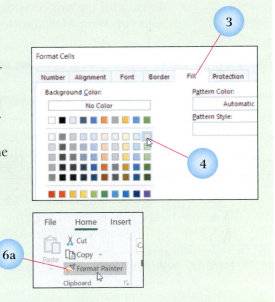

Check Your Work

Tutorial

Hiding and Unhiding Columns and Rows

Quick Steps

Hide Columns
1. Select columns.
2. Click Format button.
3. Point to *Hide & Unhide*.
4. Click *Hide Columns*.

Hide Rows
1. Select rows.
2. Click Format button.
3. Point to *Hide & Unhide*.
4. Click *Hide Rows*.

Hint Set the column width to 0 and the column is hidden. Set the row height to 0 and the row is hidden.

Hiding and Unhiding Columns and Rows

If a worksheet contains columns and/or rows of data that is not being used or should not be viewed, consider hiding the columns and/or rows. To hide columns in a worksheet, select the columns, click the Format button in the Cells group on the Home tab, point to *Hide & Unhide*, and then click *Hide Columns*. To hide rows, select the rows, click the Format button in the Cells group, point to *Hide & Unhide*, and then click *Hide Rows*. To make a hidden column visible, select the columns to the left and the right of the hidden column, click the Format button in the Cells group, point to *Hide & Unhide*, and then click *Unhide Columns*. To make a hidden row visible, select the rows above and below the hidden row, click the Format button in the Cells group, point to *Hide & Unhide*, and then click *Unhide Rows*.

If the first row or column is hidden, use the Go To feature to make it visible. To do this, click the Find & Select button in the Editing group on the Home tab and then click *Go To* at the drop-down list. At the Go To dialog box, type *A1* in the *Reference* text box and then click OK. At the worksheet, click the Format button in the Cells group, point to *Hide & Unhide*, and then click *Unhide Columns* or click *Unhide Rows*.

The mouse can also be used to unhide columns or rows. If a column or row is hidden, the light-gray boundary line in the column or row header displays as a slightly thicker gray line. To unhide a column, position the mouse pointer on the slightly thicker gray line in the column header until the mouse pointer changes into a left-and-right-pointing arrow with a double line in the middle. (Make sure the mouse pointer displays with two lines between the arrows. If a single line displays, only the size of the visible column will change.) Click and hold down the left mouse button, drag to the right until the column displays at the desired width, and then release the mouse button. Unhide a row in a similar manner. Position the mouse pointer on the slightly thicker gray line in the row header until the mouse pointer changes into an up-and-down-pointing arrow with a double line in the middle. Drag down until the row is visible and then release the mouse button. If two or more adjacent columns or rows are hidden, unhide each column or row separately.

Activity 4f Hiding and Unhiding Columns and Rows

1. With **3-HBCJobs** open, hide the row for Linstrom Enterprises and the row for Summit Services by completing the following steps:
   a. Click the row 7 header to select the entire row.
   b. Press and hold down the Ctrl key and then click the row 11 header to select the entire row.
   c. Click the Format button in the Cells group on the Home tab, point to the *Hide & Unhide* option, and then click the *Hide Rows* option at the side menu.

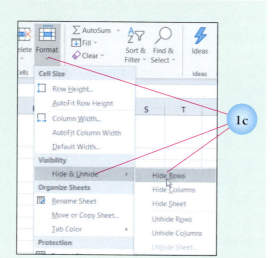

2. Hide the column containing the dollar amounts by completing the following steps:
   a. Click in cell D3 to make it the active cell.
   b. Click the Format button in the Cells group, point to the *Hide & Unhide* option, and then click the *Hide Columns* option at the side menu.
3. Save and then print **3-HBCJobs**.
4. Unhide the rows by completing the following steps:
   a. Select rows 6 through 12.
   b. Click the Format button in the Cells group, point to *Hide & Unhide*, and then click *Unhide Rows*.
   c. Click in cell A4.
5. Unhide column D by completing the following steps:
   a. Position the mouse pointer on the thicker gray line between columns C and E in the column header until the pointer turns into a left-and-right-pointing arrow with a double line in the middle.
   b. Click and hold down the left mouse button, drag to the right until *Width: 9.29* displays in a box above the mouse pointer, and then release the mouse button.

6. Save, print, and then close **3-HBCJobs**.

Check Your Work

Chapter Summary

- Change column width using the mouse on column boundary lines or using options at the Column Width dialog box. Change row height using the mouse on row boundary lines or using options at the Row Height dialog box.

- Insert a row or column in a worksheet with the Insert button in the Cells group on the Home tab or with options at the Insert dialog box.

- Delete a selected row or column or multiple rows or columns by clicking the Delete button in the Cells group.

- Delete a specific cell by clicking the Delete button arrow and then clicking *Delete Cells* at the drop-down list. At the Delete dialog box, specify if only the cell should be deleted or an entire row or column.

- Delete the cell contents by pressing the Delete key or clicking the Clear button in the Editing group on the Home tab and then clicking *Clear Contents*.

- Apply font formatting with buttons and options in the Font group on the Home tab. Use the Mini toolbar to apply font formatting to selected data in a cell.

- Apply alignment formatting with buttons in the Alignment group on the Home tab.

- Use the Themes button in the Themes group on the Page Layout tab to apply a theme to cells in a worksheet, which includes formatting such as color, font, and effects. Use the other buttons in the Themes group to customize the theme.

- Format numbers in cells with buttons in the Number group on the Home tab or with options at the Format Cells dialog box with the Number tab selected.

- Apply formatting to cells in a worksheet with options at the Format Cells dialog box, which includes the Number, Alignment, Font, Border, and Fill tabs.

- Press the F4 function key or the keyboard shortcut Ctrl + Y to repeat the last action performed.

- Use the Format Painter button in the Clipboard group on the Home tab to apply formatting to several locations in a worksheet.

- Hide selected columns or rows in a worksheet by clicking the Format button in the Cells group on the Home tab, pointing to *Hide & Unhide*, and then clicking *Hide Columns* or *Hide Rows*.

- To make a hidden column visible, select the columns to the left and right, click the Format button in the Cells group, point to *Hide & Unhide*, and then click *Unhide Columns*.

- To make a hidden row visible, select the rows above and below, click the Format button in the Cells group, point to *Hide & Unhide*, and then click *Unhide Rows*.

Commands Review

FEATURE	RIBBON TAB, GROUP	BUTTON	KEYBOARD SHORTCUT
bold text	Home, Font	**B**	Ctrl + B
borders	Home, Font		
bottom-align (in row)	Home, Alignment		
center-align (in column)	Home, Alignment		

FEATURE	RIBBON TAB, GROUP	BUTTON	KEYBOARD SHORTCUT
clear cell or cell contents	Home, Editing		
column width	Home, Cells		
decrease font size	Home, Font		
decrease indent	Home, Alignment		
delete cells, rows, or columns	Home, Cells		
fill color	Home, Font		
font	Home, Font		
font color	Home, Font		
font size	Home, Font		
Format Painter	Home, Clipboard		
hide & unhide	Home, Cells		
increase font size	Home, Font		
increase indent	Home, Alignment		
insert cells, rows, or columns	Home, Cells		
italicize text	Home, Font		Ctrl + I
left-align (in column)	Home, Alignment		
merge and center cells	Home, Alignment		
middle-align (in row)	Home, Alignment		
number format	Home, Number		
orientation	Home, Alignment		
repeat last action			F4 or Ctrl + Y
right-align (in column)	Home, Alignment		
row height	Home, Cells		
themes	Page Layout, Themes		
top-align (in row)	Home, Alignment		
underline text	Home, Font		Ctrl + U
wrap text	Home, Alignment		

Microsoft® Excel®

Enhancing a Worksheet

Performance Objectives

Upon successful completion of Chapter 4, you will be able to:

1. Change the margins in a worksheet
2. Center a worksheet horizontally and vertically on the page
3. Change page orientation and paper size
4. Insert and remove page breaks in a worksheet
5. Print column and row titles on multiple pages
6. Scale data
7. Insert a background picture
8. Print gridlines and row and column headings
9. Set and clear a print area
10. Insert headers and footers
11. Customize a print job
12. Complete a spelling check
13. Use the Undo and Redo buttons
14. Find and replace data and cell formatting
15. Sort data
16. Filter data

Excel contains features you can use to enhance and control the formatting of a worksheet. In this chapter, you will learn how to change worksheet margins, orientation, size, and scale; print column and row titles; print gridlines; and center a worksheet horizontally and vertically on the page. You will also learn how to complete a spelling check on the text in a worksheet, find and replace specific data and formatting in a worksheet, and sort and filter data.

 Data Files

Before beginning chapter work, copy the EL1C4 folder to your storage medium and then make EL1C4 the active folder.

The online course includes additional training and assessment resources.

You will format a yearly budget worksheet by inserting formulas; changing margins, page orientation, and paper size; inserting a page break; printing column headings on multiple pages; scaling data to print on one page; inserting a background picture; inserting headers and footers; and identifying a print area and customizing a print job.

 Tutorial

Changing Page
Layout Options

Formatting a Worksheet Page

An Excel worksheet has default page formatting. For example, a worksheet has left and right margins of 0.7 inch and top and bottom margins of 0.75 inch. In addition, a worksheet prints in portrait orientation and its paper size is 8.5 inches by 11 inches. These defaults, along with additional settings, can be changed and/or controlled with options on the Page Layout tab.

Changing Margins

The Page Setup group on the Page Layout tab contains buttons for changing the margins and the page orientation and size. In addition, it contains buttons for establishing a print area, inserting a page break, applying a picture background, and printing titles.

Margins

Quick Steps

Change Worksheet Margins
1. Click Page Layout tab.
2. Click Margins button.
3. Click predesigned margin.

OR
1. Click Page Layout tab.
2. Click Margins button.
3. Click *Custom Margins* at drop-down list.
4. Change top, left, right, and/or bottom measurements.
5. Click OK.

Change the worksheet margins by clicking the Margins button in the Page Setup group on the Page Layout tab. This displays a drop-down list of predesigned margin choices. If one of the predesigned choices applies the desired margins, click that option. To customize the margins, click the *Custom Margins* option at the bottom of the Margins button drop-down list. This displays the Page Setup dialog box with the Margins tab selected, as shown in Figure 4.1.

Figure 4.1 Page Setup Dialog Box with the Margins Tab Selected

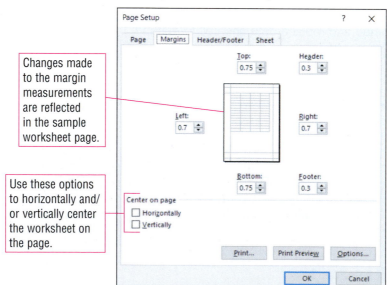

Changes made to the margin measurements are reflected in the sample worksheet page.

Use these options to horizontally and/or vertically center the worksheet on the page.

A worksheet page showing the cells and margins displays in the dialog box. As the top, bottom, left, or right margin measurements are increased or decreased, the sample worksheet page reflects the change. The measurement from the top of the page to the header can be increased or decreased with the *Header* measurement box and the measurement from the footer to the bottom of the page can be changed with the *Footer* measurement box. (Headers and footers are covered later in this chapter.)

Quick Steps

Center Worksheet Horizontally and/or Vertically

1. Click Page Layout tab.
2. Click Margins button.
3. Click *Custom Margins.*
4. Click *Horizontally* option and/or click *Vertically* check box.
5. Click OK.

Centering a Worksheet Horizontally and/or Vertically

By default, a worksheet prints in the upper left corner of the page. A worksheet can be centered on the page by changing the margins. However, an easier method for centering a worksheet is to use the *Horizontally* and/or *Vertically* check boxes that appear in the Page Setup dialog box with the Margins tab selected. Choose one or both of these check boxes and the worksheet page in the preview section displays how the worksheet will print on the page.

Activity 1a   **Changing Margins and Horizontally and Vertically Centering a Worksheet**   **Part 1 of 12**

1. Open **RPBudget** and then save it with the name **4-RPBudget**.
2. Insert the following formulas in the worksheet:
   a. Insert a SUM function in cell N5 that sums the range B5:M5. Copy the formula to the range N6:N10.
   b. Insert a SUM function in cell B11 that sums the range B5:B10. Copy the formula to the range C11:N11.
   c. Insert a SUM function in cell N14 that sums the range B14:M14. Copy the formula to the range N15:N19.
   d. Insert a SUM function in cell B20 that sums the range B14:B19. Copy the formula to the range C20:N20.
   e. Insert a formula in cell B21 that subtracts the total expenses from the income. (Make cell B21 active and then type the formula =b11-b20. Copy this formula to the range C21:N21.
   f. Apply the Accounting format with no digits after the decimal point to cell N5 and cell N14.
3. Click the Page Layout tab.
4. Click the Margins button in the Page Setup group and then click *Custom Margins* at the drop-down list.

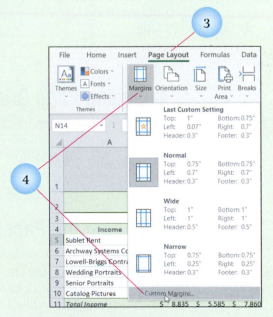

5. At the Page Setup dialog box with the Margins tab selected, click the *Top* measurement box up arrow until *3.5* displays.

6. Click the *Bottom* measurement box up arrow until *1.5* displays.

7. Preview the worksheet by clicking the Print Preview button at the bottom of the Page Setup dialog box. The worksheet appears to be a little low on the page so you decide to horizontally and vertically center it by completing the following steps:

   a. Click the <u>Page Setup</u> hyperlink below the galleries in the *Settings* category in the Print backstage area.

   b. Click the Margins tab at the Page Setup dialog box.

   c. In the *Top* and *Bottom* measurement boxes, change the measurements to *1*.

   d. Click the *Horizontally* check box to insert a check mark.

   e. Click the *Vertically* check box to insert a check mark.

   f. Click OK to close the dialog box.

   g. Look at the preview of the worksheet (notice the entire worksheet is not visible) and then click the Back button to return to the worksheet.

8. Save **4-RPBudget**.

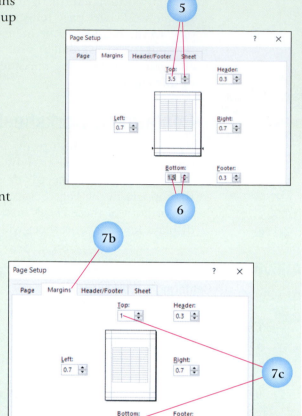

Changing Page Orientation

 Orientation

Click the Orientation button in the Page Setup group and a drop-down list displays with two choices: *Portrait* and *Landscape*. The two choices are represented by sample pages. A sample page that is taller than it is wide shows how the default orientation (*Portrait*) prints data on the page. The other choice, *Landscape*, rotates the data and prints it on a page that is wider than it is tall.

Changing the Paper Size

By default, an Excel worksheet paper size is 8.5 inches by 11 inches. Change this default size by clicking the Size button in the Page Setup group. At the drop-down list that appears, notice that the default setting is *Letter* and that the measurement *8.5″ × 11″* displays below *Letter*. This drop-down list also contains a number of paper sizes, such as *Executive* and *Legal*, and a number of envelope sizes.

 Size

1. With **4-RPBudget** open, click the Orientation button in the Page Setup group on the Page Layout tab and then click *Landscape* at the drop-down list.

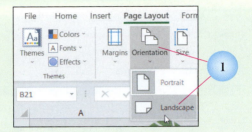

2. Click the Size button in the Page Setup group and then click *Legal* at the drop-down list.

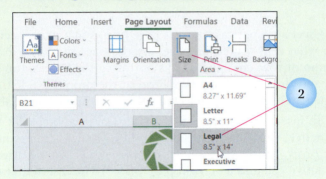

3. Preview the worksheet by clicking the File tab and then clicking the *Print* option. After viewing the worksheet in the Print backstage area, press the Esc key to return to the worksheet.
4. Save **4-RPBudget**.

 Check Your Work

 Tutorial

Using Page Break Preview

Inserting and Removing Page Breaks

The default left and right margins of 0.7 inch allow approximately 7 inches of cells across the page (8.5 inches minus 1.4 inches equals 7.1 inches). If a worksheet contains more than 7 inches of cells across the page, a vertical page break is inserted and the remaining columns are moved to the next page. A page break displays as a dashed line along cell borders. Figure 4.2 shows the page break in **4-RPBudget** when the paper size is set to *Letter*.

A page break also displays horizontally in a worksheet. By default, a worksheet can contain approximately 9.5 inches of cells down the page. This is because the paper size is set by default at 11 inches. With the default top and bottom margins of 0.75 inch, this allows 9.5 inches of cells to print vertically on one page.

Quick Steps

Insert Page Break
1. Select column or row.
2. Click Page Layout tab.
3. Click Breaks button.
4. Click *Insert Page Break*.

Figure 4.2 Page Break

	January	February	March	April	May	June	July	August	September	October	November	December	Total
Income													
Sublet Rent	$ 1,100	$ 1,100	$ 1,100	$ 1,100	$ 1,100	$ 1,100	$ 1,100	$ 1,100	$ 1,100	$ 1,100	$ 1,100	$ 1,100	$ 13,200
Archway Systems Contract	235	235	235	235	235	235	235	235	235	235	235	235	2,820
Lowell-Briggs Contract	750	750	525	525	-	-	450	450	450	575	575	575	5,625
Wedding Portraits	4,500	2,000	1,500	2,800	4,000	8,250	7,500	6,850	4,500	3,500	3,500	7,000	55,900
Senior Portraits	2,250	1,500	4,500	5,000	3,250	1,000	300	500	650	650	400	400	20,400
Catalog Pictures	-	-	-	-	500	500	500	500	500	-	-	-	2,500
Total Income	$ 8,835	$ 5,585	$ 7,860	$ 9,660	$ 9,085	$ 11,085	$ 10,085	$ 9,635	$ 7,435	$ 6,060	$ 5,810	$ 9,310	$ 100,445
Expenses													
Mortgage	$ 4,230	$ 4,230	$ 4,230	$ 4,230	$ 4,230	$ 4,230	$ 4,230	$ 4,230	$ 4,230	$ 4,230	$ 4,230	$ 4,230	$ 50,760
Utilities	625	550	600	425	400	500	650	700	700	500	550	650	6,850
Insurance	375	375	375	375	375	375	375	375	375	375	375	375	4,500
Equipment Purchases	525	1,250	950	3,500	-	-	-	-	-	-	-	-	6,225
Supplies	750	750	1,500	1,250	1,500	2,500	2,250	1,750	950	850	850	2,000	16,900

page break

Breaks

Excel automatically inserts page breaks in a worksheet. To have more control over what cells print on a page, insert a page break. To insert a page break, select a column or row, click the Breaks button in the Page Setup group on the Page Layout tab, and then click *Insert Page Break* at the drop-down list. A page break is inserted immediately left of the selected column or immediately above the selected row.

To insert both horizontal and vertical page breaks at the same time, make a cell active, click the Breaks button in the Page Setup group, and then click *Insert Page Break*. This causes a horizontal page break to be inserted immediately above the active cell and a vertical page break to be inserted at the left of the active cell. To remove a page break, select the column or row or make the cell active, click the Breaks button in the Page Setup group, and then click *Remove Page Break* at the drop-down list.

A page break that is automatically inserted by Excel may not be visible in a worksheet. One way to display the page break is to display the worksheet in the Print backstage area. Return to the worksheet and the page break will display in the worksheet.

Page Break Preview

Hint You can edit a worksheet in Page Break Preview.

Excel provides a page break view that displays worksheet pages and page breaks. To display this view, click the Page Break Preview button in the view area at the right side of the Status bar or click the View tab and then click the Page Break Preview button in the Workbook Views group. This causes the worksheet to display similarly to the worksheet shown in Figure 4.3. The word *Page* along with the page number appears in gray behind the cells in the worksheet. A dashed blue line indicates a page break inserted automatically by Excel and a solid blue line indicates a page break inserted manually.

Normal

Move a page break by positioning the mouse pointer on the blue line, clicking and holding down the left mouse button, dragging the line to the desired location, and then releasing the mouse button. To return to Normal view, click the Normal button in the view area on the Status bar or click the View tab and then click the Normal button in the Workbook Views group.

Figure 4.3 Worksheet in Page Break Preview

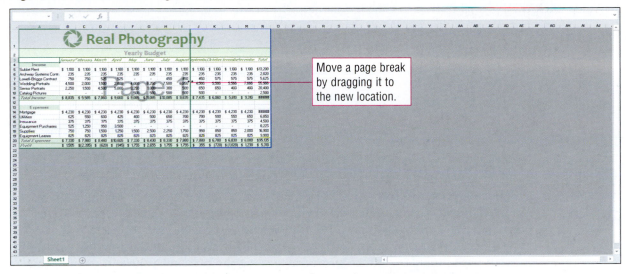

Move a page break by dragging it to the new location.

Activity 1c Inserting a Page Break in a Worksheet

1. With **4-RPBudget** open, click the Size button in the Page Setup group on the Page Layout tab and then click *Letter* at the drop-down list.
2. Click the Margins button and then click *Custom Margins* at the drop-down list.
3. At the Page Setup dialog box with the Margins tab selected, click in the *Horizontally* check box to remove the check mark, click in the *Vertically* check box to remove the check mark, and then click OK to close the dialog box.
4. Insert a page break between columns I and J by completing the following steps:
   a. Select column J.
   b. Click the Breaks button in the Page Setup group and then click *Insert Page Break* at the drop-down list. Click in any cell in column I.
5. View the worksheet in Page Break Preview by completing the following steps:
   a. Click the Page Break Preview button in the view area at the right side of the Status bar.
   b. View the pages and page breaks in the worksheet.
   c. You decide to include the first six months of the year on one page. To do this, position the mouse pointer on the vertical blue line until the mouse pointer displays as a left-and-right-pointing arrow, click and hold down the left mouse button, drag the line left so it is between columns G and H, and then release the mouse button.

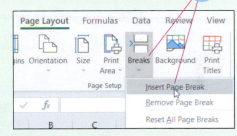

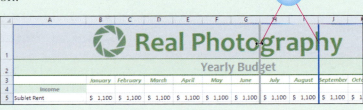

d. Click the Normal button in the view area on the Status bar.

5d

6. Save **4-RPBudget**.

Check Your Work

Tutorial

Printing Column
Headers on
Multiple Pages

 Print Titles

Printing Column and Row Titles on Multiple Pages

The columns and rows in a worksheet usually have titles. For example, in 4-RPBudget, the column titles include *Income, Expenses, January, February, March,* and so on. The row titles include the income and expenses categories. If a worksheet prints on more than one page, having column and/or row titles print on each page provides context for understanding the text and values in columns and rows. To do this, click the Print Titles button in the Page Setup group on the Page Layout tab. This displays the Page Setup dialog box with the Sheet tab selected, as shown in Figure 4.4.

At the Page Setup dialog box with the Sheet tab selected, specify the range of row cells to print on every page in the *Rows to repeat at top* text box. Type a cell range using a colon. For example, to print the range A1:J1 on every page, type *a1:j1* in the *Rows to repeat at top* text box. Type the range of column cells to print on every page in the *Columns to repeat at left* text box. To make rows and columns easy to identify on the printed page, specify that row and/or column headings print on each page.

Quick Steps

Print Column and
Row Titles
1. Click Page Layout
   tab.
2. Click Print Titles
   button.
3. Type row range in
   *Rows to repeat at
   top* option.
4. Type column range
   in *Columns to repeat
   at left* option.
5. Click OK.

Figure 4.4 Page Setup Dialog Box with the Sheet Tab Selected

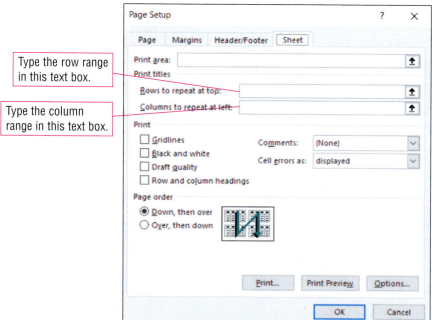

Type the row range in this text box.

Type the column range in this text box.

1. With **4-RPBudget** open, click the Page Layout tab and then click the Print Titles button in the Page Setup group.
2. At the Page Setup dialog box with the Sheet tab selected, click in the *Columns to repeat at left* text box.
3. Type a1:a21.
4. Click OK to close the dialog box.
5. Save and then print **4-RPBudget**.

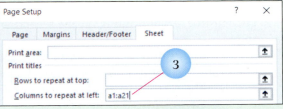

Check Your Work

 Tutorial

Changing Print
Scaling

 Width

Scaling Data

Use buttons in the Scale to Fit group on the Page Layout tab to adjust the printed output by a percentage to fit the number of pages specified. For example, if a worksheet contains too many columns to print on one page, click the *Width* option box arrow in the Scale to Fit group on the Page Layout tab and then click *1 page*. This reduces the size of the data so all the columns appear and print on one page. Manually adjust the scale of a worksheet by clicking the up or down arrows in the *Scale* measurement box or by typing a percentage in the *Scale* measurement box and then pressing the Enter key.

1. With **4-RPBudget** open, display the Page Setup dialog box with the Sheet tab selected.
2. Select and then delete the text in the *Columns to repeat at left* text box and then click the OK button.
3. Click the *Width* option box arrow in the Scale to Fit group on the Page Layout tab and then click the *1 page* option at the drop-down list.

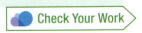

4. Display the Print backstage area, notice that all the cells that contain data appear on one page in the worksheet, and then return to the worksheet.
5. Change the margins by completing the following steps:
   a. Click the Margins button in the Page Setup group and then click *Custom Margins* at the drop-down list.
   b. At the Page Setup dialog box with the Margins tab selected, select the current number in the *Top* measurement box and then type 3.5.
   c. Select the current number in the *Left* measurement box and then type 0.3.
   d. Select the current number in the *Right* measurement box and then type 0.3.
   e. Click OK to close the Page Setup dialog box.
6. Specify that you want row titles to print on each page by completing the following steps:
   a. Click the Print Titles button in the Page Setup group on the Page Layout tab.
   b. Click in the *Rows to repeat at top* text box and then type a3:n3.
   c. Click OK to close the dialog box.

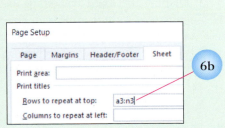

7. Save and then print **4-RPBudget**. (The worksheet prints on two pages and the row titles are repeated on the second page.)
8. At the worksheet, return to the default margins by clicking the Page Layout tab, clicking the Margins button, and then clicking the *Normal* option at the drop-down list.
9. Prevent titles from printing on the second and subsequent pages by completing the following steps:
   a. Click the Print Titles button in the Page Setup group.
   b. At the Page Setup dialog box with the Sheet tab selected, select and then delete the text in the *Rows to repeat at top* text box.
   c. Click OK to close the dialog box.
10. Change the scaling back to the default by completing the following steps:
    a. Click the *Width* option box arrow in the Scale to Fit group and then click *Automatic* at the drop-down list.
    b. Click the *Scale* measurement box up arrow until *100%* displays in the box.
11. Save **4-RPBudget**.

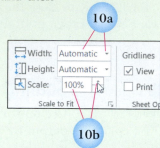

Check Your Work

Inserting a Background Picture

Quick Steps

Insert Background Picture
1. Click Page Layout tab.
2. Click Background button.
3. Navigate to picture and double-click picture.

Background

Insert a picture as a background for a worksheet with the Background button in the Page Setup group on the Page Layout tab. The picture displays only on the screen and does not print. To insert a picture, click the Background button in the Page Setup group and then click the *From a file* option at the Insert Pictures window. At the Sheet Background dialog box, navigate to the folder containing the picture and then double-click the picture. To remove the picture from the worksheet, click the Delete Background button.

Activity 1f Inserting a Background Picture   Part 6 of 12

1. With **4-RPBudget** open, insert a background picture by completing the following steps:
   a. Click the Background button in the Page Setup group on the Page Layout tab.
   b. At the Insert Pictures window, click the *From a file* option.
   c. At the Sheet Background dialog box, navigate to your EL1C4 folder and then double-click **Ship**.
   d. Scroll down the worksheet until the ship is visible.
2. Display the Print backstage area, notice that the picture does not appear in the preview worksheet, and then return to the worksheet.
3. Remove the picture by clicking the Delete Background button in the Page Setup group on the Page Layout tab.
4. Save **4-RPBudget**.

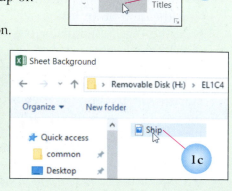

Tutorial

Printing Gridlines
and Row and
Column Headings

**Print Gridlines
and/or Row and
Column Headings**
1. Click Page Layout tab.
2. Click *Print* check
   boxes in *Gridlines* and/
   or *Headings* section in
   Sheet Options group.
OR
1. Click Page Layout tab.
2. Click Sheet Options
   dialog box launcher.
3. Click *Gridlines* and/
   or *Row and column
   headings* check boxes.
4. Click OK.

Printing Gridlines and Row and Column Headings

By default, the gridlines that create the cells in a worksheet and the row numbers and column letters that label the cells do not print. The Sheet Options group on the Page Layout tab contains check boxes for gridlines and headings. The *View* check boxes for gridlines and headings contain check marks. At these settings, gridlines and row and column headings show on the screen but do not print. To print gridlines and headings, insert check marks in the *Print* check boxes. Complex worksheets may be easier to read with the gridlines printed.

The display and printing of gridlines and headings can also be controlled with options at the Page Setup dialog box with the Sheet tab selected. Display this dialog box by clicking the Sheet Options group dialog box launcher. To print gridlines and headings, insert check marks in the check boxes in the *Print* section of the dialog box. The *Print* section contains two additional options: *Black and white* and *Draft quality*. When printing with a color printer, insert a check mark in the *Black and white* check box to print the worksheet in black and white. Insert a check mark in the *Draft quality* option to print a draft of the worksheet. With this option checked, some types of formatting, such as shading and fill, do not print.

Activity 1g **Printing Gridlines and Row and Column Headings** **Part 7 of 12**

1. With **4-RPBudget** open, click in the *Print* check box below *Gridlines* in the Sheet Options group on the Page Layout tab to insert a check mark.
2. Click in the *Print* check box below *Headings* in the Sheet Options group to insert a check mark.
3. Click the Margins button in the Page Setup group and then click *Custom Margins* at the drop-down list.
4. At the Page Setup dialog box with the Margins tab selected, click in the *Horizontally* check box to insert a check mark.
5. Click in the *Vertically* check box to insert a check mark.
6. Click OK to close the dialog box.
7. Save and then print **4-RPBudget**.
8. Click in the *Print* check box below *Headings* in the Sheet Options group to remove the check mark.
9. Click in the *Print* check box below *Gridlines* in the Sheet Options group to remove the check mark.
10. Save **4-RPBudget**.

 **Check Your Work**

 Tutorial

Setting a Print Area

 Print Area

Printing a Specific Area of a Worksheet

Use the Print Area button in the Page Setup group on the Page Layout tab to select and print specific areas of a worksheet. To do this, select the cells to print, click the Print Area button in the Page Setup group, and then click *Set Print Area* at the drop-down list. This inserts a border around the selected cells. Display the Print backstage area and click the Print button to print the cells within the border.

More than one print area can be specified in a worksheet. To do this, select the first group of cells, click the Print Area button in the Page Setup group, and then click *Set Print Area*. Select the next group of cells, click the Print Area button, and then click *Add to Print Area*. Clear a print area by clicking the Print Area button in the Page Setup group and then clicking *Clear Print Area* at the drop-down list.

Each area specified as a print area prints on a separate page. To print nonadjacent print areas on the same page, consider hiding columns and/or rows in the worksheet to bring the areas together.

Activity 1h Printing Specific Areas

1. With **4-RPBudget** open, print the first half of the year's income and expenses by completing the following steps:
   a. Select the range A3:G21.
   b. Click the Print Area button in the Page Setup group on the Page Layout tab and then click *Set Print Area* at the drop-down list.

   c. With the border surrounding the range A3:G21, click the File tab, click the *Print* option, and then click the Print button at the Print backstage area.
   d. Clear the print area by clicking the Print Area button in the Page Setup group and then clicking *Clear Print Area* at the drop-down list.
2. Suppose you want to print the income and expenses information as well as the totals for April. To do this, hide columns and select a print area by completing the following steps:
   a. Select columns B through D.
   b. Click the Home tab.
   c. Click the Format button in the Cells group, point to *Hide & Unhide*, and then click *Hide Columns*.
   d. Click the Page Layout tab.
   e. Select the range A3:E21. (Columns A and E are now adjacent.)
   f. Click the Print Area button in the Page Setup group and then click *Set Print Area* at the drop-down list.
3. Click the File tab, click the *Print* option, and then click the Print button.
4. Clear the print area by ensuring that the range A3:E21 is selected, clicking the Print Area button in the Page Setup group, and then clicking *Clear Print Area* at the drop-down list.
5. Unhide the columns by completing the following steps:
   a. Click the Home tab.
   b. Select columns A and E. (These columns are adjacent.)
   c. Click the Format button in the Cells group, point to *Hide & Unhide*, and then click *Unhide Columns*.
   d. Deselect the text by clicking in any cell containing data in the worksheet.
6. Save **4-RPBudget**.

Check Your Work

Tutorial

Inserting Headers and Footers

Inserting Headers and Footers

Text that prints at the top of each worksheet page is called a *header* and text that prints at the bottom of each worksheet page is called a *footer*. Create a header and/or footer with the Header & Footer button in the Text group on the Insert tab in Page Layout view or with options at the Page Setup dialog box with the Header/Footer tab selected.

Header & Footer

Quick Steps

Insert Header or Footer

1. Click Insert tab.
2. Click the Text button.
3. Click Header & Footer button.
4. Click Header button and then click predesigned header or click Footer button and then click predesigned footer.

OR

1. Click Insert tab.
2. Click the Text button.
3. Click Header & Footer button.
4. Click header or footer elements.

To create a header with the Header & Footer button, click the Insert tab, click the Text button and then click the Header & Footer button. This displays the worksheet in Page Layout view and displays the Header & Footer Tools Design tab. Use buttons on this tab, shown in Figure 4.5, to insert predesigned headers and/or footers or to insert header and footer elements such as page numbers, date, time, path name, and file name. A different header or footer can be created on the first page of the worksheet or one header or footer can be created for even pages and another for odd pages.

At the Print backstage area, preview headers and footers before printing. Click the File tab and then click the *Print* option to display the Print backstage area. A preview of the worksheet is shown at the right side of the backstage area. If the worksheet will print on more than one page, view the different pages by clicking the Next Page button or the Previous Page button. These buttons are below and to the left of the preview worksheet at the Print backstage area. Two buttons display in the bottom right corner of the Print backstage area. Click the Zoom to Page button to zoom in or out of the preview of the worksheet. Click the Show Margins button to display margin guidelines and handles on the preview page. The handles, which appear as black squares, can be used to increase or decrease the page margins and column widths. To do this, position the mouse pointer on the desired handle, click and hold down the left mouse button, drag to the new position, and then release the mouse button.

Figure 4.5 Header & Footer Tools Design Tab

Activity 1i Inserting a Header in a Worksheet

1. With **4-RPBudget** open, create a header by completing the following steps:
   a. Click the Insert tab.
   b. Click the Text button and then click the Header & Footer button.

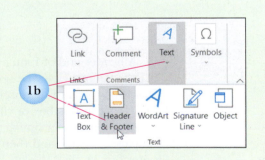

c. Click the Header button at the left side of the Header & Footer Tools Design tab and then click *Page 1, 4-RPBudget* at the drop-down list. (This inserts the page number in the middle header box and the workbook name in the right header box.)

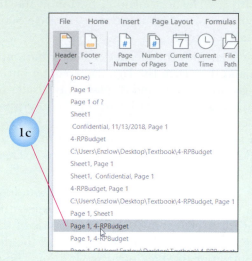

2. Preview the worksheet by completing the following steps:
   a. Click the File tab and then click the *Print* option.
   b. At the Print backstage area, look at the preview worksheet at the right side of the backstage area.
   c. View the next page of the worksheet by clicking the Next Page button below and to the left of the preview worksheet.

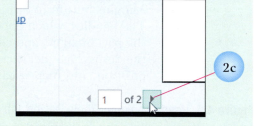

   d. View the first page by clicking the Previous Page button left of the Next Page button.
   e. Click the Zoom to Page button in the lower right corner of the backstage area. (Notice that the preview page has zoomed in on the worksheet.)
   f. Click the Zoom to Page button again.
   g. Click the Show Margins button in the lower right corner of the backstage area. (Notice the guidelines and handles that display on the preview page.)

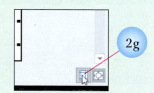

   h. Click the Show Margins button to remove the guidelines and handles.
   i. Click the Back button to return to the worksheet.
3. Save **4-RPBudget**.

Check Your Work

A header and/or footer can also be inserted by working in Page Layout view. In Page Layout view, the text *Add header* appears at the top of the worksheet page. Click this text and the insertion point is positioned in the middle header box. Type the header in this box or click in the left box or right box and then type the header. Create a footer in a similar manner. Scroll down the worksheet until the bottom of the page is visible and then click the text *Add footer*. Type the footer in the center footer box or click the left box or right box and then type the footer.

1. With **4-RPBudget** open, make sure the workbook displays in Page Layout view.
2. Scroll down the worksheet until the text *Add footer* is visible and then click the text.

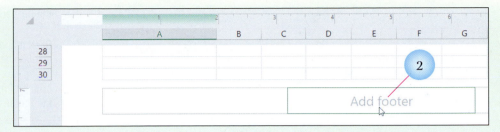

3. Type your first and last names.
4. Click in the left footer box, click the Header & Footer Tools Design tab, and then click the Current Date button in the Header & Footer Elements group. (This inserts a date code. The date will display when you click outside the footer box.)
5. Click in the right footer box and then click the Current Time button in the Header & Footer Elements group. (This inserts the time as a code. The time will display when you click outside the footer box.)
6. View the header and footer at the Print backstage area and then return to the worksheet.
7. Modify the header by completing the following steps:
   a. Scroll to the beginning of the worksheet and display the header text.
   b. Click the page number in the middle header box. (This displays the Header & Footer Tools Design tab, changes the header to a field, and selects the field.)
   c. Press the Delete key to delete the header.
   d. Click the header text in the right header box and then press the Delete key.
   e. With the insertion point positioned in the right header box, insert the page number by clicking the Header & Footer Tools Design tab and then clicking the Page Number button in the Header & Footer Elements group.
   f. Click in the left header box and then click the File Name button in the Header & Footer Elements group.

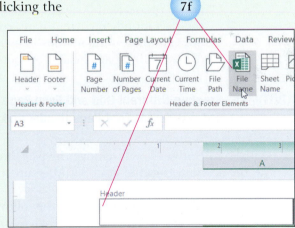

8. Click in any cell in the worksheet that contains data.
9. View the header and footer at the Print backstage area and then return to the worksheet.
10. Save **4-RPBudget**.

Check Your Work ▶

Headers and footers can also be inserted and customized using options at the Page Setup dialog box with the Header/Footer tab selected, as shown in Figure 4.6. Display this dialog box by clicking the Page Layout tab and then clicking the Page Setup group dialog box launcher. At the Page Setup dialog box, click the Header/Footer tab. If a worksheet contains headers or footers, they will appear in the dialog box. Use the check box options in the lower left corner of the dialog box to insert different odd and even page headers and/or footers or to insert a different

Figure 4.6 Page Setup Dialog Box with the Header/Footer Tab Selected

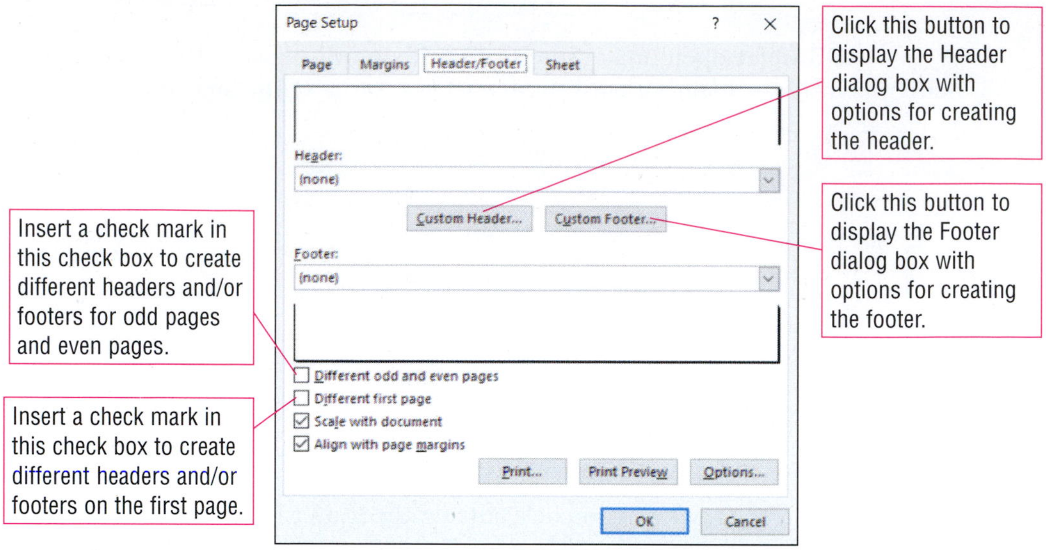

Insert a check mark in this check box to create different headers and/or footers for odd pages and even pages.

Insert a check mark in this check box to create different headers and/or footers on the first page.

Click this button to display the Header dialog box with options for creating the header.

Click this button to display the Footer dialog box with options for creating the footer.

first page header and/or footer. The bottom two check box options are active by default. These defaults scale the header and footer text with the worksheet text and align the header and footer with the page margins.

To create different odd and even page headers, click the *Different odd and even pages* check box to insert a check mark and then click the Custom Header button. This displays the Header dialog box with the Odd Page Header tab selected. Type or insert the odd page header data in the *Left section*, *Center section*, or *Right section* text box and then click the Even Page Header tab. Type or insert the even page header data in the desired section text box and then click OK. Use the buttons above the section boxes to format the header text and insert information such as the page number, current date, current time, file name, worksheet name, and so on. Complete similar steps to create different odd and even page footers and a different first page header or footer.

Activity 1k **Creating Different Odd and Even Page Headers and Footers and a Different First Page Header and Footer**

1. With **4-RPBudget** open, remove the page break by clicking the Page Layout tab, clicking the Breaks button in the Page Setup group, and then clicking *Reset All Page Breaks* at the drop-down list.
2. Change the margins by completing the following steps:
   a. Click the Margins button in the Page Setup group on the Page Layout tab and then click *Custom Margins* at the drop-down list.
   b. At the Page Setup dialog box with the Margins tab selected, select the current number in the *Left* measurement box and then type 3.
   c. Select the current number in the *Right* measurement box and then type 3.
   d. Click OK to close the dialog box.

3. Click the Page Setup group dialog box launcher on the Page Layout tab.

4. At the Page Setup dialog box, click the Header/Footer tab.

5. At the Page Setup dialog box with the Header/Footer tab selected, click the *Different odd and even pages* check box to insert a check mark and then click the Custom Header button.

6. At the Header dialog box with the Odd Page Header tab selected, click the Format Text button (above the *Left section* text box).

7. At the Font dialog box, click *12* in the *Size* list box and then click OK.

8. At the Header dialog box with the file name code (&[File]) highlighted in the *Left section* text box, type Yearly Budget.

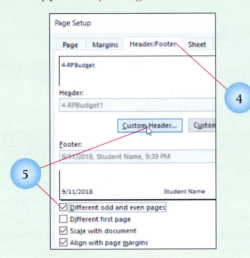

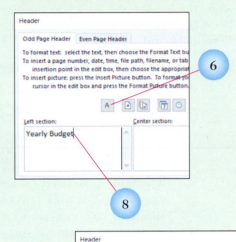

9. Click the Even Page Header tab, click in the *Left section* text box, and then click the Insert Page Number button.

10. Click in the *Right section* text box and then type Yearly Budget.

11. Select the text *Yearly Budget*, click the Format Text button, click *12* in the *Size* list box, and then click OK.

12. Click OK to close the Header dialog box.

13. Click the Custom Footer button. At the Footer dialog box with the Odd Page Footer tab selected, delete the data in the *Left section* text box and then select and delete the data in the *Right section* text box. (The footer should contain only your name.)

14. Select your name, click the Format Text button, click *12* in the *Size* list box, and then click OK.

15. Click the Even Page Footer tab, type your name in the *Center section* text box, select your name, and then change the font size to 12 points.

16. Click OK to close the Footer dialog box and then click OK to close the Page Setup dialog box. (View the header and footer in the Print backstage area and then return to the worksheet.)

17. Click the Page Setup group dialog box launcher on the Page Layout tab.

18. At the Page Setup dialog box, click the Header/Footer tab.

19. Click the *Different odd and even pages* check box to remove the check mark.

20. Click the *Different first page* check box to insert a check mark and then click the Custom Header button.

21. At the Header dialog box with the Header tab selected, click the First Page Header tab.
22. Click in the *Right section* text box and then click the Insert Page Number button.
23. Click OK to close the Header dialog box and then click OK to close the Page Setup dialog box.
24. View the header and footer in the Print backstage area and then return to the worksheet.
25. Save **4-RPBudget**.

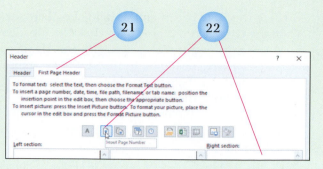

> **Check Your Work** >

Customizing Print Jobs

Use options in the *Settings* category at the Print backstage area to specify what to print. By default, the active worksheet prints. Change this by clicking the first gallery in the *Settings* category. At the drop-down list, specify if the entire workbook is to print (which is useful when a workbook contains multiple worksheets) or only selected cells. With the other galleries in the *Settings* category, specify if pages are to print on one side or both sides of the paper (this depends on the printer) and if they are to be collated. With other options, specify the worksheet orientation, size, and margins and whether the worksheet is to be scaled to fit all the columns or rows on one page.

With the *Pages* text boxes in the *Settings* category, specify the pages of the worksheet to be printed. For example, to print pages 2 and 3 of the active worksheet, type 2 in the *Pages* measurement box in the *Settings* category and then type 3 in the *to* measurement box. Or click the up- and down-pointing arrows to select page numbers.

Activity 1I Printing Specific Pages of a Worksheet   **Part 12 of 12**

1. With **4-RPBudget** open, print the first two pages of the worksheet by completing the following steps:
   a. Click the File tab and then click the *Print* option.
   b. At the Print backstage area, click in the *Pages* measurement box below the first gallery in the *Settings* category and then type 1.
   c. Click in the *to* measurement box in the *Settings* category and then type 2.
   d. Click the Print button.

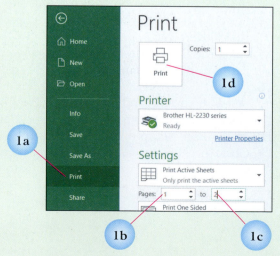

2. Print selected cells by completing the following steps:
   a. Display the worksheet in Normal view.
   b. Select the range A3:D11.
   c. Click the File tab and then click the *Print* option.
   d. At the Print backstage area, select and then delete the number in the *Pages* measurement box and the number in the *to* measurement box. (These are the numbers you inserted in Steps 1b and 1c.)
   e. Click the first gallery in the *Settings* category (displays with *Print Active Sheets*) and then click *Print Selection* at the drop-down list.
   f. Click the Print button.
3. Save and then close **4-RPBudget**.

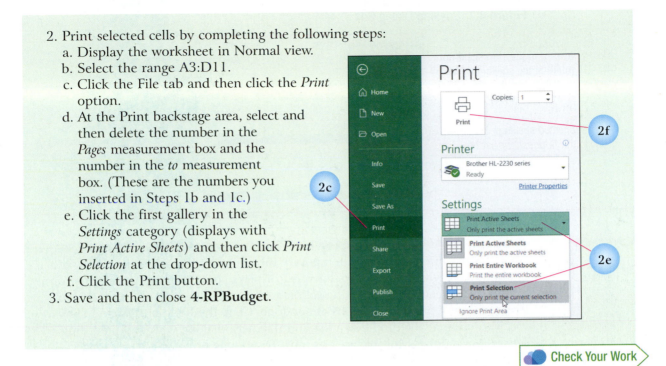

Check Your Work

Activity 2 **Format a Sales and Commissions Worksheet**   **3 Parts**

You will format a sales commission worksheet by inserting a formula, completing a spelling check, and finding and replacing data and cell formatting.

Tutorial

Checking Spelling

 Spelling

Quick Steps

Checking Spelling
1. Click Review tab.
2. Click Spelling button.
3. Replace or ignore selected words.

Checking Spelling

Excel provides a spelling check feature that verifies the spelling of text in a worksheet. The spelling check uses an electronic dictionary to identify misspelled words and suggest alternatives. Before checking the spelling in a worksheet, make the first cell active. The spelling check reviews the worksheet from the active cell to the last cell in the worksheet that contains data.

To use the spelling check, click the Review tab and then click the Spelling button in the Proofing group. Figure 4.7 shows the Spelling dialog box. At this dialog box, tell Excel to ignore a word or to replace a misspelled word with a word from the *Suggestions* list box using one of the available buttons.

Tutorial

Using Undo and Redo

 Undo

 Redo

Using Undo and Redo

Excel includes an Undo button on the Quick Access Toolbar that reverses certain commands or deletes the last data typed in a cell. For example, apply formatting to cells in a worksheet and then click the Undo button on the Quick Access Toolbar and the formatting is removed. To reapply the formatting, click the Redo button on the Quick Access Toolbar.

Figure 4.7 Spelling Dialog Box

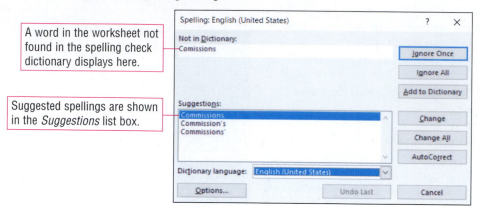

A word in the worksheet not found in the spelling check dictionary displays here.

Suggested spellings are shown in the *Suggestions* list box.

💡**Hint** Ctrl + Z is the keyboard shortcut to undo a command and Ctrl + Y is the keyboard shortcut to redo a command.

Excel maintains actions in temporary memory. To undo an action, click the Undo button arrow and a drop-down list displays containing the actions performed on the worksheet. Click a specific action at the drop-down list and that action along with any preceding actions are undone. Click the Redo button and click a specific action at the drop-down list and that action along with any preceding actions are redone. Multiple actions must be undone or redone in sequence.

Activity 2a Spell Checking and Formatting a Worksheet

Part 1 of 3

1. Open **MRSales** and then save it with the name **4-MRSales**.
2. Complete a spelling check on the worksheet by completing the following steps:
   a. If necessary, make cell A1 active.
   b. Click the Review tab.
   c. Click the Spelling button in the Proofing group.
   d. Click the Change button as needed to correct misspelled words in the worksheet. (When the spelling check stops at the proper names *Pirozzi* and *Yonemoto*, click the Ignore All button.)
   e. At the message stating the spelling check is complete, click OK.
3. Insert a formula and then copy the formula without the formatting by completing the following steps:
   a. Make cell G4 active and then insert a formula that multiplies the sale price by the commission percentage.
   b. Copy the formula to the range G5:G26.
   c. Some of the cells contain shading that you do not want removed, so click the Auto Fill Options button at the bottom right of the selected cells and then click the *Fill Without Formatting* option at the drop-down list.

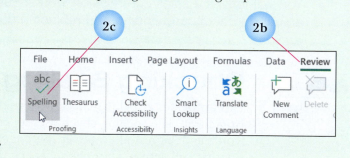

4. Make cell G27 active and then insert the sum of the range G4:G26.
5. Apply the Accounting format with no digits after the decimal point to cell G4 and cell G27.

6. Apply a theme by clicking the Page Layout tab, clicking the Themes button, and then clicking *Ion* at the drop-down gallery.
7. After looking at the worksheet with the Ion theme applied, you decide that you want to return to the original formatting. To do this, click the Undo button on the Quick Access Toolbar.

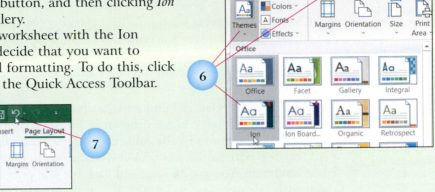

8. Save **4-MRSales**.

Check Your Work

Tutorial
Finding Data

Tutorial
Replacing Data

Tutorial
Replacing Formatting

Finding and Replacing Data and Cell Formatting

Use Excel's find feature to look for specific data and either replace it with nothing or replace it with other data. This feature is particularly helpful for finding data quickly in a large worksheet. Excel also includes a find and replace feature. Use this feature to look for specific data in a worksheet and replace it with other data.

To find specific data in a worksheet, click the Find & Select button in the Editing group on the Home tab and then click *Find* at the drop-down list. This displays the Find and Replace dialog box with the Find tab selected, as shown in Figure 4.8. Type the find data in the *Find what* text box and then click the Find Next button. Continue clicking the Find Next button to move to the next occurrence of the data. If the Find and Replace dialog box blocks the view of the worksheet, use the mouse pointer on the title bar to drag the dialog box to a different location.

To find specific data in a worksheet and replace it with other data, click the Find & Select button in the Editing group on the Home tab and then click *Replace* at the drop-down list. This displays the Find and Replace dialog box with the

Quick Steps

Find Data
1. Click Find & Select button.
2. Click *Find*.
3. Type data in *Find what* text box.
4. Click Find Next button.

Find & Select

Figure 4.8 Find and Replace Dialog Box with the Find Tab Selected

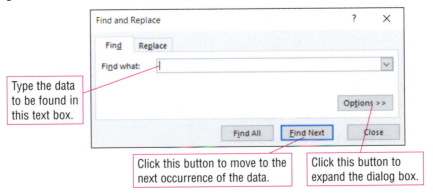

Type the data to be found in this text box.

Click this button to move to the next occurrence of the data.

Click this button to expand the dialog box.

Replace tab selected, as shown in Figure 4.9. Enter the find data in the *Find what* text box. Press the Tab key or click in the *Replace with* text box and then enter the replace data in the *Replace with* text box.

Click the Find Next button to find the next occurrence of the data. Click the Replace button to replace the data and find the next occurrence. To replace all the occurrences of the data in the *Find what* text box with the data in the *Replace with* text box, click the Replace All button. Click the Close button to close the Replace dialog box.

Display additional find and replace options by clicking the Options button. This expands the dialog box, as shown in Figure 4.10. By default, Excel will look for any data that contains the same characters as the data entered in the *Find what* text box without concern for the characters before or after the entered data. For example, in Activity 2b, you will look for sale prices of $450,000 and replace them with sale prices of $475,000. If you do not specify that you want to find only cells that contain *450000*, Excel will stop at any cell containing *450000*. For example, Excel will stop at a cell containing *$1,450,000* and a cell containing *$2,450,000*. To specify that the only data to be contained in the cell is what is entered in the *Find what* text box, click the Options button to expand the dialog box and then insert a check mark in the *Match entire cell contents* check box.

If the *Match case* option is active (contains a check mark), Excel will look for only that data that matches the case of the data entered in the *Find what* text box. Remove the check mark from this check box and Excel will find the data entered in the *Find what* text box in any case. By default, Excel will search in the current worksheet. If the workbook contains more than one worksheet, change the *Within* option to *Workbook*. By default, Excel searches by rows in a worksheet. This can be changed to by columns with the *Search* option.

Figure 4.9 Find and Replace Dialog Box with the Replace Tab Selected

Figure 4.10 Expanded Find and Replace Dialog Box

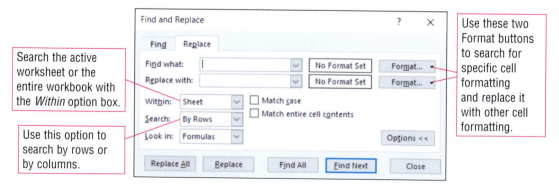

1. With **4-MRSales** open, find all occurrences of *Land* in the worksheet and replace them with *Acreage* by completing the following steps:

   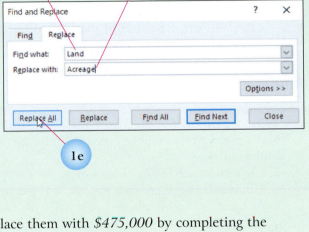

   a. Click the Find & Select button in the Editing group on the Home tab and then click *Replace* at the drop-down list.
   b. At the Find and Replace dialog box with the Replace tab selected, type *Land* in the *Find what* text box.
   c. Press the Tab key. (This moves the insertion point to the *Replace with* text box.)
   d. Type *Acreage*.
   e. Click the Replace All button.
   f. At the message stating that four replacements were made, click OK.
   g. Click the Close button to close the Find and Replace dialog box.

2. Find all occurrences of *$450,000* and replace them with *$475,000* by completing the following steps:

   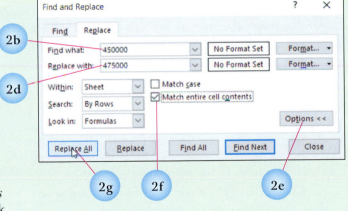

   a. Click the Find & Select button in the Editing group and then click *Replace* at the drop-down list.
   b. At the Find and Replace dialog box with the Replace tab selected, select any text in the *Find what* text box and then type *450000*.
   c. Press the Tab key.
   d. Type *475000*.
   e. Click the Options button to display additional options. (If additional options are already visible, skip this step.)
   f. Click the *Match entire cell contents* check box to insert a check mark.
   g. Click the Replace All button.
   h. At the message stating that two replacements were made, click OK.
   i. At the Find and Replace dialog box, click the *Match entire cell contents* check box to remove the check mark.
   j. Click the Close button to close the Find and Replace dialog box.

3. Save **4-MRSales**.

Check Your Work

Use the Format buttons at the expanded Find and Replace dialog box (see Figure 4.10 (on page 100)) to search for specific cell formatting and replace it with other formatting. Click the Format button arrow and a drop-down list displays. Click the *Format* option and the Find Format dialog box displays with the Number, Alignment, Font, Border, Fill, and Protection tabs. Specify formatting at this dialog box. Click the *Choose Format From Cell* option from the Format button drop-down list or click the Choose Format From Cell button in the Find Format dialog box and the mouse pointer displays with a pointer tool attached. Click in the cell containing the desired formatting and the formatting displays in the *Preview* box left of the Format button. Click the *Clear Find Format* option at the Find button drop-down list and any formatting in the *Preview* box is removed.

Activity 2c Finding and Replacing Cell Formatting

Part 3 of 3

1. With **4-MRSales** open, search for a light-turquoise fill color and replace it with a light-green fill color by completing the following steps:

   a. Click the Find & Select button in the Editing group on the Home tab and then click *Replace* at the drop-down list.

   b. At the Find and Replace dialog box with the Replace tab selected, make sure the dialog box is expanded. (If not, click the Options button.)

   c. Select and then delete any text in the *Find what* text box.

   d. Select and then delete any text in the *Replace with* text box.

   e. Make sure the boxes immediately before the two Format buttons display with the text *No Format Set*. (If not, click the Format button arrow and then click the *Clear Find Format* or *Clear Replace Format* option at the drop-down list. Do this for each Format button.)

   f. Click the top Format button.

   g. At the Find Format dialog box, click the Fill tab.

   h. Click the More Colors button.

   i. At the Colors dialog box with the Standard tab selected, click the light-turquoise color, as shown at the right.

   j. Click OK to close the Colors dialog box.

   k. Click OK to close the Find Format dialog box.

   l. Click the bottom Format button.

   m. At the Replace Format dialog box with the Fill tab selected, click the light-green color (last column, second row), as shown at the right.

   n. Click OK to close the dialog box.

   o. At the Find and Replace dialog box, click the Replace All button.

   p. At the message stating that 10 replacements were made, click OK.

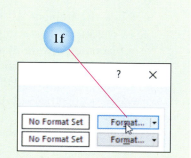

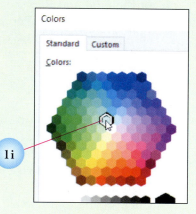

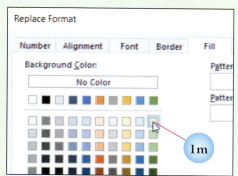

2. Search for a light-gray fill color and replace it with a light-yellow fill color by completing the following steps:
   a. At the Find and Replace dialog box, click the top Format button.
   b. At the Find Format dialog box with the Fill tab selected, click the light-gray color (fourth column, second row), as shown at the right.
   c. Click OK to close the Find Format dialog box.
   d. Click the bottom Format button.
   e. At the Replace Format dialog box with the Fill tab selected, click the yellow color (eighth column, second row), as shown below and to the right.
   f. Click OK to close the dialog box.
   g. At the Find and Replace dialog box, click the Replace All button.
   h. At the message stating that 78 replacements were made, click OK.

3. Search for 11-point Calibri formatting and replace it with 10-point Arial formatting by completing the following steps:
   a. With the Find and Replace dialog box open, clear formatting from the top Format button by clicking the top Format button arrow and then clicking the *Clear Find Format* option at the drop-down list.
   b. Clear formatting from the bottom Format button by clicking the bottom Format button arrow and then clicking *Clear Replace Format*.
   c. Click the top Format button.
   d. At the Find Format dialog box, click the Font tab.
   e. Scroll down the *Font* list box and then click *Calibri*.
   f. Click *11* in the *Size* list box.
   g. Click OK to close the dialog box.
   h. Click the bottom Format button.
   i. At the Replace Format dialog box with the Font tab selected, scroll down the *Font* list box and then click *Arial*.
   j. Click *10* in the *Size* list box.
   k. Click OK to close the dialog box.
   l. At the Find and Replace dialog box, click the Replace All button.
   m. At the message stating that 174 replacements were made, click OK.
   n. At the Find and Replace dialog box, clear formatting from both Format buttons.
   o. Click the Close button to close the Find and Replace dialog box.

4. Save, print, and then close **4-MRSales**.

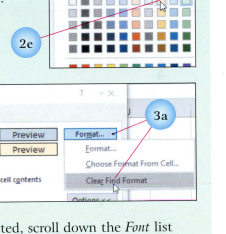

Check Your Work

Activity 3 Insert a Formula and Sort and Filter Data in a Billing Worksheet

4 Parts

You will insert a formula in a weekly billing worksheet and then sort and filter specific data in the worksheet.

Tutorial

Sorting Data

Sorting Data

Excel is primarily a spreadsheet program but it also includes some basic database functions, such as sorting data in alphabetic or numeric order. To sort data in a worksheet, use the Sort & Filter button in the Editing group on the Home tab.

 Sort & Filter

To sort data in a worksheet, select the cells containing the data to be sorted, click the Sort & Filter button in the Editing group and then click the option representing the desired sort. The sort option names vary depending on the data in selected cells. For example, if the first column of selected cells contains text, the sort options at the drop-down list are *Sort A to Z* and *Sort Z to A*. If the selected cells contain dates, the sort options at the drop-down list are *Sort Oldest to Newest* and *Sort Newest to Oldest*. If the cells contain numbers or values, the sort options are *Sort Smallest to Largest* and *Sort Largest to Smallest*. If more than one column is selected in a worksheet, Excel sorts the data in the first selected column.

Quick Steps

Sort Data
1. Select cells.
2. Click Sort & Filter button.
3. Click sort option at drop-down list.

Activity 3a Sorting Data

Part 1 of 4

1. Open **APTBilling** and then save it with the name **4-APTBilling**.
2. Insert a formula in cell F4 that multiplies the rate by the hours. Copy the formula to the range F5:F29.
3. Sort the data in the first column in descending order by completing the following steps:
   a. Make cell A4 active.
   b. Click the Sort & Filter button in the Editing group on the Home tab.
   c. Click the *Sort Largest to Smallest* option at the drop-down list.
4. Sort in ascending order by clicking the Sort & Filter button and then clicking *Sort Smallest to Largest* at the drop-down list.
5. Save **4-APTBilling**.

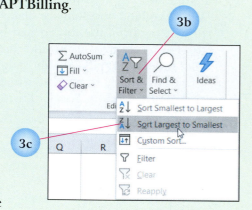

Check Your Work

Completing a Custom Sort

Quick Steps

Complete Custom Sort
1. Select cells.
2. Click Sort & Filter button.
3. Click *Custom Sort* at drop-down list.
4. Specify options at Sort dialog box.
5. Click OK.

To sort data in a column other than the first column, use options at the Sort dialog box. Select one column in a worksheet, click the Sort & Filter button, and then click the desired sort option; only the data in that column is sorted. If this data is related to data to the left or right that relationship is broken. For example, after sorting the range C4:C29 in 4-APTBilling, the client number, treatment, hours, and total no longer match the date.

Use options at the Sort dialog box to sort data and maintain the relationship among all the cells. To sort using the Sort dialog box, select the cells to be sorted, click the Sort & Filter button, and then click *Custom Sort*. This displays the Sort dialog box, shown in Figure 4.11.

Figure 4.11 Sort Dialog Box

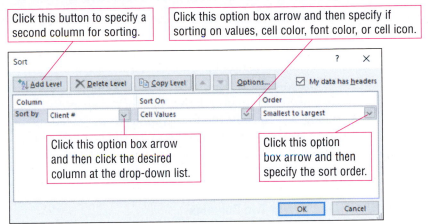

Click this button to specify a second column for sorting.

Click this option box arrow and then specify if sorting on values, cell color, font color, or cell icon.

Click this option box arrow and then click the desired column at the drop-down list.

Click this option box arrow and then specify the sort order.

The data that displays in the *Sort by* option box will vary depending on what is selected. Generally, the data that displays is the title of the first column of selected cells. If the selected cells do not have a title, the data may display as *Column A*. Use this option to specify what column is to be sorted. Using the Sort dialog box to sort data in a column maintains the relationship among the data.

Activity 3b Sorting Data Using the Sort Dialog Box   Part 2 of 4

1. With **4-APTBilling** open, sort the rates in the range E4:E29 in descending order and maintain the relationship to the other data by completing the following steps:
   a. Select the range A3:F29.
   b. Click the Sort & Filter button and then click *Custom Sort*.
   c. At the Sort dialog box, click the *Sort by* option box arrow and then click *Rate* at the drop-down list.
   d. Click the *Order* option box arrow and then click *Largest to Smallest* at the drop-down list.

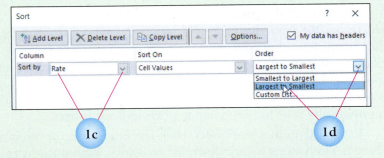

   e. Click OK to close the Sort dialog box.
   f. Deselect the cells.
2. Sort the dates in ascending order (oldest to newest) by completing steps similar to those in Step 1.
3. Save and then print **4-APTBilling**.

Check Your Work

Sorting More Than One Column

When sorting data in cells, data in more than one column can be sorted. For example, in Activity 3c, you will sort the dates from oldest to newest and the client numbers from lowest to highest. In this sort, the dates are sorted first and then the client numbers are sorted in ascending order within the same date.

To sort data in more than one column, select all the columns in the worksheet that need to remain relative and then display the Sort dialog box. At the Sort dialog box, specify the first column to be sorted in the *Sort by* option box, click the *Add Level* button, and then specify the second column in the first *Then by* option box. To sort multiple columns, add additional *Then by* option boxes by clicking the *Add Level* button.

Activity 3c **Sorting Data in Two Columns**   **Part 3 of 4**

1. With **4-APTBilling** open, select the range A3:F29.
2. Click the Sort & Filter button and then click *Custom Sort*.
3. At the Sort dialog box, click the *Sort by* option box arrow and then click *Date* at the drop-down list. (Skip this step if *Date* already displays in the *Sort by* option box.)
4. Make sure *Oldest to Newest* displays in the *Order* option box.
5. Click the Add Level button.
6. Click the *Then by* option box arrow and then click *Client #* at the drop-down list.
7. Click OK to close the dialog box.
8. Deselect the cells.
9. Save and then print **4-APTBilling**.

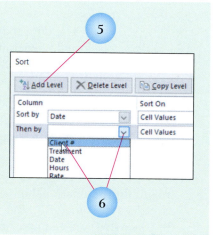

> Check Your Work

> Tutorial

Filtering Data

Ǭuick Steps

Filter List
1. Select cells.
2. Click Sort & Filter button.
3. Click *Filter* at drop-down list.
4. Click filter arrow in heading to filter.
5. Click option at drop-down list.

Filtering Data

A restriction called a *filter* can be placed temporarily on data in a worksheet to isolate specific data. To turn on filtering, make a cell containing data active, click the Sort & Filter button in the Editing group on the Home tab, and then click *Filter* at the drop-down list. This turns on filtering and causes a filter arrow to appear with each column label in the worksheet, as shown in Figure 4.12. Data does not need to be selected before turning on filtering because Excel automatically searches for column labels in a worksheet.

To filter data in a worksheet, click the filter arrow in the heading to be filtered. This causes a drop-down list to display with options to filter all the records, create a custom filter, or select an entry that appears in one or more of the cells in the column. When data is filtered, the filter arrow changes to a funnel icon. The funnel icon indicates that rows in the worksheet have been filtered. To turn off filtering, click the Sort & Filter button and then click *Filter*.

If a column contains numbers, click the filter arrow and point to *Number Filters* and a side menu displays with options for filtering numbers. For example, numbers can be filtered that are equal to, greater than, or less than a specified number; the top 10 numbers can be filtered; and numbers can be filtered that are above or below a specified number.

Figure 4.12 Filtering Data

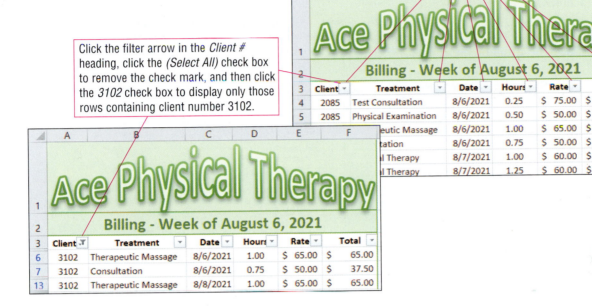

Turn on filtering and filter arrows appear with column headings.

Click the filter arrow in the *Client #* heading, click the *(Select All)* check box to remove the check mark, and then click the *3102* check box to display only those rows containing client number 3102.

Activity 3d Filtering Data

Part 4 of 4

1. With **4-APTBilling** open, click in cell A4.
2. Turn on filtering by clicking the Sort & Filter button in the Editing group on the Home tab and then clicking *Filter* at the drop-down list.
3. Filter rows for client number 3102 by completing the following steps:
   a. Click the filter arrow in the *Client #* heading.
   b. Click the *(Select All)* check box to remove the check mark. (This also removes the check marks for all the items in the list.)
   c. Scroll down the list box and then click *3102* to insert a check mark in the check box.
   d. Click OK.
4. Redisplay all the rows containing data by completing the following steps:
   a. Click the funnel icon in the *Client #* heading.
   b. Click the *(Select All)* check box to insert a check mark. (This also inserts check marks for all the items in the list.)
   c. Click OK.

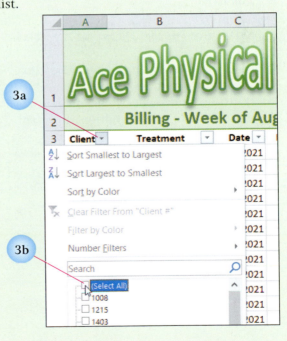

Chapter 4 | Enhancing a Worksheet   **107**

5. Filter a list of clients who receive physical therapy by completing the following steps:
   a. Click the filter arrow in the *Treatment* heading.
   b. Click the *(Select All)* check box to remove the check mark.
   c. Click the *Physical Therapy* check box to insert a check mark.
   d. Click OK.
6. Redisplay all the rows containing data by completing the following steps:
   a. Click the funnel icon in the *Treatment* heading.
   b. Click the *Clear Filter From "Treatment"* option.
7. Display the two highest rates by completing the following steps:
   a. Click the filter arrow in the *Rate* heading.
   b. Point to *Number Filters* and then click *Top 10* at the side menu.
   c. At the Top 10 AutoFilter dialog box, select the *10* in the middle measurement box and then type *2*.
   d. Click OK to close the dialog box.
8. Redisplay all the rows that contain data by completing the following steps:
   a. Click the funnel icon in the *Rate* heading.
   b. Click the *Clear Filter From "Rate"* option.
9. Display totals greater than $60 by completing the following steps:
   a. Click the filter arrow in the *Total* heading.
   b. Point to *Number Filters* and then click *Greater Than*.
   c. At the Custom AutoFilter dialog box, type *60* and then click OK.
10. Print the worksheet by clicking the File tab, clicking the *Print* option, and then clicking the Print button.
11. Turn off the filtering feature by clicking the Sort & Filter button and then clicking *Filter* at the drop-down list.
12. Save and then close **4-APTBilling**.

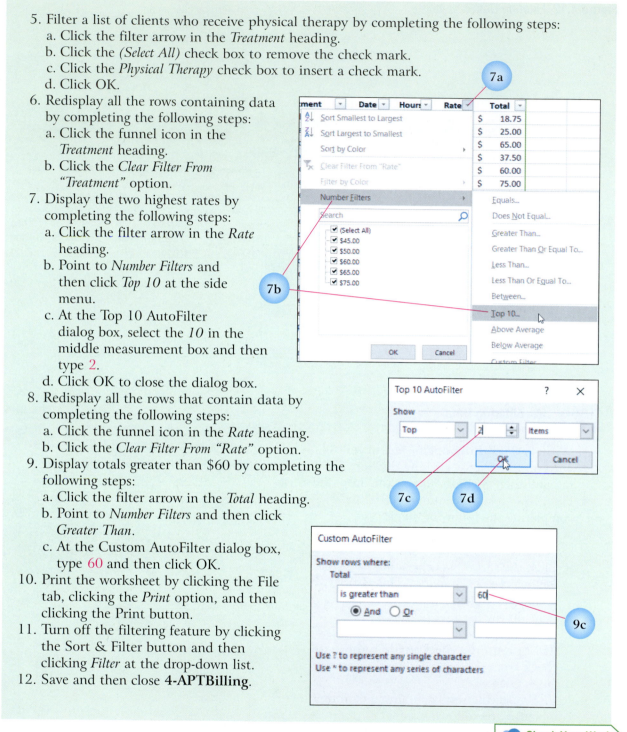

Check Your Work

Chapter Summary

- The Page Setup group on the Page Layout tab contains buttons for changing the margins and page orientation and size, as well as buttons for establishing the print area, inserting a page break, applying a picture background, and printing titles.

- The default left and right margins are 0.7 inch and the default top and bottom margins are 0.75 inch. Change these default margins with the Margins button in the Page Setup group on the Page Layout tab.

- Display the Page Setup dialog box with the Margins tab selected by clicking the Margins button in the Page Setup group on the Page Layout tab and then clicking *Custom Margins* at the drop-down list.

- Center a worksheet on the page with the *Horizontally* and *Vertically* check boxes at the Page Setup dialog box with the Margins tab selected.

- Click the Orientation button in the Page Setup group on the Page Layout tab to display the two orientation choices: *Portrait* and *Landscape*.

- Insert a page break by selecting the column or row, clicking the Breaks button in the Page Setup group on the Page Layout tab, and then clicking *Insert Page Break* at the drop-down list.

- To insert both horizontal and vertical page breaks at the same time, make a cell active, click the Breaks button, and then click *Insert Page Break* at the drop-down list.

- Preview the page breaks in a worksheet by clicking the Page Break Preview button in the view area on the Status bar or clicking the View tab and then clicking the Page Break Preview button in the Workbook Views group.

- Use options at the Page Setup dialog box with the Sheet tab selected to specify printing column and/or row titles on each page. Display this dialog box by clicking the Print Titles button in the Page Setup group on the Page Layout tab.

- Use buttons in the Scale to Fit group on the Page Layout tab to scale data to fit on a specific number of pages.

- Use the Background button in the Page Setup group on the Page Layout tab to insert a worksheet background picture. A background picture displays on the screen but does not print.

- Use options in the Sheet Options group on the Page Layout tab to specify whether to view and/or print gridlines and headings.

- Specify the print area by selecting cells, clicking the Print Area button in the Page Setup group on the Page Layout tab, and then clicking *Set Print Area* at the drop-down list. Add another print area by selecting the cells, clicking the Print Area button, and then clicking *Add to Print Area* at the drop-down list.

- Create a header and/or footer with the Header & Footer button in the Text group on the Insert tab, in Page Layout view, or with options at the Page Setup dialog box with the Header/Footer tab selected.

- Customize odd and even page headers and footers at the Page Setup dialog box with the Header/Footer tab selected.

- Customize a print job with options at the Print backstage area.

- To check spelling in a worksheet, click the Review tab and then click the Spelling button.

- Click the Undo button on the Quick Access Toolbar to reverse the most recent action and click the Redo button to redo a previously reversed action.
- Use options at the Find and Replace dialog box with the Find tab selected to find specific data and/or formatting in a worksheet.
- Use options at the Find and Replace dialog box with the Replace tab selected to find specific data and/or formatting and replace it with other data and/or formatting.
- Sort data in a worksheet with options at the Sort & Filter button in the Editing group on the Home tab.
- Create a custom sort with options at the Sort dialog box. Display this dialog box by clicking the Sort & Filter button and then clicking *Custom Sort* at the drop-down list.
- Temporarily isolate data by filtering it. Turn on the filter feature by clicking the Sort & Filter button in the Editing group on the Home tab and then clicking *Filter* at the drop-down list. This inserts a filter arrow with each column label. Click a filter arrow and then use options at the drop-down list to specify the filter data.

Commands Review

FEATURE	RIBBON TAB, GROUP	BUTTON, OPTION	KEYBOARD SHORTCUT
background picture	Page Layout, Page Setup		
filter data	Home, Editing		
Find and Replace dialog box with Find tab selected	Home, Editing	, *Find*	Ctrl + F
Find and Replace dialog box with Replace tab selected	Home, Editing	, *Replace*	Ctrl + H
header and footer	Insert, Text		
insert page break	Page Layout, Page Setup	, *Insert Page Break*	
margins	Page Layout, Page Setup		
orientation	Page Layout, Page Setup		
Page Layout view	View, Workbook Views		
Page Setup dialog box with Margins tab selected	Page Layout, Page Setup	, *Custom Margins*	
Page Setup dialog box with Sheet tab selected	Page Layout, Page Setup		
preview page break	View, Workbook Views		
print area	Page Layout, Page Setup		
redo an action			Ctrl + Y
remove page break	Page Layout, Page Setup	, *Remove Page Break*	

FEATURE	RIBBON TAB, GROUP	BUTTON, OPTION	KEYBOARD SHORTCUT
scale height	Page Layout, Scale to Fit		
scale to fit	Page Layout, Scale to Fit		
scale width	Page Layout, Scale to Fit		
size	Page Layout, Page Setup		
sort data	Home, Editing		
spelling check	Review, Proofing		F7
undo an action			Ctrl + Z

Microsoft® Excel Level 1

Unit 2

Enhancing the Display of Workbooks

Microsoft® Excel®

Moving Data within and between Workbooks

Performance Objectives

Upon successful completion of Chapter 5, you will be able to:

1 Insert and delete worksheets

2 Move, copy, and paste cells within and between worksheets

3 Move, rename, and format sheet tabs

4 Hide and unhide worksheets

5 Print a workbook containing multiple worksheets

6 Change the zoom

7 Split a worksheet into windows and freeze/unfreeze panes

8 Name a range of cells and use a range in a formula

9 Open multiple workbooks

10 Arrange, size, hide/unhide, and move workbooks

11 Move, copy, and paste data between workbooks

12 Link data between worksheets

13 Copy and paste data between programs

Up to this point, the workbooks you have worked in have consisted of single worksheets. In this chapter, you will learn to create a workbook with several worksheets and complete tasks such as copying and pasting data within and between worksheets. Moving and pasting or copying and pasting selected cells within and between worksheets is useful for rearranging data and saving time. You will also work with multiple workbooks and complete tasks such as arranging, sizing, and moving workbooks and opening and closing multiple workbooks.

 Data Files

Before beginning chapter work, copy the EL1C5 folder to your storage medium and then make EL1C5 the active folder.

 The online course includes additional training and assessment resources.

You will open an account workbook containing multiple worksheets and then insert and delete worksheets and move, copy, and paste data between worksheets. You will rename and apply color to sheet tabs, hide and unhide a worksheet, and format and print multiple worksheets in the workbook.

Creating a Workbook with Multiple Worksheets

Hint Creating multiple worksheets within a workbook is helpful for saving related data.

An Excel workbook contains one worksheet by default, but additional worksheets can be added. Add additional worksheets to a workbook to store related data, such as a worksheet for expenses for individual salespeople in the company and another worksheet for the monthly payroll for all the departments within the company. Another example is to record sales statistics for each quarter in individual worksheets within a workbook.

Tutorial

Inserting and Renaming Worksheets

New sheet

Quick Steps

Insert Worksheet
Click New sheet button.
OR
Press Shift + F11.

Delete Worksheet
1. Click sheet tab.
2. Click Delete button arrow.
3. Click *Delete Sheet*.
4. Click Delete button.

Inserting a New Worksheet

Insert a new worksheet in a workbook by clicking the New sheet button to the right of the Sheet1 tab at the bottom of the worksheet area. A new worksheet can also be inserted in a workbook with the keyboard shortcut Shift + F11. A new sheet tab is inserted to the right of the active tab. To move between worksheets, click the desired tab. The active sheet tab displays with a white background and the worksheet name displays in green. Any inactive tabs display with a light-gray background and gray text.

Deleting a Worksheet

If a worksheet is no longer needed in a workbook, delete it by clicking the sheet tab, clicking the Delete button arrow in the Cells group on the Home tab, and then clicking *Delete Sheet* at the drop-down list. Another method for deleting a worksheet is to right-click the sheet tab and then click *Delete* at the shortcut menu. When deleting a worksheet, Excel displays a deletion confirmation message. At this message, click the Delete button.

Selecting Multiple Worksheets

To work with more than one worksheet at a time, select the worksheets. With multiple worksheets selected, the same formatting can be applied to cells or the selected worksheets can be deleted. To select adjacent sheet tabs, click the first tab, press and hold down the Shift key, click the last tab, and then release the Shift key. To select nonadjacent sheet tabs, click the first tab, press and hold down the Ctrl key, click any other tabs to be selected, and then release the Ctrl key.

Copying, Cutting, and Pasting Cells

Cells in a workbook may need to be copied or moved to different locations within a worksheet or to another worksheet in the workbook. Move or copy cells in a worksheet or between worksheets or workbooks by selecting the cells and then using the Cut, Copy, and/or Paste buttons in the Clipboard group on the Home tab.

Copying and Pasting Selected Cells

Copying selected cells can be useful in worksheets that contain repetitive data. To copy cells, select the cells and then click the Copy button in the Clipboard group on the Home tab. This causes a moving dashed line border (called a *marquee*) to appear around the selected cells. To copy cells to another worksheet, click the sheet tab, click in the cell where the first selected cell is to be pasted, and then click the Paste button in the Clipboard group. Remove the moving marquee from selected cells by pressing the Esc key or double-clicking in any cell.

Selected cells in the same worksheet can be copied using the mouse and the Ctrl key. To do this, select the cells to be copied and then position the mouse pointer on any border around the selected cells until the pointer appears with a four-headed arrow attached. Press and hold down the Ctrl key, click and hold down the left mouse button, drag the outline of the selected cells to the new location, release the left mouse button, and then release the Ctrl key.

Activity 1a Inserting, Deleting, Selecting, Copying, Pasting, and Formatting Worksheets

Part 1 of 7

1. Open **RPFacAccts** and then save it with the name **5-RPFacAccts**.
2. Insert a new worksheet in the workbook by completing the following steps:
   a. Click the 2ndHalfSales sheet tab to make it active.
   b. Click the New sheet button to the right of the 2ndHalfSales sheet tab. (This inserts a new worksheet to the right of the 2ndHalfSales worksheet with the name Sheet4.)
3. Delete two sheet tabs by completing the following steps:
   a. Click the 1stHalfSales sheet tab.
   b. Press and hold down the Shift key, click the 2ndHalfSales sheet tab, and then release the Shift key. (These tabs must be adjacent. If they are not, press and hold down the Ctrl key when clicking the 2ndHalfSales sheet tab.)
   c. With the two sheet tabs selected, click the Delete button arrow in the Cells group on the Home tab and then click *Delete Sheet* at the drop-down list.
   d. At the message stating that Microsoft will permanently delete the sheets, click the Delete button.

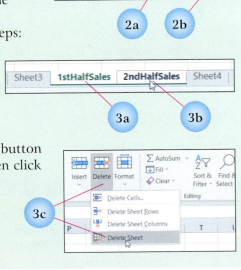

4. Copy cells from Sheet1 to Sheet4 by completing the following steps:
   a. Click the Sheet1 tab to make it the active worksheet.
   b. Select the range A1:A3 (the first three rows of data).
   c. Click the Copy button.
   d. Click the Sheet4 tab to make it the active tab.
   e. With A1 the active cell, click the Paste button.

5. Make the following changes to the new worksheet:
   a. Click in cell A3 and then type First Quarter Summary 2021.
   b. Change the width of column A to 20.00 characters.
   c. Change the width of columns B, C, and D to 12.00 characters.
   d. Type the following text in the specified cells:

B4	January
C4	February
D4	March
A5	Checks amount
A6	Deposit amount
A7	End-of-month balance

   e. Select the range B4:D4, click the Bold button and then click the Center button.
   f. Select the range B5:D7 and then apply the Comma format (using the Comma Style button in the Number group on the Home tab) with two digits after the decimal point.

6. Apply formatting to the cells in all four worksheets by completing the following steps:
   a. Click the Sheet1 tab to make it active and then click in cell A1 to make it the active cell.
   b. Press and hold down the Shift key, click the Sheet4 tab, and then release the Shift key. (This selects all four worksheets.)
   c. With cell A1 active, change the row height to 51.00 points.
   d. Click in cell A3.
   e. Change the font size to 14 points.
   f. Click each remaining sheet tab (Sheet2, Sheet3, and Sheet4) and notice the formatting changes applied to all the cells.

7. Change the column width for the three worksheets by completing the following steps:
   a. Click the Sheet1 tab to make it active.
   b. Press and hold down the Shift key, click the Sheet3 tab, and then release the Shift key.
   c. Select columns E, F, and G and then change the column width to 10.00 characters.
   d. Click the Sheet2 tab and then click the Sheet3 tab. Notice that the width of columns E, F, and G has changed to 10.00 characters. Click the Sheet4 tab and notice that the column width did not change.

8. Save 5-RPFacAccts.

Check Your Work

Using Paste Options

Tutorial
Using Paste Options

(Ctrl) ▾
Paste Options

When pasting cells in a worksheet, specify how the cells are pasted by clicking the Paste button arrow and then clicking a paste option button at the drop-down list. Click the Paste button (not the button arrow) and a Paste Options button displays in the lower right corner of the pasted cell(s). Display a list of paste options by clicking the button or pressing the Ctrl key. This causes a drop-down list to display, as shown in Figure 5.1. The same option buttons display when the

Figure 5.1 Paste Options Buttons

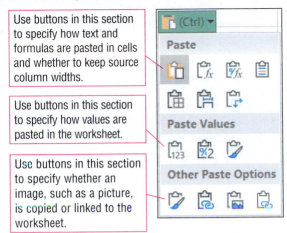

Use buttons in this section to specify how text and formulas are pasted in cells and whether to keep source column widths.

Use buttons in this section to specify how values are pasted in the worksheet.

Use buttons in this section to specify whether an image, such as a picture, is copied or linked to the worksheet.

Paste button arrow is clicked. Hover the mouse pointer over a button in the drop-down list and the descriptive name of the button displays along with the keyboard shortcut. Use buttons in this drop-down list to specify what is pasted.

 Tutorial

Moving Cells

Moving Selected Cells

Selected cells and cell contents can be moved within and between worksheets. Move selected cells using the Cut and Paste buttons in the Clipboard group on the Home tab or by dragging with the mouse.

Quick Steps

Move and Paste Cells
1. Select cells.
2. Click Cut button.
3. Click cell.
4. Click Paste button.

To move selected cells with buttons on the Home tab, select the cells and then click the Cut button in the Clipboard group. Click in the cell where the first selected cell is to be inserted and then click the Paste button in the Clipboard group.

💡 **Hint** Ctrl + X is the keyboard shortcut to cut selected data. Ctrl + V is the keyboard shortcut to paste data.

To move selected cells with the mouse, select the cells and then position the mouse pointer on any border of the selected cells until the pointer appears with a four-headed arrow attached. Click and hold down the left mouse button, drag the outline of the selected cells to the new location, and then release the mouse button.

Activity 1b Copying and Moving Cells and Pasting Cells Using Paste Options   Part 2 of 7

1. With **5-RPFacAccts** open, copy cells from Sheet2 to Sheet3 using the Paste Options button by completing the following steps:
   a. Click the Sheet2 tab to make it active.
   b. Select the range C7:E9.
   c. Click the Copy button.
   d. Click the Sheet3 tab.
   e. Click in cell C7.
   f. Click the Paste button.

g. Click the Paste Options button in the lower right corner of the pasted cells and then click the Keep Source Column Widths button at the drop-down list.

h. Make Sheet2 active and then press the Esc key to remove the moving marquee.

2. Click the Sheet1 tab.

3. You realize that the sublet rent deposit was recorded on the wrong day. The correct day is January 9. To move the cells containing information on the deposit, complete the following steps:

   a. Click in cell A13 and then insert a row. (The new row should appear above the row containing *Rainier Suppliers*.)

   b. Select the range A7:F7.

   c. Click the Cut button.

   d. Click in cell A13.

   e. Click the Paste button.

   f. Change the date of the deposit from January 1 to January 9.

   g. Select row 7 and then delete it.

4. Move cells using the mouse by completing the following steps:

   a. Click the Sheet2 tab.

   b. Click in cell A13 and then insert a new row.

   c. Using the mouse, select the range A7:F7.

   d. Position the mouse pointer on any boundary of the selected cells until it apppears with a four-headed arrow attached. Click and hold down the left mouse button, drag the outline of the selected cells to row 13, and then release the mouse button.

11	11-Feb	517	Stationery Plus	Paper supplies	266.43
12	12-Feb	518	Clear Source	Developer supplies	123.74
13					
14	Feb	519	Rainier Suppliers	era supplies	119.62
15	17-Feb	520	A1 Wedding Supplies	Photo albums	222.58

e. Change the date of the deposit to February 13.

   f. Delete row 7.

5. Save **5-RPFacAccts**.

Check Your Work

Copying and Pasting Using the Clipboard Task Pane

Quick Steps

Copy and Paste Multiple Items
1. Click Clipboard group task pane launcher.
2. Select cells.
3. Click Copy button.
4. Repeat Steps 2 and 3 as desired.
5. Make cell active.
6. Click item in Clipboard task pane to be inserted in worksheet.
7. Repeat Step 6 as desired.

Use the Clipboard task pane to copy and paste multiple items. To use the task pane, click the Clipboard group task pane launcher in the lower right corner of the Clipboard group on the Home tab. The Clipboard task pane displays at the left side of the screen similarly to what is shown in Figure 5.2.

Select data or an object to be copied and then click the Copy button in the Clipboard group. Continue selecting cells, text, or other items and clicking the Copy button. To paste an item into a worksheet, make the desired cell active and then click the item in the Clipboard task pane. If the copied item is text, the first 50 characters appear in the task pane. To paste all the selected items into a single location, make the desired cell active and then click the Paste All button in the task pane. When all the items have been pasted into the worksheet, click the Clear All button to remove any remaining items from the task pane.

Figure 5.2 Clipboard Task Pane

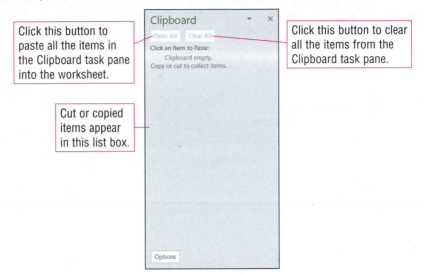

Click this button to paste all the items in the Clipboard task pane into the worksheet.

Click this button to clear all the items from the Clipboard task pane.

Cut or copied items appear in this list box.

Activity 1c Copying and Pasting Cells Using the Clipboard Task Pane

Part 3 of 7

1. With **5-RPFacAccts** open, select cells for copying by completing the following steps:
   a. Display the Clipboard task pane by clicking the Clipboard group task pane launcher. (If the Clipboard task pane contains any copied data, click the Clear All button.)
   b. Click the Sheet1 tab.
   c. Select the range C15:E16.
   d. Click the Copy button.
   e. Select the range C19:E19.
   f. Click the Copy button.
2. Paste the copied cells by completing the following steps:
   a. Click the Sheet2 tab.
   b. Click in cell C15.
   c. Click the item in the Clipboard task pane representing *General Systems Developer*.
   d. Click the Sheet3 tab.
   e. Click in cell C15.
   f. Click the item in the Clipboard task pane representing *General Systems Developer*.
   g. Click in cell C19.
   h. Click the item in the Clipboard task pane representing *Parkland City Services*.
3. Click the Clear All button at the top of the Clipboard task pane.
4. Close the Clipboard task pane by clicking the Close button (contains an *X*) in the upper right corner of the task pane.
5. Save **5-RPFacAccts**.

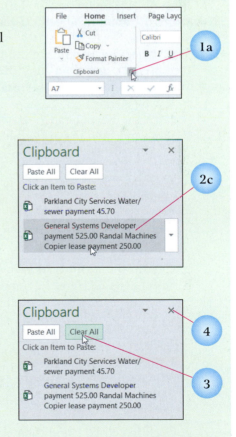

Check Your Work

Pasting Values Only

When pasting cells that contain a value and a formula, specify what is to be pasted using button options from the Paste button or Paste Options button drop-down list. Use the buttons in the *Paste Values* section of the drop-down list to insert only the value, the value with numbering formatting, or the value with source formatting.

Activity 1d Copying and Pasting Values

1. With **5-RPFacAccts** open, make Sheet1 the active tab.
2. Click in cell G6, type the formula =(f6-e6)+g5, and then press the Enter key.
3. Copy the formula in cell G6 to the range G7:G20.
4. Copy as a value (and not a formula) the final balance from Sheet1 to Sheet2 by completing the following steps:
   a. Click in cell G20.
   b. Click the Copy button.
   c. Click the Sheet2 tab.
   d. Click in cell G5 and then click the Paste button arrow.
   e. At the drop-down list, click the Values button in the *Paste Values* section of the drop-down list. (This inserts the value and not the formula.)

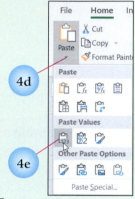

5. Click in cell G6, insert a formula that determines the balance (see Step 2), and then copy the formula to the range G7:G20.
6. Copy the amount in cell G20 and then paste the value only in cell G5 in Sheet3.
7. With Sheet3 active, make cell G6 active, insert a formula that determines the balance (see Step 2), and then copy the formula to the range G7:G20.
8. Insert formulas and apply formatting to cells in the three worksheets by completing the following steps:
   a. Click the Sheet1 tab.
   b. Press and hold down the Shift key, click the Sheet3 tab, and then release the Shift key.
   c. Click in cell D21, click the Bold button and then type Total.
   d. Click in cell E21 and then click the AutoSum button. (This inserts the formula =SUM(E13:E20).)
   e. Change the formula to =SUM(E7:E20) and then press the Enter key.
   f. Click in cell F21 and then click the AutoSum button. (This inserts the formula =SUM(F12:F20).)
   g. Change the formula to =SUM(F6:F20) and then press the Enter key.
   h. Select cells E21 and F21 and then click the Accounting Number Format button. Click in cell G5 and then click the Accounting Number Format button. (Cell G5 in Sheet1 already contains the Accounting format but cells G5 in Sheet2 and Sheet3 do not.)
   i. Click the Sheet2 tab and notice the text and formulas inserted in the worksheet, click the Sheet3 tab and notice the text and formulas, and then click the Sheet4 tab (to deselect the tabs).

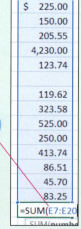

9. Copy values from Sheet1 to Sheet4 by completing the following steps:
   a. Click the Sheet1 tab.
   b. Click in cell E21 and then click the Copy button.
   c. Click the Sheet4 tab.

d. Click in cell B5 and then click the Paste button.

e. Click the Paste Options button and then click the Values button in the *Paste Values* section of the drop-down list.

f. Click the Sheet1 tab.

g. Click in cell F21 and then click the Copy button.

h. Click the Sheet4 tab.

i. Click in cell B6, click the Paste button arrow, and then click the Values button at the drop-down list.

j. Click the Sheet1 tab.

k. Click in cell G20 and then click the Copy button.

l. Click the Sheet4 tab.

m. Click in cell B7, click the Paste button arrow, and then click the Values button at the drop-down list.

10. Complete steps similar to those in Step 9 to insert amounts and balances for February (from Sheet2) and March (from Sheet3).

11. Select the range B5:D5 and then click the Accounting Number Format button.

12. Save **5-RPFacAccts**.

▶ Check Your Work ▶

Moving, Copying, and Deleting a Worksheet

Quick Steps

Move or Copy Worksheet
1. Right-click sheet tab.
2. Click *Move or Copy*.
3. At Move or Copy dialog box, click worksheet name in *Before sheet* list box.
4. Click OK.
OR
Drag sheet tab to new position. (To copy, press and hold down Ctrl key while dragging.)

Managing Worksheets

Right-click a sheet tab and a shortcut menu displays with options for managing worksheets, as shown in Figure 5.3. For example, remove a worksheet by clicking the *Delete* option. Move or copy a worksheet by clicking the *Move or Copy* option. Clicking this option causes a Move or Copy dialog box to display with options for specifying where to move or copy the selected sheet. By default, Excel names worksheets in a workbook *Sheet1, Sheet2, Sheet3,* and so on. To rename a worksheet, click the *Rename* option (which selects the default sheet name) and then type the new name.

In addition to the shortcut menu options, the mouse can be used to move or copy worksheets. To move a worksheet, position the mouse pointer on the sheet tab, click and hold down the left mouse button (a page icon displays next to the mouse pointer), drag the page icon to the new position, and then release the mouse button. For example, to move the Sheet2 tab after the Sheet3 tab, position the mouse pointer on the Sheet2 tab, click and hold down the left mouse button, drag the page icon after the Sheet3 tab, and then release the mouse button. To copy a worksheet, press and hold down the Ctrl key and then drag the sheet tab.

Figure 5.3 Sheet Tab Shortcut Menu

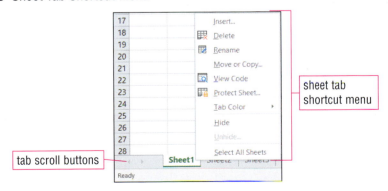

Quick Steps

Apply Color to Sheet Tab
1. Right-click sheet tab.
2. Point to *Tab Color*.
3. Click color at color palette.

Use the *Tab Color* option at the shortcut menu to apply a color to a sheet tab. Right-click a sheet tab, point to *Tab Color* at the shortcut menu, and then click a color at the color palette.

Activity 1e Selecting, Moving, Renaming, and Changing the Color of Sheet Tabs   Part 5 of 7

1. With **5-RPFacAccts** open, move Sheet4 by completing the following steps:
   a. Right-click the Sheet4 tab and then click *Move or Copy* at the shortcut menu.
   b. At the Move or Copy dialog box, make sure *Sheet1* is selected in the *Before sheet* list box and then click OK.

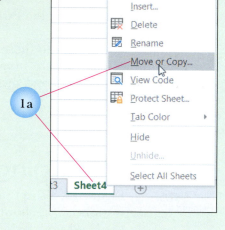

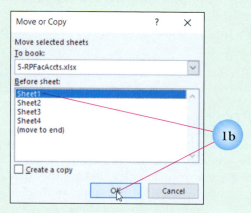

2. Rename Sheet4 by completing the following steps:
   a. Right-click the Sheet4 tab and then click *Rename*.
   b. Type Summary and then press the Enter key.
3. Complete steps similar to those in Step 2 to rename Sheet1 to *January*, Sheet2 to *February*, and Sheet3 to *March*.
4. Change the color of the Summary sheet tab by completing the following steps:
   a. Right-click the Summary sheet tab.
   b. Point to *Tab Color* at the shortcut menu.
   c. Click the *Red* color option (second option in the *Standard Colors* section).
5. Follow steps similar to those in Step 4 to change the January sheet tab to Blue (eighth option in the *Standard Colors* section), the February sheet tab to Purple (last option in the *Standard Colors* section), and the March sheet tab to Green (sixth option in the *Standard Colors* section).
6. Save **5-RPFacAccts**.

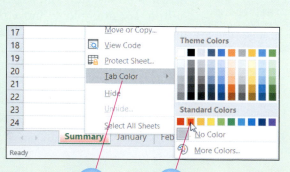

Check Your Work

124   Excel Level 1 | Unit 2   Chapter 5 | Moving Data within and between Workbooks

Tutorial

Hiding and Unhiding
a Worksheet

 Format

Quick Steps

Hide Worksheet
1. Click Format button.
2. Point to *Hide & Unhide*.
3. Click *Hide Sheet*.
OR
1. Right-click sheet tab.
2. Click *Hide* at shortcut menu.

Unhide Worksheet
1. Click Format button.
2. Point to *Hide & Unhide*.
3. Click *Unhide Sheet*.
4. Double-click hidden worksheet in Unhide dialog box.
OR
1. Right-click sheet tab.
2. Click *Unhide* at shortcut menu.
3. Double-click hidden worksheet in Unhide dialog box.

Hiding and Unhiding a Worksheet in a Workbook

In a workbook with multiple worksheets, a worksheet can be hidden that contains data that should not appear or print with the workbook. To hide a worksheet in a workbook, click the Format button in the Cells group on the Home tab, point to *Hide & Unhide*, and then click *Hide Sheet*. A worksheet can also be hidden by right-clicking a sheet tab and then clicking the *Hide* option at the shortcut menu.

To make a hidden worksheet visible, click the Format button in the Cells group, point to *Hide & Unhide* and then click *Unhide Sheet*, or right-click a sheet tab and then click *Unhide* at the shortcut menu. At the Unhide dialog box, shown in Figure 5.4, double-click the name of the worksheet to be unhidden.

Figure 5.4 Unhide Dialog Box

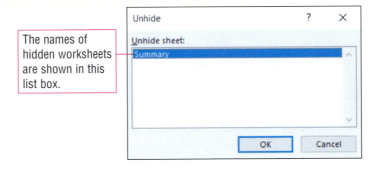

The names of hidden worksheets are shown in this list box.

Activity 1f Hiding and Unhiding a Worksheet and Formatting Multiple Worksheets   Part 6 of 7

1. With **5-RPFacAccts** open, hide the Summary worksheet by completing the following steps:
   a. Click the Summary tab.
   b. Click the Format button in the Cells group on the Home tab, point to *Hide & Unhide*, and then click *Hide Sheet*.

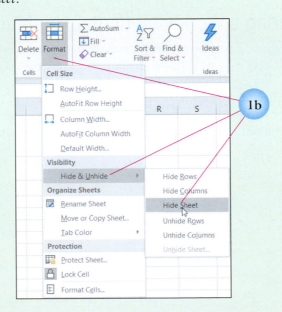

2. Unhide the worksheet by completing the following steps:

   a. Click the Format button, point to *Hide & Unhide*, and then click *Unhide Sheet*.

   b. At the Unhide dialog box, make sure *Summary* is selected in the *Unhide sheet* list box and then click OK.

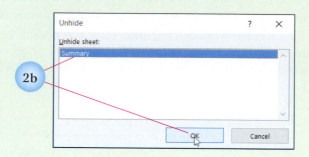

3. Insert a header for each worksheet by completing the following steps:

   a. With the Summary tab active, press and hold down the Shift key, click the March tab, and then release the Shift key. (This selects all four tabs.)

   b. Click the Insert tab.

   c. Click the Header & Footer button in the Text group.

   d. Click the Header button in the Header & Footer group on the Header & Footer Tools Design tab and then click the option at the drop-down list that prints your name at the left side of the page (if a name other than your own appears at the left side of the page, select the name and then type your first and last names), the page number in the middle, and the date at the right.

4. With all the sheet tabs selected, center each worksheet horizontally and vertically on the page. **Hint: Do this at the Page Setup dialog box with the Margins tab selected.**

5. With all the sheet tabs still selected, change to landscape orientation. **Hint: Do this with the Orientation button on the Page Layout tab.**

6. Save **5-RPFacAccts**.

 Tutorial

Printing Multiple Worksheets

Printing a Workbook Containing Multiple Worksheets

By default, Excel prints the currently displayed worksheet. To print all the worksheets in a workbook, display the Print backstage area, click the first gallery in the *Settings* category, click *Print Entire Workbook* at the drop-down list, and then click the Print button. Print specific worksheets in a workbook by selecting the tabs of the worksheets to be printed. With the sheet tabs selected, display the Print backstage area and then click the Print button.

Quick Steps

Print All Worksheets in Workbook
1. Click File tab.
2. Click *Print* option.
3. Click first gallery in *Settings* category.
4. Click *Print Entire Workbook*.
5. Click Print button.

1. With **5-RPFacAccts** open, click the File tab and then click the *Print* option.
2. At the Print backstage area, click the first gallery in the *Settings* category and then click *Print Entire Workbook* at the drop-down list.
3. Click the Print button.
4. Save and then close **5-RPFacAccts**.

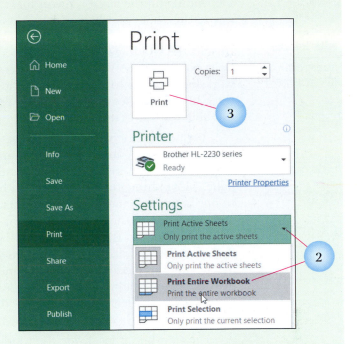

Check Your Work

Activity 2 Write Formulas Using Ranges in an Equipment Usage Workbook

2 Parts

You will open an equipment usage workbook, view the document at different zoom percentages, and then split the window, freeze panes and edit cells. You will also name ranges and then use the range names to write formulas in the workbook.

 Tutorial

Changing the Zoom

 Zoom

 100%

 Zoom to Selection

Changing the Zoom

The View tab contains a Zoom group with three buttons for changing zoom settings. Click the Zoom button in the Zoom group to open the Zoom dialog box, which contains options for changing the zoom percentage. Click the 100% button in the Zoom group to return the view to 100%, which is the default. Select a range of cells and then click the Zoom to Selection button to scale the zoom setting so the selected range fills the worksheet area.

Use the zoom slider bar at the right side of the Status bar to change the zoom percentage. Click the Zoom Out button (displays with a minus symbol [–]) to decrease the zoom percentage or click the Zoom In button (displays with a plus symbol [+]) to increase the zoom percentage. Another method for increasing or decreasing zoom percentage is to click and drag the zoom slider bar button on the slider bar.

Splitting a
Worksheet

Freezing and
Unfreezing Panes

 Split

Quick Steps

Split Worksheet
1. Click View tab.
2. Click Split button.

 Freeze Panes

💡 **Hint** Remove a
split line by double-
clicking anywhere
on the split line that
divides the panes.

Splitting a Worksheet and Freezing and Unfreezing Panes

Depending on the size of a worksheet and the screen display settings, all cells in a worksheet may not be visible in the worksheet area at one time. (An example of this will be seen in Activity 2a.) To more easily view all the data, it can be helpful to split the window into panes. Split a worksheet window into panes with the Split button in the Window group on the View tab. Click the Split button and the worksheet splits into four panes, as shown in Figure 5.5. The panes are separated by thick light-gray lines called *split lines*. To remove split lines from a worksheet, click the Split button to deactivate it.

A window pane will display the active cell. As the insertion point is moved through the pane, another active cell may display. This additional active cell displays when the insertion point passes over one of the split lines that creates the pane. Move through a worksheet and both active cells may display. Make a change to one active cell and the change is made in the other as well. To display only one active cell, freeze the window panes by clicking the Freeze Panes button in the Window group on the View tab and then clicking *Freeze Panes* at the drop-down list. Maintain the display of column headings while editing or typing text in cells by clicking the Freeze Panes button and then clicking *Freeze Top Row*. Maintain the display of row headings by clicking the Freeze Panes button and then clicking *Freeze First Column*. Unfreeze window panes by clicking the Freeze Panes button and then clicking *Unfreeze Panes* at the drop-down list.

The split lines that divide the window can be adjusted using the mouse. To do this, position the mouse pointer on a split line until the pointer turns into a left-and-right-pointing arrow with a double line in the middle. Click and hold down the left mouse button, drag the outline of the split line to the desired location, and then release the mouse button. To move both the horizontal and vertical split lines at the same time, position the mouse pointer on the intersection of the split lines until the pointer turns into a four-headed arrow. Click and hold down the left mouse button, drag the split lines to the desired location, and then release the mouse button.

Figure 5.5 Split Window

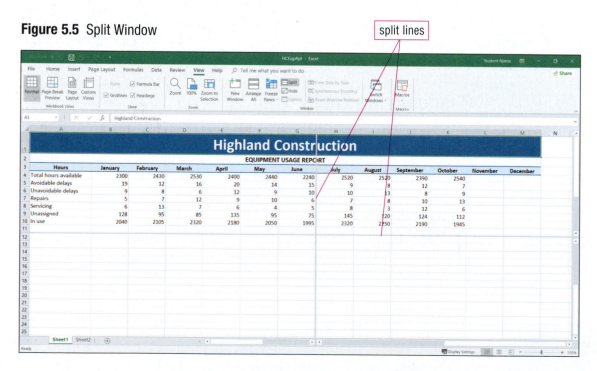

1. Open **HCEqpRpt** and then save it with the name **5-HCEqpRpt**.
2. Increase the Zoom percentage by clicking the Zoom In button at the right of the zoom slider bar two times.
3. Select the range G3:I10, click the View tab, and then click the Zoom to Selection button in the Zoom group.
4. Click the Zoom button in the Zoom group, click the *75%* option at the Zoom dialog box, and then click OK.
5. Click the 100% button in the Zoom group.
6. Make cell A1 active and then split the window by clicking the Split button in the Window group on the View tab. (This splits the window into four panes.)
7. Drag the vertical split line by completing the following steps:
   a. Position the mouse pointer on the vertical split line until the pointer turns into a left-and-right-pointing arrow with a double line in the middle.
   b. Click and hold down the left mouse button, drag to the left until the vertical split line is immediately to the right of the first column, and then release the mouse button.

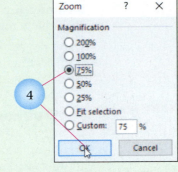

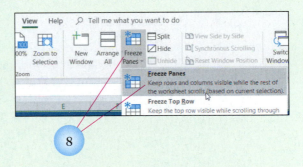

8. Freeze the window panes by clicking the Freeze Panes button in the Window group on the View tab and then clicking *Freeze Panes* at the drop-down list.
9. Make cell L4 active and then type the following data in the specified cells:

L4	2310	M4	2210
L5	12	M5	5
L6	5	M6	7
L7	9	M7	8
L8	11	M8	12
L9	95	M9	120
L10	2005	M10	1830

10. Unfreeze the window panes by clicking the Freeze Panes button and then clicking *Unfreeze Panes* at the drop-down list.
11. Remove the panes by clicking the Split button in the Window group to deactivate it.
12. Save **5-HCEqpRpt**.

Check Your Work

Naming and Using
a Range

Quick Steps

Name Range
1. Select cells.
2. Click in Name box.
3. Type range name.
4. Press Enter key.

Define Name

💡**Hint** Another method for moving to a range is to click the Find & Select button in the Editing group on the Home tab and then click *Go To*. At the Go To dialog box, double-click the range name.

Naming and Using a Range

A group of adjacent cells is referred to as a *range*. A range of cells can be formatted, moved, copied, or deleted. A range can also be named and then the insertion point can be moved to the range or the named range can be used as part of a formula.

To name a range, select the cells and then click in the Name box to the left of the Formula bar. Type a name for the range (do not use spaces) and then press the Enter key. To move the insertion point to a specific range and select the range, click the Name box arrow and then click the range name at the drop-down list.

A range can also be named using the Define Name button in the Defined Names group on the Formulas tab. Clicking the Define Name button displays the New Name dialog box. At the New Name dialog box, type a name for the range and then click OK.

A range name can be used in a formula. For example, to insert in a cell the average of all the cells in a range named *Profit*, make the cell active and then type the formula =*AVERAGE(Profit)*. Use a named range in the current worksheet or in another worksheet within the workbook.

Activity 2b Naming a Range and Using a Range in a Formula

Part 2 of 2

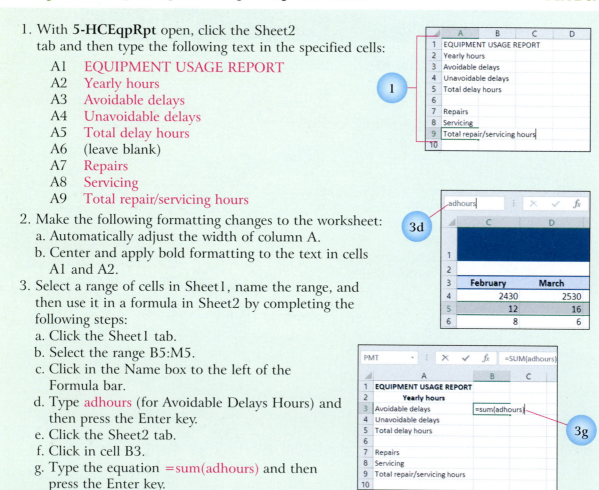

1. With **5-HCEqpRpt** open, click the Sheet2 tab and then type the following text in the specified cells:

   A1 EQUIPMENT USAGE REPORT
   A2 Yearly hours
   A3 Avoidable delays
   A4 Unavoidable delays
   A5 Total delay hours
   A6 (leave blank)
   A7 Repairs
   A8 Servicing
   A9 Total repair/servicing hours

2. Make the following formatting changes to the worksheet:
   a. Automatically adjust the width of column A.
   b. Center and apply bold formatting to the text in cells A1 and A2.

3. Select a range of cells in Sheet1, name the range, and then use it in a formula in Sheet2 by completing the following steps:
   a. Click the Sheet1 tab.
   b. Select the range B5:M5.
   c. Click in the Name box to the left of the Formula bar.
   d. Type adhours (for Avoidable Delays Hours) and then press the Enter key.
   e. Click the Sheet2 tab.
   f. Click in cell B3.
   g. Type the equation =sum(adhours) and then press the Enter key.

4. Click the Sheet1 tab and then complete the following steps:
   a. Select the range B6:M6.
   b. Click the Formulas tab.
   c. Click the Define Name button in the Defined Names group.
   d. At the New Name dialog box, type *udhours* and then click OK.
   e. Click the Sheet2 tab, make sure cell B4 is active, type the equation =sum(udhours), and then press the Enter key.

5. Click the Sheet1 tab and then complete the following steps:
   a. Select the range B7:M7 and then name the range *rhours*.
   b. Click the Sheet2 tab, make cell B7 active, type the equation =sum(rhours), and then press the Enter key.
   c. Click the Sheet1 tab.
   d. Select the range B8:M8 and then name the range *shours*.
   e. Click the Sheet2 tab, make sure cell B8 is active, type the equation =sum(shours), and then press the Enter key.

6. With Sheet2 still active, make the following changes:
   a. Make cell B5 active.
   b. Double-click the AutoSum button.
   c. Make cell B9 active.
   d. Double-click the AutoSum button.

7. Click the Sheet1 tab and then move to the adhours range by clicking the Name box arrow and then clicking *adhours* at the drop-down list.

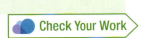

8. Select both sheet tabs, change to landscape orientation, scale the contents to fit on one page (by changing the width to *1 page* on the Page Layout tab), and then insert a custom footer with your name, the page number, and the date.

9. With both sheet tabs selected, print both worksheets in the workbook.

10. Save and then close **5-HCEqpRpt**.

> **Check Your Work**

Activity 3 Arrange, Size, and Copy Data between Workbooks   3 Parts

> You will open, arrange, hide, unhide, size, and move multiple workbooks. You will also copy cells from one workbook and paste the contents in another workbook.

> **Tutorial**

Working with Windows and Hiding and Unhiding Workbooks

Working with Windows

In Excel, multiple workbooks can be opened, a new window with the current workbook can be opened, and the open workbooks can be arranged in the Excel window. With multiple workbooks open, cell entries can be cut and pasted or copied and pasted from one workbook to another using the techniques discussed earlier in this chapter. The exception is that the destination workbook must be active before using the Paste command.

Opening Multiple Workbooks

With multiple workbooks or more than one version of the current workbook open, data can be moved or copied between workbooks and the contents of several workbooks can be compared. When a new workbook or a new window of the current workbook is opened, it is placed on top of the original workbook.

New Window

Open a new window of the current workbook by clicking the View tab and then clicking the New Window button in the Window group. Excel adds a colon followed by the number *2* to the end of the workbook title and adds a colon followed by the number *1* to the end of the originating workbook name.

Open multiple workbooks at one time at the Open dialog box. Select adjacent workbooks by clicking the name of the first workbook to be opened, pressing and holding down the Shift key, clicking the name of the last workbook to be opened, releasing the Shift key, and then clicking the Open button. If the workbooks are nonadjacent, click the name of the first workbook to be opened, press and hold down the Ctrl key, and then click the names of any other workbooks to be opened.

Switch Windows

To see what workbooks are currently open, click the View tab and then click the Switch Windows button in the Window group. The names of the open workbooks display in a drop-down list and the workbook name preceded by a check mark is the active workbook. To make another workbook active, click the workbook name at the drop-down list.

Another method for determining which workbooks are open is to hover the mouse over the Excel button on the taskbar. This causes a thumbnail to display of each open workbook. If more than one workbook is open, the Excel button on the taskbar displays additional layers in a cascaded manner. The layer behind the Excel button displays only a portion of the edge at the right of the button. Hovering the mouse over the Excel button on the taskbar displays thumbnails of all the workbooks above the button. To make another workbook active, click the thumbnail that represents the workbook.

Arranging Workbooks

If more than one workbook is open, arrange the workbooks at the Arrange Windows dialog box, shown in Figure 5.6. To display this dialog box, click the Arrange All button in the Window group on the View tab. At the Arrange Windows dialog box, click *Tiled* to display a portion of each open workbook. Figure 5.7 displays four tiled workbooks.

Arrange All

Quick Steps
Arrange Workbooks
1. Click View tab.
2. Click Arrange All button.
3. At Arrange Windows dialog box, click arrangement.
4. Click OK.

Figure 5.6 Arrange Windows Dialog Box

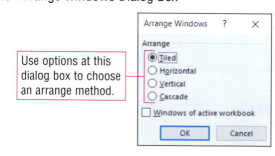

Use options at this dialog box to choose an arrange method.

Choose the *Horizontal* option at the Arrange Windows dialog box to display the open workbooks across the screen. Choose the *Vertical* option to display the open workbooks up and down the screen. Choose the last option, *Cascade*, to display the Title bar of each open workbook. Figure 5.8 shows four cascaded workbooks.

Select the arrange option for displaying multiple workbooks based on which parts of the workbooks are most important to view simultaneously. For example, the tiled workbooks in Figure 5.7 display the company names of the workbooks.

Figure 5.7 Tiled Workbooks

Figure 5.8 Cascaded Workbooks

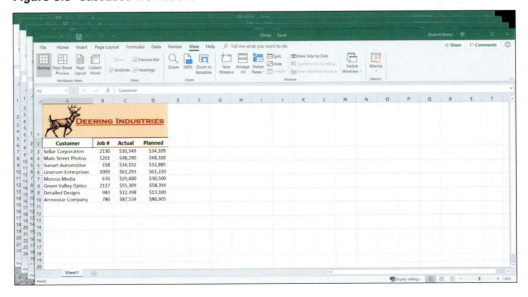

Hiding and Unhiding Workbooks

Hide

Unhide

Use the Hide button in the Window group on the View tab to hide the active workbook. If a workbook has been hidden, redisplay it by clicking the Unhide button in the Window group. At the Unhide dialog box, make sure the specific workbook is selected in the list box and then click OK.

Activity 3a Opening, Arranging, Hiding and Unhiding Workbooks
Part 1 of 3

1. Open several workbooks at the same time by completing the following steps:
   a. Display the Open dialog box with EL1C5 the active folder.
   b. Click the workbook *DIJobs*.
   c. Press and hold down the Ctrl key, click *EPSales*, click *FinCon*, click *RPFacAccts*, and then release the Ctrl key.
   d. Click the Open button in the dialog box.
2. Make **DIJobs** the active workbook by clicking the View tab, clicking the Switch Windows button, and then clicking *DIJobs* at the drop-down list.
3. Tile the workbooks by completing the following steps:
   a. Click the View tab and then click the Arrange All button in the Window group.
   b. At the Arrange Windows dialog box, make sure *Tiled* is selected and then click OK.
4. Cascade the workbooks by completing the following steps:
   a. Click the Arrange All button in the **DIJobs** workbook.
   b. At the Arrange Windows dialog box, click *Cascade* and then click OK.
5. Hide and unhide workbooks by completing the following steps:
   a. Make sure **DIJobs** is the active workbook. (The file name displays on top of each workbook file.)
   b. Click the Hide button in the Window group on the View tab.
   c. Make sure **RPFacAccts** is the active workbook. (The file name displays at the top of each workbook file.)
   d. Click the Hide button in the Window group on the View tab.
   e. At the active workbook, click the View tab and then click the Unhide button.
   f. At the Unhide dialog box, click *RPFacAccts* in the list box and then click OK.
   g. Click the Unhide button.
   h. At the Unhide dialog box, make sure **DIJobs** is selected in the list box and then click OK.
6. Close all the open workbooks (without saving changes) except **DIJobs**.
7. Open a new window with the current workbook by clicking the New Window button in the Window group on the View tab. (Notice that the new window contains the workbook name followed by a hyphen and the number *2*.)
8. Switch back and forth between the two versions of the workbook.
9. Make **DIJobs-2** the active window and then close the workbook.

Sizing and Moving Workbooks

Maximize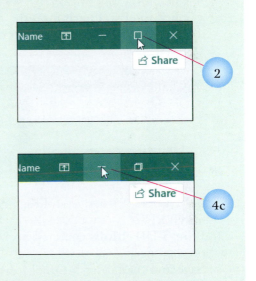

Minimize

Close

Restore Down

Change the size of the window using the Maximize and Minimize buttons in the upper right corner of the active workbook. The Maximize button is in the upper right corner of the active workbook immediately to the left of the Close button. (The Close button is the button containing the *X*.) The Minimize button is immediately to the left of the Maximize button.

If all the open workbooks are arranged, clicking the Maximize button causes the active workbook to expand to fill the screen. In addition, the Maximize button changes to the Restore Down button. To return the active workbook back to its original size, click the Restore Down button.

Click the Minimize button in the active workbook and the workbook is reduced and displays as a layer behind the Excel button on the taskbar. To maximize a workbook that has been minimized, click the Excel button on the taskbar and then click the thumbnail representing the workbook.

Activity 3b Minimizing, Maximizing, and Restoring Workbooks

Part 2 of 3

1. Make sure **DIJobs** is open.
2. Maximize **DIJobs** by clicking the Maximize button in the upper right corner of the screen immediately to the left of the Close button.
3. Open **EPSales** and **FinCon**.
4. Make the following changes to the open workbooks:
   a. Tile the workbooks.
   b. Click the **DIJobs** Title bar to make it the active workbook.
   c. Minimize **DIJobs** by clicking the Minimize button at the right side of the Title bar.
   d. Make **EPSales** the active workbook and then minimize it.
   e. Minimize **FinCon**.
5. Click the Excel button on the taskbar, click the **DIJobs** thumbnail, and then close the workbook without saving changes.
6. Complete steps similar to Step 5 to close the other two workbooks.

Moving, Linking, Copying, and Pasting Data between Workbooks

With more than one workbook open, data can be moved, linked, copied, and/or pasted from one workbook to another. To move, link, copy, and/or paste data between workbooks, use the cutting and pasting options discussed earlier in this chapter together with the information about windows.

Moving and Copying Data

Data can be moved or copied within a worksheet, between worksheets, and between workbooks and documents created in other programs, such as Word, PowerPoint, and Access. The Paste Options button provides a variety of options for pasting data in a worksheet, another workbook, or a document created in another program. In addition to being pasted, data can be linked and data can be pasted as an object or a picture object.

Activity 3c Copying Selected Cells from One Open Worksheet to Another   Part 3 of 3

1. Open **DIFebJobs**.
2. If you just completed Activity 3b, click the Maximize button so the worksheet fills the entire worksheet window.
3. Save the workbook and name it **5-DIFebJobs**.
4. With **5-DIFebJobs** open, open **DIJobs**.
5. Select and then copy text from **DIJobs** to **5-DIFebJobs** by completing the following steps:
   a. With **DIJobs** the active workbook, select the range A3:D10.
   b. Click the Copy button.
   c. Click the Excel button on the taskbar and then click the **5-DIFebJobs** thumbnail.
   d. Make cell A8 active and then click the Paste button.

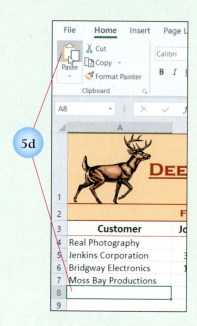

   e. Make cell E7 active and then drag the fill handle to cell E15.
6. Print **5-DIFebJobs** centered horizontally and vertically on the page.
7. Save and then close **5-DIFebJobs**.
8. Close **DIJobs**.

> 🔵 Check Your Work

Activity 4 Linking and Copying Data within and between Worksheets and Word   2 Parts

You will open a workbook containing four worksheets with quarterly expenses data, copy and link cells between the worksheets, and then copy and paste the worksheets into Word as picture objects.

Linking Data

In addition to being copied and pasted, data can be copied and then linked within or between worksheets or workbooks. Linking data is useful for maintaining consistency and control over critical data in worksheets or workbooks. When data is linked, a change made in a linked cell is automatically made to the other cells in the link. Links can be made with individual cells or with a range of cells. When linking data, the worksheet that contains the original data is called the *source worksheet* and the worksheet that relies on the source worksheet for the data in the link is called the *dependent worksheet*.

Ö̓uick Steps

Link Data between Worksheets
1. Select cells.
2. Click Copy button.
3. Click sheet tab.
4. Click in cell.
5. Click Paste button arrow.
6. Click Paste Link button.

To create a link, make active the cell containing the data to be linked (or select the cells) and then click the Copy button in the Clipboard group on the Home tab. Make active the worksheet where the cells are to be linked, click the Paste button arrow, and then click the Paste Link button in the *Other Paste Options* section in the drop-down list. Another method for creating a link is to click the Paste button, click the Paste Options button, and then click the Paste Link button in the *Other Paste Options* section in the drop-down list.

Activity 4a Linking Cells between Worksheets   **Part 1 of 2**

1. Open **DWQtrlyExp** and then save it with the name **5-DWQtrlyExp**.
2. Link cells in the first-quarter worksheet to the other three worksheets by completing the following steps:
   a. With the 1st Qtr tab active, select the range C4:C10.
   b. Click the Copy button.
   c. Click the 2nd Qtr tab.
   d. Make cell C4 active.
   e. Click the Paste button arrow and then click the Paste Link button in the *Other Paste Options* section in the drop-down list.
   f. Click the 3rd Qtr tab and then make cell C4 active.
   g. Click the Paste button arrow and then click the Paste Link button.
   h. Click the 4th Qtr tab and then make cell C4 active.
   i. Click the Paste button.
   j. Click the Paste Options button and then click the Paste Link button in the *Other Paste Options* section in the drop-down list.

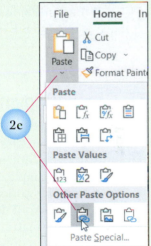

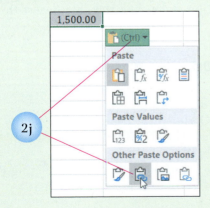

3. Click the 1st Qtr tab and then press the Esc key to remove the moving marquee.

4. Insert a formula in each worksheet that subtracts the budget amount from the variance amount by completing the following steps:
   a. Make sure the first-quarter worksheet is visible.
   b. Press and hold down the Shift key and then click the 4th Qtr tab. (This selects all four tabs.)
   c. Make cell D4 active, type the formula =c4-b4, and then press the Enter key.
   d. Copy the formula in cell D4 to the range D5:D10.
   e. Make cell D4 active and then apply the Accounting format with two digits after the decimal point and a dollar symbol.
   f. Click the 2nd Qtr tab and notice that the formula was inserted and copied in this worksheet.
   g. Click the other sheet tabs and notice the amounts in column D.
   h. Click the 1st Qtr tab.

uarter		
Budget	**Variance**	
$ 126,000.00	4,000.00	
54,500.00	(3,500.00)	
10,100.00	1,850.00	
6,000.00	(350.00)	
4,500.00	360.00	
2,200.00	(230.00)	
1,500.00	50.00	

4d

5. With the first-quarter worksheet active, make the following changes to the specified linked cells:

   C4: Change *$126,000* to *$128,000*

   C5: Change *54,500* to *56,000*

   C9: Change *2,200* to *2,400*

6. Click the 2nd Qtr tab and notice that the values in cells C4, C5, and C9 automatically changed (because they were linked to the first-quarter worksheet).
7. Click the other tabs and notice that the values changed.
8. Save **5-DWQtrlyExp** and then print all four worksheets in the workbook.

> **Check Your Work**

> Tutorial

Copying and Pasting Data between Programs

Copying and Pasting Data between Programs

Microsoft Office is a suite that allows *integration*, which is the combining of data from files created by two or more programs into one file. Integration can occur by copying and pasting data between files created in different programs. For example, a worksheet can be created in Excel and specific data can be selected in the worksheet and then copied to a Word document. When pasting Excel data in a Word document, choose from among these formatting options: keep the source formatting, use destination styles, link the data, insert the data as a picture, or keep only the text.

Activity 4b Copying and Pasting Excel Data into a Word Document   Part 2 of 2

1. With **5-DWQtrlyExp** open, open the Word program.
2. In Word, open the document **DWQtrlyRpt** in your EL1C5 folder.
3. Save the Word document with the name **5-DWQtrlyRpt**.
4. Click the Excel button on the taskbar.
5. Copy the first-quarter data into the Word document by completing the following steps:
   a. Click the 1st Qtr tab.
   b. Select the range A2:D10.
   c. Click the Copy button.
   d. Click the Word button on the taskbar.

e. In the **5-DWQtrlyRpt** document, press Ctrl + End to move the insertion point below the heading.

f. Click the Paste button arrow. (This displays a drop-down list of paste option buttons.)

g. Move the mouse over the various buttons in the drop-down list to see how each option inserts the data in the document.

h. Click the Picture button. (This inserts the data as a picture object.)

i. Press Ctrl + End and then press the Enter key two times. (This moves the insertion point below the data.)

j. Click the Excel button on the taskbar.

6. Click the 2nd Qtr tab and then complete steps similar to those in Step 5 to copy and paste the second-quarter data into the Word document. Press Ctrl + End and then press the Enter key two times.

7. Click the 3rd Qtr tab and then complete steps similar to those in Step 5 to copy and paste the third-quarter data to the Word document. Press Ctrl + End and then press the Enter key two times.

8. Click the 4th Qtr tab and then complete steps similar to those in Step 5 to copy and paste the fourth-quarter data to the Word document. (The data will display on two pages.)

9. Print the document by clicking the File tab, clicking the *Print* option, and then clicking the Print button at the Print backstage area.

10. Save and close **5-DWQtrlyRpt** and then close Word.

11. In Excel, press the Esc key to remove the moving marquee and then make cell A1 active.

12. Save and then close **5-DWQtrlyExp**.

> Check Your Work

Chapter Summary

- By default, an Excel workbook contains one worksheet. Add a new worksheet to a workbook by clicking the New sheet button or using the keyboard shortcut Shift + F11.

- Delete a worksheet with the Delete button in the Cells group on the Home tab or by right-clicking a sheet tab and then clicking *Delete* at the shortcut menu.

- To manage more than one worksheet at a time, first select the worksheets. Use the mouse together with the Shift key to select adjacent sheet tabs and use the mouse together with the Ctrl key to select nonadjacent sheet tabs.

- Copy or move selected cells and cell contents in and between worksheets using the Cut, Copy, and/or Paste buttons in the Clipboard group on the Home tab or by dragging with the mouse.

- Move selected cells with the mouse by dragging the outline of the selected cells to the new position.

- Copy selected cells with the mouse by pressing and holding down the Ctrl key while dragging the cells to the new position.

- When pasting data, specify how cells are to be pasted by clicking the Paste button arrow or pasting the cells and then clicking the Paste Options button. Clicking either button displays a drop-down list of paste option buttons. Click a button at the drop-down list.

- Use the Clipboard task pane to copy and paste data within and between worksheets and workbooks. Display the Clipboard task pane by clicking the Clipboard group task pane launcher.

- Manage worksheets by right-clicking a sheet tab and then clicking an option at the shortcut menu. Options include removing and renaming a worksheet.

- The mouse can be used to move or copy worksheets. To move a worksheet, drag the sheet tab with the mouse. To copy a worksheet, press and hold down the Ctrl key and then drag the sheet tab with the mouse.

- Use the *Tab Color* option at the sheet tab shortcut menu to apply a color to a sheet tab.

- Hide and unhide a worksheet by clicking the Format button in the Cells group on the Home tab and then clicking the desired option at the drop-down list or by right-clicking the sheet tab and then clicking the option at the shortcut menu.

- To print all the worksheets in a workbook, display the Print backstage area, click the first gallery in the *Settings* category, and then click *Print Entire Workbook* at the drop-down list. Print specific worksheets by selecting their tabs.

- Use buttons in the Zoom group on the View tab or the zoom slider bar at the right side of the Status bar to change the zoom percentage.

- Split the worksheet window into panes with the Split button in the Window group on the View tab. To remove a split from a worksheet, click the Split button to deactivate it.

- Freeze window panes by clicking the Freeze Panes button in the Window group on the View tab and then clicking *Freeze Panes* at the drop-down list. Unfreeze window panes by clicking the Freeze Panes button and then clicking *Unfreeze Panes* at the drop-down list.

- A selected group of cells is referred to as a *range*. A range can be named and used in a formula. Name a range by typing the name in the Name box to the left of the Formula bar or at the New Name dialog box.

- To open multiple workbooks that are adjacent, display the Open dialog box, click the name of the first workbook, press and hold down the Shift key, click the name of the last workbook, release the Shift key, and then click the Open button. To open workbooks that are nonadjacent, click the name of the first workbook, press and hold down the Ctrl key, click the names of the desired workbooks, release the Ctrl key, and then click the Open button.

- To see a list of open workbooks, click the View tab and then click the Switch Windows button in the Window group.

- Arrange multiple workbooks in a window with options at the Arrange Windows dialog box.

- Hide the active workbook by clicking the Hide button in the Window group on the View tab and unhide a workbook by clicking the Unhide button.

- Click the Maximize button in the upper right corner of the active workbook to make the workbook fill the entire window area. Click the Minimize button to reduce the workbook and display it as a layer behind the Excel button on the taskbar. Click the Restore Down button to return the workbook to its previous size.

- Data can be moved, copied, linked, and/or pasted between workbooks using options at the Paste Options button. Also, a workbook can be pasted as a link in a different Microsoft Office program, such a Word or PowerPoint. Changing the data in one program will change linked data that exists in a different program.

Commands Review

FEATURE	RIBBON TAB, GROUP	BUTTON, OPTION	KEYBOARD SHORTCUT
100% view	View, Zoom		
Arrange Windows dialog box	View, Window		
Clipboard task pane	Home, Clipboard		
copy selected cells	Home, Clipboard		Ctrl + C
cut selected cells	Home, Clipboard		Ctrl + X
freeze window panes	View, Window	, *Freeze Panes*	
hide workbook	View, Window		
hide worksheet	Home, Cells	, *Hide & Unhide*, *Hide Sheet*	
insert new worksheet			Shift + F11
maximize window			
minimize window			
New Name dialog box	Formulas, Defined Names		
new window	View, Window		
paste selected cells	Home, Clipboard		Ctrl + V
restore down			
split window into panes	View, Window		
switch windows	View, Window		
unfreeze window panes	View, Window	, *Unfreeze Panes*	
unhide workbook	View, Window		
unhide worksheet	Home, Cells	, *Hide & Unhide*, *Unhide Sheet*	
Zoom dialog box	View, Zoom		

Performance Objectives

Upon successful completion of Chapter 6, you will be able to:

1. Pin and unpin workbooks at the *Recent* option list

2. Copy and move worksheets between workbooks

3. Apply and modify a cell style

4. Modify, remove, and delete a cell style

5. Insert and use hyperlinks

6. Modify, edit, and remove hyperlinks

7. Create financial forms using templates

8. Insert, edit, delete, and show comments

9. Insert formulas using financial functions

After you have worked with Excel for a period of time, you will have accumulated several workbook files. Frequently used workbooks can be pinned at the Open and Home backstage areas so you can access them without needing to browse for them. In this chapter, you will also learn more methods for creating and maintaining workbooks, such as copying or moving worksheets from one workbook to another, applying cell styles and globally changing the style, inserting hyperlinks in a workbook, and using an Excel template to create a workbook. Inserting, posting, editing, and deleting comments will also be covered.

 Data Files

Before beginning chapter work, copy the EL1C6 folder to your storage medium and then make EL1C6 the active folder.

The online course includes additional training and assessment resources.

> ## Activity 1 Copy and Move Worksheets into an Equipment Rental Workbook
> 3 Parts
>
> You will manage workbooks at the Open backstage area and then open multiple workbooks and copy and move worksheets between the workbooks.

Tutorial

Managing the *Recent* Option List

Managing the *Recent* Option List

As workbooks are opened and closed, Excel keeps a list of the most recently opened workbooks. To view this list, click the File tab and then click the *Open* option. This displays the Open backstage area, similar to what is shown in Figure 6.1. (The workbook names you see may vary from those in the figure.) Generally, the names of the 50 most recently opened workbooks are shown in the *Recent* option list and are organized in categories such as *Today*, *Yesterday*, and *Last Week*. To open a workbook, scroll down the list and then click the workbook name. The Excel opening screen and Home backstage area also display a list of the most recently opened workbooks.

Figure 6.1 Open Backstage Area

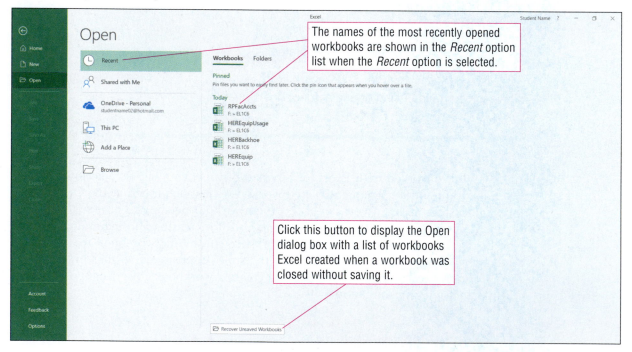

The names of the most recently opened workbooks are shown in the *Recent* option list when the *Recent* option is selected.

Click this button to display the Open dialog box with a list of workbooks Excel created when a workbook was closed without saving it.

Pinning and Unpinning a Workbook

Quick Steps

Pinning/Unpinning Document
1. Click File tab.
2. Click push pin icon at right of workbook name.
OR
1. Click File tab.
2. Click *Open* option.
3. Click push pin icon at right of workbook name.

A workbook that is opened on a regular basis can be pinned to the *Recent* option list so that it can be found more easily. To pin a workbook to the *Recent* option list at the Open backstage area, hover the mouse pointer over the workbook name and then click the small left-pointing push pin icon to the right of the workbook name. The left-pointing push pin changes to a down-pointing push pin and the pinned workbook appears at the top of the list in the *Pinned* category. A workbook can also be pinned at the Home backstage area. Click the push pin icon next to a workbook name and then workbook will display in the *Pinned* tab.

To "unpin" a workbook from the *Recent* option list at the Open backstage area or the *Pinned* tab at the Home backstage area, click the push pin icon to change it from a down-pointing pin to a left-pointing pin. More than one workbook can be pinned to a list. Another method for pinning and unpinning a workbook is to use the shortcut menu. Right-click a workbook name and then click the *Pin to list* or *Unpin from list* option.

In addition to workbooks, folders can be pinned for easier access. To pin a frequently-used folder, display the Open backstage area and then click the *Folders* option. Recently opened folders are listed and grouped into categories such as *Today*, *Yesterday*, and *Last Week* to reflect the time they were last accessed. Click the push pin icon to the right of a folder and it will be pinned to the top of the list.

Recovering an Unsaved Workbook

If a workbook is closed without having been saved, it can be recovered with the Recover Unsaved Workbooks button below the *Recent* option list. Click this button and the Open dialog box displays with the names of the workbooks that Excel has saved automatically. At this dialog box, double-click the workbook name to open it.

Clearing the *Recent* Option List and the Recent List

Clear the contents (except pinned workbooks) of the *Recent* option list by right-clicking a workbook name in the list and then clicking *Clear unpinned Workbooks* at the shortcut menu. At the message asking to confirm removal of the items, click Yes. To clear a folder from the Open backstage area, right-click a folder in the list and then click *Remove from list* at the shortcut menu.

Activity 1a **Managing Workbooks at the Open Backstage Area**   Part 1 of 3

1. Open Excel.
2. Click the File tab and then click the *Open* option.
3. Make sure the *Recent* option below the heading *Open* is selected. Notice the workbook names that display in the *Recent* option list.
4. Navigate to your EL1C6 folder, open **HEREquip**, and then save it with the name **6-HEREquip**.
5. Close **6-HEREquip**.
6. Open **HEREquipUsage** and then close it.

7. Open **HERBackhoe** and then close it.
8. Pin the three workbooks to the *Recent* option list (you will use them in Activity 1b) by completing the following steps:
   a. Click the File tab and then click the *Open* option. (This displays the Open backstage area with the *Recent* option selected.)
   b. Click the left-pointing push pin icon at the right of **6-HEREquip**. (This changes the pin from left pointing to down pointing and moves the workbook to the top of the list in the *Pinned* category.)

c. Click the left-pointing push pin icon at the right of **HEREquipUsage**.
d. Right-click **HERBackhoe** and then click *Pin to list* at the shortcut menu.
e. Click the Back button to exit the Open backstage area.

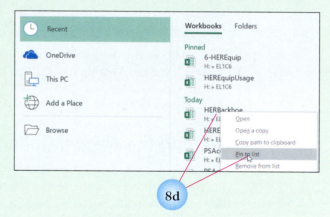

9. Open **6-HEREquip** by clicking the File tab, clicking the *Open* option, and then clicking **6-HEREquip** in the *Recent* option list.

Managing Worksheets

Individual worksheets can be moved or copied within the same workbook or to another existing workbook. Exercise caution when moving sheets, since any calculations and charts based on the data in a worksheet might become inaccurate if a worksheet is moved. To duplicate a sheet in the same workbook, press and hold down the Ctrl key, click the sheet tab and hold down the left mouse button, drag to the new location, and then release the mouse button and the Ctrl key.

Tutorial

Copying a Worksheet to Another Workbook

Copying a Worksheet to Another Workbook

To copy a worksheet to another workbook, open both the source and the destination workbooks. Right-click the sheet tab and then click *Move or Copy* at the shortcut menu. At the Move or Copy dialog box, shown in Figure 6.2, select the name of the destination workbook in the *To book* option drop-down list, select the name of the worksheet the copied worksheet will be placed before in the *Before sheet* list box, click the *Create a copy* check box, and then click OK.

Figure 6.2 Move or Copy Dialog Box

Copy Worksheet to
Another Workbook
1. Right-click sheet tab.
2. Click *Move or Copy.*
3. Select destination
   workbook.
4. Select worksheet
   location.
5. Click *Create a copy*
   check box.
6. Click OK.

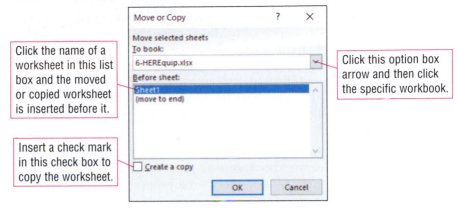

Click the name of a worksheet in this list box and the moved or copied worksheet is inserted before it.

Click this option box arrow and then click the specific workbook.

Insert a check mark in this check box to copy the worksheet.

Activity 1b Copying Worksheets to Another Workbook

Part 2 of 3

1. With **6-HEREquip** open, open **HEREquipUsage**.
2. Copy the Front Loader worksheet by completing the following steps:
   a. With **HEREquipUsage** the active workbook, right-click the Front Loader tab and then click *Move or Copy* at the shortcut menu.
   b. Click the *To book* option box arrow and then click **6-HEREquip.xlsx** at the drop-down list.
   c. Click *(move to end)* in the *Before sheet* list box.
   d. Click the *Create a copy* check box to insert a check mark.
   e. Click OK. (Excel switches to the **6-HEREquip** workbook and inserts the copied Front Loader worksheet after Sheet1.)

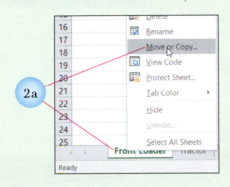

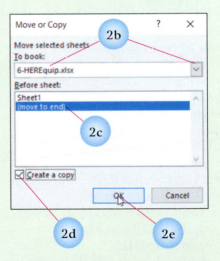

3. Complete steps similar to those in Step 2 to copy the Tractor worksheet to the **6-HEREquip** workbook.
4. Complete steps similar to those in Step 2 to copy the Forklift worksheet to the **6-HEREquip** workbook and insert the Forklift worksheet before the Tractor worksheet.
5. Save **6-HEREquip**.
6. Make **HEREquipUsage** the active workbook and then close it.

Check Your Work

Moving a Worksheet to Another Workbook

Quick Steps

Move Worksheet to Another Workbook
1. Right-click sheet tab.
2. Click *Move or Copy.*
3. Select destination workbook.
4. Select worksheet location.
5. Click OK.

To move a worksheet to another workbook, open both the source and the destination workbooks. Make active the worksheet to be moved in the source workbook, right-click the sheet tab, and then click *Move or Copy* at the shortcut menu. At the Move or Copy dialog box, shown in Figure 6.2 (on page 147), select the name of the destination workbook in the *To book* drop-down list, select the name of the worksheet the moved worksheet will be placed before in the *Before sheet* list box, and then click OK. To reposition a sheet tab, drag the tab to the new position.

Be careful when moving a worksheet to another workbook file. If formulas in the source workbook depend on the contents of the cells in the worksheet that is moved, they will no longer work properly.

Activity 1c   Moving a Worksheet to Another Workbook

Part 3 of 3

1. With **6-HEREquip** open, open **HERBackhoe**.
2. Move Sheet1 from **HERBackhoe** to **6-HEREquip** by completing the following steps:
   a. With **HERBackhoe** the active workbook, right-click the Sheet1 tab and then click *Move or Copy* at the shortcut menu.
   b. Click the *To book* option box arrow and then click **6-HEREquip.xlsx** at the drop-down list.
   c. Click *(move to end)* in the *Before sheet* list box.
   d. Click OK.
3. With **6-HEREquip** open, make the following changes:
   a. Rename Sheet1 as *Equipment Hours.*
   b. Rename Sheet1 (2) as *Backhoe.*
4. Create a range for the front loader total hours available by completing the following steps:
   a. Click the Front Loader tab.
   b. Select the range B4:E4.
   c. Click in the Name box.
   d. Type FrontLoaderHours.
   e. Press the Enter key.
5. Complete steps similar to those in Step 4 to create the following ranges:
   a. In the Front Loader worksheet, select the range B10:E10 and name it *FrontLoaderHoursInUse.*
   b. Click the Forklift tab and then select the range B4:E4 and name it *ForkliftHours.* Also select the range B10:E10 and name it *ForkliftHoursInUse.*
   c. Click the Tractor tab and then select the range B4:E4 and name it *TractorHours.* Also select the range B10:E10 and name it *TractorHoursInUse.*
   d. Click the Backhoe tab and then select the range B4:E4 and name it *BackhoeHours.* Also select the range B10:E10 and name it *BackhoeHoursInUse.*

6. Click the Equipment Hours tab to make it the active worksheet and then insert a formula that calculates the total hours for the front loader by completing the following steps:
   a. Make cell C4 active.
   b. Type =sum(Fr.
   c. When you type *Fr*, a drop-down list displays with the front loader ranges. Double-click *FrontLoaderHours*.
   d. Type) (the closing parenthesis).

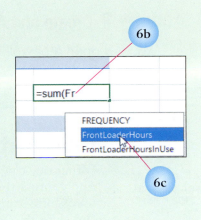

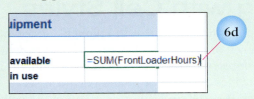

   e. Press the Enter key.
7. Complete steps similar to those in Step 6 to insert ranges in the following cells:
   a. Make cell C5 active and then insert a formula that calculates the total in-use hours for the front loader.
   b. Make cell C8 active and then insert a formula that calculates the total hours available for the forklift.
   c. Make cell C9 active and then insert a formula that calculates the total in-use hours for the forklift.
   d. Make cell C12 active and then insert a formula that calculates the total hours available for the tractor.
   e. Make cell C13 active and then insert a formula that calculates the total in-use hours for the tractor.
   f. Make cell C16 active and then insert a formula that calculates the total hours available for the backhoe.
   g. Make cell C17 active and then insert a formula that calculates the total in-use hours for the backhoe.
8. Make the following changes to specific worksheets:
   a. Click the Front Loader tab and then change the number in cell E4 from *415* to *426* and the number in cell C6 from *6* to *14*.
   b. Click the Forklift tab and then change the number in cell E4 from *415* to *426* and the number in cell D8 from *4* to *12*.
9. Select all the sheet tabs and then create a header that prints your name at the left of each worksheet, the page number in the middle, and the current date at the right.
10. Save and then print all the worksheets in **6-HEREquip**.
11. Close the workbook. (Make sure all the workbooks are closed.)
12. Make the following changes to the Open backstage area:
    a. Click the File tab and then click the *Open* option.
    b. Make sure the *Recent* option is selected.
    c. Unpin **6-HEREquip** from the *Recent* option list by clicking the down-pointing push pin icon at the right of **6-HEREquip**. (This changes the down-pointing push pin to a left-pointing push pin and moves the workbook down the list.)
    d. Unpin **HERBackhoe** and **HEREquipUsage**.
13. Click the Back button to exit the Open backstage area.

Check Your Work

Formatting with Cell Styles

💡*Hint* Cell styles are based on the workbook theme.

Formatting can be applied in a worksheet to highlight or accentuate certain cells. Apply formatting to a cell or selected cells with a cell style, which is a predefined set of formatting attributes, such as font, font size, alignment, borders, shading, and so forth. Excel provides a gallery of predesigned cell styles in the Styles group on the Home tab. Click the Cell Styles button to open the gallery. (On a wide-screen monitor, the gallery may already be open and some of the styles will be displayed. Click the More Styles arrow button at the right of the gallery to see all the available styles.)

Tutorial

Applying Cell Styles

Applying a Cell Style

To apply a style, select the cell(s), click the Cell Styles button in the Styles group on the Home tab, and then click the style at the drop-down gallery, shown in Figure 6.3. Hover the mouse pointer over a style in the drop-down gallery and the cell or selected cells display with the formatting applied.

🕐*uick Steps*

Apply Cell Style
1. Select cell(s).
2. Click Cell Styles button.
3. Click style.

Cell Styles

Figure 6.3 Cell Styles Button Drop-Down Gallery

Choose an option at this drop-down gallery to apply a predesigned style to a cell or selected cells in the worksheet.

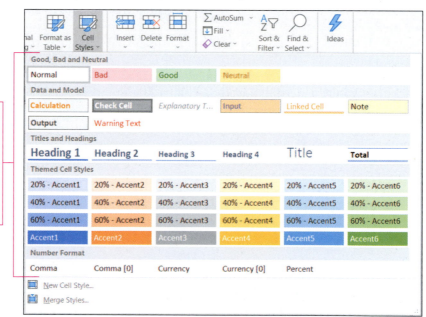

1. Open **OEPayroll** and then save it with the name **6-OEPayroll**.
2. With Sheet1 the active worksheet, insert the necessary formulas to calculate gross pay, withholding tax amount, social security tax amount, and net pay. *Hint: Refer to Activity 3c in Chapter 2 for assistance*. Select the range D4:G4 and then click the Accounting Number Format button to insert dollar symbols.
3. Make Sheet2 active and then insert a formula that calculates the amount due. *Hint: The formula in cell F4 will be =D4*(1+E4).* Make cell F4 active and then click the Accounting Number Format button to insert a dollar symbol.
4. Make Sheet3 active and then insert a formula in the *Due Date* column that calculates the purchase date plus the number of days in the *Terms* column. *Hint: The formula in cell F4 will be =D4+E4.*
5. Apply cell styles to cells by completing the following steps:
   a. Make Sheet1 active and then select cells A11 and A12.
   b. Click the Cell Styles button in the Styles gallery in the Styles group on the Home tab.
   c. At the drop-down gallery, hover the mouse pointer over different styles to see how the formatting affects the selected cells.
   d. Click the *Check Cell* option (second column, first row in the *Data and Model* section).
6. Select cells B11 and B12, click the Cell Styles button, and then click the *Output* option (first column, second row in the *Data and Model* section).

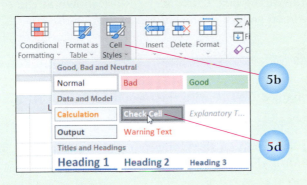
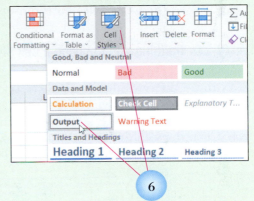

7. Save **6-OEPayroll**.

Check Your Work

Tutorial

Defining a Cell
Style

Quick Steps

Define Cell Style with Existing Formatting
1. Select cell containing formatting.
2. Click Cell Styles button.
3. Click *New Cell Style*.
4. Type name for new style.
5. Click OK.

Defining a Cell Style

Apply a style from the Cell Styles button drop-down gallery or create a new style. Using a style to apply formatting has several advantages. One key advantage is that it helps to ensure consistent formatting from one worksheet to another. To change the formatting, change the style and all the cells formatted with that style automatically reflect the change.

Two basic methods are available for defining a cell style. Define a style with formats already applied to a cell or display the Style dialog box, click the Format button, and then choose formatting options at the Format Cells dialog box. New styles are available only in the workbook in which they are created.

Figure 6.4 Style Dialog Box

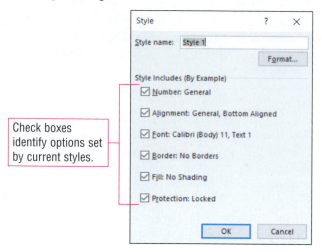

Check boxes identify options set by current styles.

To define a style with existing formatting, select the cell or cells containing the formatting, click the Cell Styles button on the Home tab, and then click the *New Cell Style* option at the bottom of the drop-down gallery. At the Style dialog box, shown in Figure 6.4, type a name for the new style in the *Style name* text box and then click OK to close the dialog box. Custom styles are shown at the top of the Cell Styles button drop-down gallery in the *Custom* section.

Activity 2b Defining and Applying a Cell Style

Part 2 of 5

1. With **6-OEPayroll** open, define a style named *C6Title* with the formatting in cell A1 by completing the following steps:
   a. Make sure Sheet1 is active and then make cell A1 active.
   b. Click the Cell Styles button in the Styles group on the Home tab and then click the *New Cell Style* option at the bottom of the drop-down gallery.

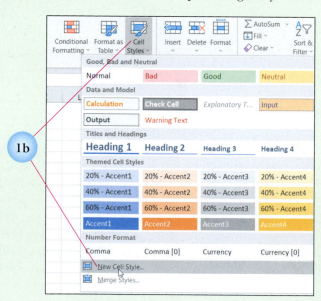

c. At the Style dialog box, type C6Title in the *Style name* text box.

d. Click OK.

2. Even though cell A1 is already formatted, the style has not been applied to it. (Later, you will modify the style and the style must be applied to the cell for the change to affect it.) Apply the C6Title style to cell A1 by completing the following steps:

a. With cell A1 active, click the Cell Styles button.

b. Click the *C6Title* style in the *Styles* gallery.

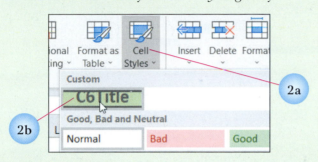

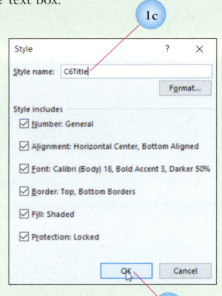

3. Apply the C6Title style to other cells by completing the following steps:

a. Click the Sheet2 tab.

b. Make cell A1 active.

c. Click the *C6Title* style at the Styles gallery. (Notice that the style does not apply row height formatting. The style applies only cell formatting.)

d. Click the Sheet3 tab.

e. Make cell A1 active.

f. Click the *C6Title* style at the Styles gallery.

g. Click the Sheet1 tab.

4. Save **6-OEPayroll**.

Check Your Work

Quick Steps

Define Cell Style
1. Click in blank cell.
2. Click Cell Styles button.
3. Click *New Cell Style*.
4. Type style name.
5. Click Format button.
6. Choose formatting options.
7. Click OK.
8. Click OK.

In addition to defining a style based on cell formatting, a custom style can be defined without first applying the formatting. To do this, display the Style dialog box, type a name for the custom style, and then click the Format button. At the Format Cells dialog box, apply the formatting and then click OK to close the dialog box. At the Style dialog box, remove the check mark from any formatting that should not be included in the style and then click OK to close the Style dialog box.

Activity 2c Defining a Cell Style without First Applying Formatting

Part 3 of 5

1. With **6-OEPayroll** open, define a custom style named *C6Subtitle* without first applying the formatting by completing the following steps:

a. With Sheet1 active, click in any empty cell.

b. Click the Cell Styles button and then click *New Cell Style* at the drop-down gallery.

c. At the Style dialog box, type C6Subtitle in the *Style name* text box.

d. Click the Format button in the Style dialog box.

e. Click the Font tab.

f. At the Format Cells dialog box with the Font tab selected, change the font to Candara, the font style to bold, the size to 12 points, and the color to White, Background 1.

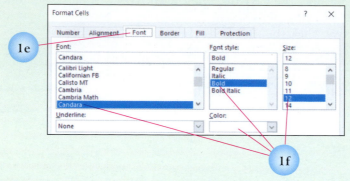

g. Click the Fill tab.

h. Click the green color shown at the right (last column, fifth row).

i. Click the Alignment tab.

j. Change the horizontal alignment to center alignment.

k. Click OK to close the Format Cells dialog box.

l. Click OK to close the Style dialog box.

2. Apply the C6Subtitle custom style by completing the following steps:

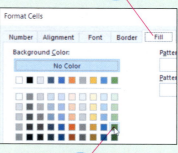

a. Make cell A2 active.

b. Click the Cell Styles button and then click the *C6Subtitle* style.

c. Click the Sheet2 tab.

d. Make cell A2 active.

e. Click the Cell Styles button and then click the *C6Subtitle* style.

f. Click the Sheet3 tab.

g. Make cell A2 active.

h. Click the Cell Styles button and then click the *C6Subtitle* style.

i. Click the Sheet1 tab.

3. Apply the following predesigned cell styles:

a. With Sheet1 the active tab, select the range A3:G3.

b. Click the Cell Styles button and then click the *Heading 3* style in the *Titles and Headings* section at the drop-down gallery.

c. Select the range A5:G5.

d. Click the Cell Styles button and then click the *20% - Accent3* style.

e. Apply the 20% - Accent3 style to the range A7:G7 and the range A9:G9.

f. Click the Sheet2 tab.

g. Select the range A3:F3 and then apply the Heading 3 style.

h. Select the range A5:F5 and then apply the 20% - Accent3 style.

i. Apply the 20% - Accent3 style to every other row of cells (the range A7:F7, A9:F9, and so on, finishing with the range A17:F17).

j. Click the Sheet3 tab.

k. Select the range A3:F3 and then apply the Heading 3 style.

l. Apply the 20% - Accent3 style to the ranges A5:F5, A7:F7, and A9:F9.

4. With Sheet3 active, change the height of row 1 to 36.00 points.

5. Make Sheet2 active and then change the height of row 1 to 36.00 points.
6. Make Sheet1 active.
7. Save **6-OEPayroll** and then print only the first worksheet.

 Check Your Work

 Tutorial

Modifying a Cell Style

Modifying a Cell Style

One of the advantages to formatting cells with a style is that when the formatting is modified and all the cells formatted with that style update automatically. Modify a predesigned style and only the style in the current workbook is affected. Open a blank workbook and the cell styles available are the default styles.

To modify a style, click the Cell Styles button in the Styles group on the Home tab and then right-click the style at the drop-down gallery. At the shortcut menu, click *Modify*. At the Style dialog box, click the Format button. Make the formatting changes at the Format Cells dialog box and then click OK. Click OK to close the Style dialog box and any cells formatted with the style automatically update.

Quick Steps

Modify Cell Style
1. Click Cell Styles button.
2. Right-click style.
3. Click *Modify*.
4. Click Format button.
5. Make formatting changes.
6. Click OK.
7. Click OK.

Activity 2d Modifying Cell Styles

Part 4 of 5

1. With **6-OEPayroll** open, modify the C6Title custom style by completing the following steps:
   a. Click in any empty cell.
   b. Click the Cell Styles button.
   c. At the drop-down gallery, right-click the *C6Title* style in the *Custom* section and then click *Modify* at the drop-down gallery.
   d. At the Style dialog box, click the Format button.
   e. At the Format Cells dialog box, click the Font tab and then change the font to Candara.
   f. Click the Alignment tab.
   g. Click the *Vertical* option box arrow and then click *Center* at the drop-down list.
   h. Click the Fill tab.
   i. Click the light blue fill color (fifth column, third row), as shown at the right.

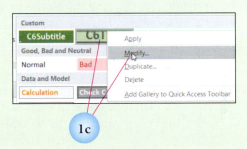

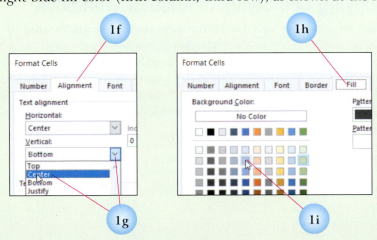

  j. Click OK to close the Format Cells dialog box.

  k. Click OK to close the Style dialog box.

2. Modify the C6Subtitle style by completing the following steps:

  a. Click in any empty cell.

  b. Click the Cell Styles button.

  c. At the drop-down gallery, right-click the *C6Subtitle* style in the *Custom* section and then click *Modify*.

  d. At the Style dialog box, click the Format button.

  e. At the Format Cells dialog box, click the Font tab and then change the font to Calibri.

  f. Click the Fill tab.

  g. Click the dark blue fill color, as shown at the right (fifth column, sixth row).

  h. Click OK to close the Format Cells dialog box.

  i. Click OK to close the Style dialog box.

3. Modify the predefined 20% - Accent3 style by completing the following steps:

  a. Click the Cell Styles button.

  b. At the drop-down gallery, right-click the *20% - Accent3* style and then click *Modify*.

  c. At the Style dialog box, click the Format button.

  d. At the Format Cells dialog box, click the Fill tab.

  e. Click the light blue fill color, as shown at the right (fifth column, second row).

  f. Click OK to close the Format Cells dialog box.

  g. Click OK to close the Style dialog box.

4. Click each sheet tab and notice the formatting changes made by the modified styles.

5. Change the name of Sheet1 to *Weekly Payroll*, the name of Sheet2 to *Invoices*, and the name of Sheet3 to *Overdue Accounts*.

6. Apply a different color to each of the three sheet tabs.

7. Save and then print all the worksheets in **6-OEPayroll**.

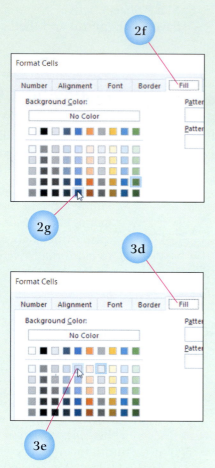

Check Your Work

 Tutorial

Copying Cell
Styles to Another
Workbook

Quick Steps

Copy Cell Styles to
Another Workbook
1. Open workbook
 containing styles.
2. Open workbook to
 be modified.
3. Click Cell Styles
 button.
4. Click *Merge Styles*
 option.
5. Double-click name
 of workbook that
 contains styles.

Copying Cell Styles to Another Workbook

Custom styles are saved with the workbook they are created in. However, styles can be copied from one workbook to another. To do this, open the workbook containing the styles and open the workbook the styles will be copied into. Click the Cell Styles button in the Styles group on the Home tab and then click the *Merge Styles* option at the bottom of the drop-down gallery. At the Merge Styles dialog box, shown in Figure 6.5, double-click the name of the workbook that contains the styles to be copied.

Figure 6.5 Merge Styles Dialog Box

Double-click the name of the workbook containing the styles to be copied.

Removing a Cell Style

Quick Steps

Remove Cell Style
1. Select cells formatted with style to be removed.
2. Click Cell Styles button.
3. Click *Normal* style.

Delete Cell Style
1. Click Cell Styles button.
2. Right-click style.
3. Click *Delete*.

Remove formatting applied by a style by applying the Normal style, which is the default. To do this, select the cells, click the Cell Styles button, and then click the *Normal* style at the drop-down gallery.

Deleting a Cell Style

To delete a style, click the Cell Styles button in the Styles group on the Home tab. At the drop-down gallery, right-click the style to be deleted and then click *Delete* at the shortcut menu. Formatting applied by the deleted style is removed from cells in the workbook. The Normal cell style cannot be deleted.

Activity 2e Copying Cell Styles to Another Workbook   **Part 5 of 5**

1. With **6-OEPayroll** open, open **OEPlans**.
2. Save the workbook and name it **6-OEPlans**.
3. Copy the styles in **6-OEPayroll** into **6-OEPlans** by completing the following steps:
   a. With **6-OEPlans** as the active workbook, click the Cell Styles button in the Styles group on the Home tab.
   b. Click the *Merge Styles* option at the bottom of the drop-down gallery.
   c. At the Merge Styles dialog box, double-click **6-OEPayroll.xlsx** in the *Merge styles from* list box.
   d. At the message asking if you want to merge styles that have the same names, click Yes.

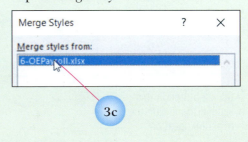

4. Apply the C6Title custom style to cell A1 and the C6Subtitle custom style to cell A2.
5. Increase the height of row 1 to 36.00 points.
6. Save, print, and then close **6-OEPlans**.
7. Close **6-OEPayroll**.

 **Check Your Work**

Activity 3 Insert, Modify, and Remove Hyperlinks

3 Parts

You will open a facilities account workbook and then insert hyperlinks to a website, to cells in other worksheets in the workbook, and to another workbook. You will modify and edit hyperlinks and then remove a hyperlink from the workbook.

Tutorial

Inserting Hyperlinks

Quick Steps

Insert Hyperlink
1. Click Insert tab.
2. Click Link button.
3. Make changes at Insert Hyperlink dialog box.
4. Click OK.

Link

Inserting Hyperlinks

A hyperlink can serve a number of purposes in a workbook: Click it to navigate to a web page on the internet or a specific location in the workbook, to display a different workbook, to open a file in a different program, to create a new document, or to link to an email address. Create a customized hyperlink by clicking in a cell in a workbook, clicking the Insert tab, and then clicking the Link button in the Links group. This displays the Insert Hyperlink dialog box, shown in Figure 6.6. At this dialog box, identify what is to be linked and the location of the link. Click the ScreenTip button to customize the hyperlink ScreenTip.

Linking to an Existing Web Page or File

At the Insert Hyperlink dialog box, link to a web page on the internet by typing a web address or by using the Existing File or Web Page button in the *Link to* section. To link to an existing web page, type the address of the web page, such as *www.paradigmeducation.com*.

By default, the automatic formatting of hyperlinks is turned on and the web address is formatted as a hyperlink. (The text is underlined and the color changes to blue.) Turn off the automatic formatting of hyperlinks at the AutoCorrect dialog box. Display this dialog box by clicking the File tab, clicking *Options*, and then clicking *Proofing* in the left panel of the Excel Options dialog box. Click the AutoCorrect Options button to display the AutoCorrect dialog box. At this dialog

Figure 6.6 Insert Hyperlink Dialog Box

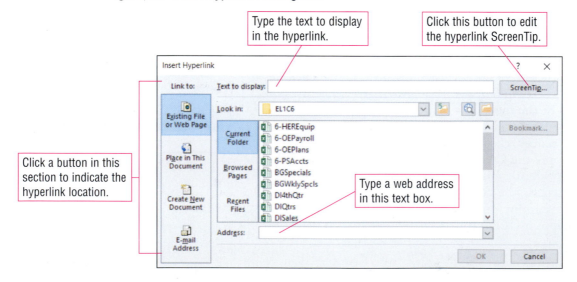

box, click the AutoFormat As You Type tab and then remove the check mark from the *Internet and network paths with hyperlinks* check box.

A hyperlink can be inserted that links to any of several sources, such as another Excel workbook, a Word document, or a PowerPoint presentation. To link an Excel workbook to a workbook or file in another application, display the Insert Hyperlink dialog box and then click the Existing File or Web Page button in the *Link to* section. Use buttons in the *Look in* section to navigate to the folder containing the file and then click the file name. Make other changes in the Insert Hyperlink dialog box as needed and then click OK.

Navigating Using Hyperlinks

Navigate to a hyperlinked location by clicking the hyperlink in the worksheet. Hover the mouse pointer over the hyperlink and a ScreenTip displays with the address of the hyperlinked location. To display specific information in the ScreenTip, click the ScreenTip button at the Insert Hyperlink dialog box, type the text in the Set Hyperlink ScreenTip dialog box, and then click OK.

Activity 3a **Linking to a Website and Another Workbook**   **Part 1 of 3**

1. Open **PSAccts** and then save it with the name **6-PSAccts**.
2. Insert a hyperlink to information about Pyramid Sales, a fictitious company (the hyperlink will connect to the publishing company website), by completing the following steps:
   a. Make cell A13 active in the Summary sheet.
   b. Click the Insert tab and then click the Link button in the Links group.
   c. At the Insert Hyperlink dialog box, if necessary, click the Existing File or Web Page button in the *Link to* section.
   d. Type www.paradigmeducation.com in the *Address* text box. (*http://* will automatically be added to the address)
   e. Select the text in the *Text to display* text box and then type Company information.
   f. Click the ScreenTip button in the upper right corner of the dialog box.

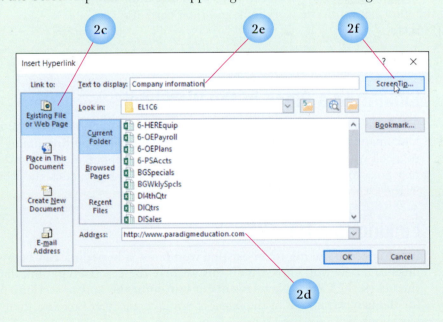

g. At the Set Hyperlink ScreenTip dialog box, type View the company website. and then click OK.

h. Click OK to close the Insert Hyperlink dialog box.

3. Navigate to the company website (in this case, the publishing company website) by clicking the <u>Company information</u> hyperlink in cell A13.

4. Close the web browser.

5. Create a link to another workbook by completing the following steps:

a. Make cell A11 active, type Semiannual sales, and then press the Enter key.

b. Make cell A11 active and then click the Link button.

c. At the Insert Hyperlink dialog box, make sure the Existing File or Web Page button is selected.

d. If necessary, click your *Look in* option box arrow and then navigate to your EL1C6 folder.

e. Double-click **PSSalesAnalysis**.

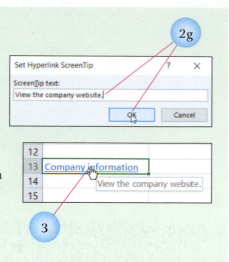

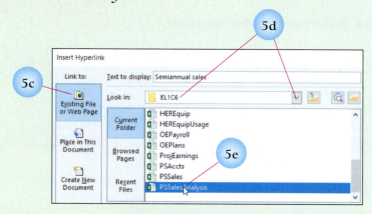

6. Click the <u>Semiannual sales</u> hyperlink to open **PSSalesAnalysis**.

7. Look at the information in the workbook and then close it.

8. Save **6-PSAccts**.

 Check Your Work

Linking to a Place in the Workbook

To create a hyperlink to another location in the workbook, click the Place in This Document button in the *Link to* section in the Edit Hyperlink dialog box. To link to a cell within the same worksheet, type the cell name in the *Type the cell reference* text box. To link to another worksheet in the workbook, click the worksheet name in the *Or select a place in this document* list box.

Linking to a New Workbook

In addition to linking to an existing workbook, a hyperlink can be inserted that links to a new workbook. To do this, display the Insert Hyperlink dialog box and then click the Create New Document button in the *Link to* section. Type a name for the new workbook in the *Name of new document* text box and then specify if the workbook will be edited now or later.

Linking Using a Graphic

A graphic—such as an image, picture, or text box—can be used to create a hyperlink to a file or website. To create a hyperlink with a graphic, select the graphic, click the Insert tab, and then click the Link button. Or right-click the graphic and then click *Link* at the shortcut menu. At the Insert Hyperlink dialog box, specify the location to be linked to and the text to display in the hyperlink.

Linking to an Email Address

At the Insert Hyperlink dialog box, a hyperlink can be inserted that links to an email address. To do this, click the E-mail Address button in the *Link to* section, type the address in the *E-mail address* text box, and then type a subject for the email in the *Subject* text box. Click in the *Text to display* text box and then type the text to display in the worksheet.

Activity 3b **Linking to a Place in a Workbook, Linking to Another Workbook, and Linking from a Graphic**   **Part 2 of 3**

1. With **6-PSAccts** open, create a link from the balance in cell B8 to the balance in cell G20 in the January worksheet by completing the following steps:
   a. Make cell B8 active.
   b. Click the Link button.
   c. At the Insert Hyperlink dialog box, click the Place in This Document button in the *Link to* section.
   d. Select the text in the *Type the cell reference* text box and then type g20.
   e. Click *January* in the *Or select a place in this document* list box.
   f. Click OK to close the Insert Hyperlink dialog box.

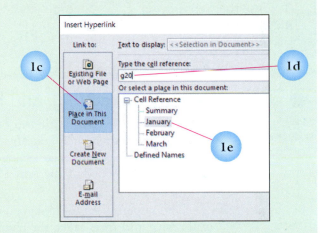

2. Make cell C8 active and then complete steps similar to those in Steps 1b through 1f except click *February* in the *Or select a place in this document* list box.
3. Make cell D8 active and then complete steps similar to those in Steps 1b through 1f except click *March* in the *Or select a place in this document* list box.
4. Click the hyperlinked amount in cell B8. (This makes cell G20 active in the January worksheet.)
5. Click the Summary sheet tab.
6. Click the hyperlinked amount in cell C8. (This makes cell G20 active in the February worksheet.)
7. Click the Summary sheet tab.
8. Click the hyperlinked amount in cell D8. (This makes cell G20 active in the March worksheet.)
9. Click the Summary sheet tab.

10. Use the first pyramid graphic image in cell A1 to create a link to the company web page by completing the following steps:

   a. Right-click the first pyramid graphic image in cell A1 and then click *Link* at the shortcut menu.

   b. At the Insert Hyperlink dialog box, if necessary, click the Existing File or Web Page button in the *Link to* section.

   c. Type www.paradigmeducation.com in the *Address* text box.

   d. Click the ScreenTip button in the upper right corner of the dialog box.

   e. At the Set Hyperlink ScreenTip dialog box, type View the company website. and then click OK.

   f. Click OK to close the Insert Hyperlink dialog box.

11. Make cell A5 active.

12. Navigate to the company website (the publishing company website) by clicking the first pyramid graphic image.

13. Close the web browser.

14. Save **6-PSAccts**.

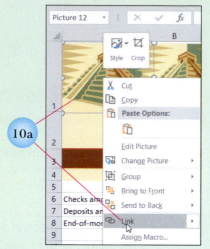

Check Your Work >

 Tutorial

Modifying, Editing, and Removing a Hyperlink

Modifying, Editing, and Removing a Hyperlink

The hyperlink text or destination can be modified. To do this, right-click the hyperlink and then click *Edit Hyperlink* at the shortcut menu. At the Edit Hyperlink dialog box, make changes and then close the dialog box. The same options are provided at the Edit Hyperlink dialog box as the Insert Hyperlink dialog box.

The hyperlinked text in a cell can also be modified. To do this, make the cell active and then make the changes, such as applying a different font or font size, changing the text color, and adding a text effect. Remove a hyperlink from a workbook by right-clicking the cell containing the hyperlink and then clicking *Remove Hyperlink* at the shortcut menu.

Activity 3c   Modifying, Editing, and Removing a Hyperlink   Part 3 of 3

1. With **6-PSAccts** open, modify the <u>Semiannual sales</u> hyperlink by completing the following steps:

   a. Position the mouse pointer on the <u>Semiannual sales</u> hyperlink in cell A11, click the right mouse button, and then click *Edit Hyperlink* at the shortcut menu.

   b. At the Edit Hyperlink dialog box, select the text *Semiannual sales* in the *Text to display* text box and then type Customer sales analysis.

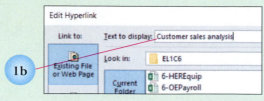

162   Excel Level 1 | Unit 2   Chapter 6 | Maintaining Workbooks

c. Click the ScreenTip button in the upper right corner of the dialog box.

d. At the Set Hyperlink ScreenTip dialog box, type Click this hyperlink to display the workbook containing customer sales analysis.

e. Click OK to close the Set Hyperlink ScreenTip dialog box.

f. Click OK to close the Edit Hyperlink dialog box.

2. Click the Customer sales analysis hyperlink.

3. After looking at the **PSSalesAnalysis** workbook, close it.

4. With cell A11 active, edit the Customer sales analysis hyperlink text by completing the following steps:

a. Click the Home tab.

b. Click the Font Color button arrow and then click the *Dark Red* color option (first option in the *Standard Colors* section).

c. Click the Bold button.

d. Click the Underline button. (This removes underlining from the text.)

5. Remove the Company information hyperlink by right-clicking in cell A13 and then clicking *Remove Hyperlink* at the shortcut menu.

6. Press the Delete key to remove the contents of cell A13.

7. Save, print only the first worksheet (the Summary worksheet), and then close **6-PSAccts**.

 Check Your Work

---

Activity 4 **Create a Billing Statement Using a Template;** **3 Parts**
Posting, Editing and Deleting Comments

You will open a Billing Statement template provided by Excel, add data, and then save the template as an Excel workbook. You will also post, edit, and delete comments in the Billing statement workbook.

 Tutorial

Using Templates

Using Excel Templates

Excel provides a number of template worksheet forms for specific uses. Use Excel templates to create a variety of worksheets with specialized formatting, such as balance sheets, billing statements, loan amortizations, sales invoices, and time cards. Display installed templates by clicking the File tab and then clicking the *New* option. This displays the New backstage area, as shown in Figure 6.7.

Click a template in the New backstage area and a preview of the template displays in a window. Click the Create button in the template window and a workbook based on the template opens and displays on the screen.

Quick Steps

Use Excel Template
1. Click File tab.
2. Click *New* option.
3. Double-click template.

Locations for personalized text are shown in placeholders in the worksheet. To enter information in the worksheet, position the mouse pointer (white plus symbol [+]) in the location the data is to be typed and then click the left mouse button. After typing the data, click the next location. The insertion point can also be moved to another cell using the commands learned in Chapter 1. For example, press the Tab key to make the next cell active or press Shift + Tab to make the previous cell active. If the computer is connected to the internet, a number of templates offered by Microsoft can be downloaded.

Figure 6.7 New Backstage Area

Use this option to search for templates online.

The templates shown in this section of the New backstage area will vary from what is shown in this figure.

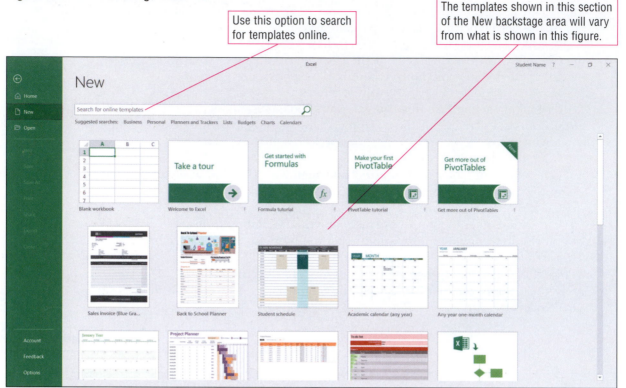

Activity 4a Preparing a Billing Statement Using a Template

Part 1 of 3

1. Click the File tab and then click the *New* option.
2. At the New backstage area, click in the search text box, type billing statement, and then press the Enter key.
3. Double-click the *Billing statement* template (see image below). If you are unable to access online templates, open the **BillingStatement** file in your EL1C6 folder.

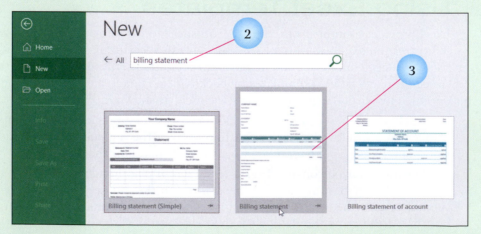

4. Make cell B1 active and then type IN-FLOW SYSTEMS.
5. Click in the cell to the right of *Street Address* (cell C2) and then type 320 Milander Way.

6. Click in each of the cells for the labels specified below and then type the text indicated:

Address 2 (cell C3): P.O. Box 2300
City, ST ZIP Code (cell C4): Boston, MA 02188
Phone (cell G2): (617) 555-3900
Fax (cell G3): (617) 555-3945
E-mail (cell G4): inflow@ppi-edu.net
Statement # (cell C6): 5432
Date (cell C7): =TODAY()
Customer ID (cell C8): 25-345
Name (cell G6): Aidan Mackenzie
Company Name (cell G7): Stanfield Enterprises
Street Address (cell G8): 9921 South 42nd Avenue
Address 2 (cell G9): P.O. Box 5540
City, ST ZIP Code (cell G10): Boston, MA 02193
Type (cell C13): System Unit
Invoice # (cell D13): 7452
Description (cell E13): Calibration Unit
Amount (cell F13): 950
Payment (cell G13): 200
Customer Name (cell C22): Stanfield Enterprises
Amount Enclosed (cell C27): 750

7. Save the completed invoice and name it **6-Billing**.

Inserting and Managing Comments

Excel includes a comment feature that allows users to post, edit, reply, and delete comments. A comment is a pop-up box that is attached to a cell and contains text pertaining to the contents of the cell, as shown in Figure 6.8. Other users can post replies to a comment, starting a dialog between users to assist in reviewing a workbook. A cell that contains a comment will show a colored comment icon in the upper right corner of a cell, alerting the reader that a comment exists. Display a comment by hovering the mouse over the cell that contains a comment. Insert and manage comments with buttons in the Comments group on the Review tab, a shown in Firgure 6.9

Inserting a New Comment

New Comment

Insert a new comment in a cell by first making the desired cell active and then clicking the New Comment button in the Comments group on the Review tab. When a new comment is inserted, a comment pop-up box will appear, with the insertion point in a text box. Type the comment in the text box that is regarding the contents of the cell.

A new comment can also be inserted using the shortcut menu. Insert a new comment using the shortcut menu by right-clicking a cell and then clicking the *New Comment* option on the shortcut menu.

Posting a Comment

Once a comment is typed into the text box of the comment pop-up box, click the Post button to post the comment. Once a comment has been posted, other users can reply to it and additional comments can be added to the worksheet.

Figure 6.8 Comment Box

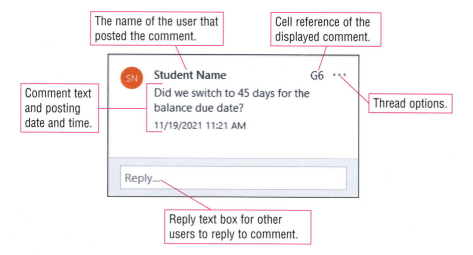

The name of the user that posted the comment.

Cell reference of the displayed comment.

Comment text and posting date and time.

Thread options.

Reply text box for other users to reply to comment.

Figure 6.9 Review Tab

1. With 6-Billing open, insert a new comment by completing the following steps:
   a. Make cell C3 active.
   b. Click the Review tab.
   c. Click the New Comment button in the Comments group.

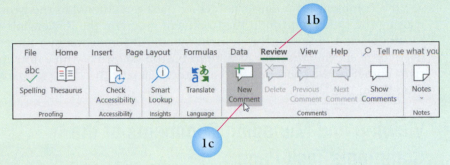

   d. Type Please enter the new P.O. Box for the Billing department here.
   e. Click the Post button.
2. Insert a new comment indicating that the contact person for Stanfield Enterprises has changed by completing the following steps:
   a. Right-click cell G6.
   b. Click the *New Comment* option at the shortcut menu.
   c. Type Check with Stanfield Enterprises to learn the name of their new contact person.
   d. Click the Post button.

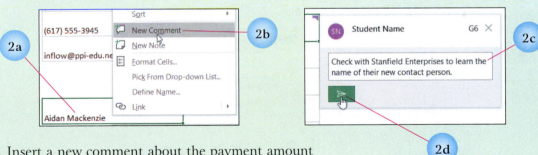

3. Insert a new comment about the payment amount by completing the following steps:
   a. Click in cell G13.
   b. Click the New Comment button.
   c. Type Ask Roger if this is the correct payment previously sent by Stanfield Enterprises.
   d. Click the Post button.
4. Insert a new comment about the balance due by completing the following steps:
   a. Click in cell B20.
   b. Click the New Comment button.
   c. Type Did we switch to 45 days for the balance due date?
   d. Click the Post button.
5. Save **6-Billing**.

Editing and Deleting a Comment

After a comment has been posted, it can be edited by using the Edit button in the comment box. Click in a cell that contains a posted comment and then position the mouse pointer anywhere inside the comment box and an Edit button appears in the lower right corner of the comment box. Click the Edit button and then use the mouse and keyboard to make edits to the comment text.

 Delete

If a comment is no longer needed or has been entered in the wrong cell, delete it using the Delete button in the Comment group on the Review tab or using the *Delete Comment* option at the shortcut menu. All comments in a thread can be deleted by clicking the Thread options button (shown as three dots in the upper right corner of the comment box) and then clicking the *Delete thread* option at the drop-down list.

Viewing and Managing Comments at the Comments Task Pane

 Show Comments

Quick Steps

Open Comments Task Pane
1. Click Review tab.
2. Click Show Comments button.

In a large worksheet, locating every cell that contains a comment may be difficult. To view all comments at a glance, open the Comments task pane, as shown in firgure 6.10. Open the Comments task pane by clicking the Show Comments button in the Comments group on the Review tab. Comments will appear in the Comments task pane in order first by row number, then by column letter. Comments can be edited, deleted and replied to in the Comments task pane. If a worksheet contains more comments than can be shown at one time in the Comments task pane, a scroll bar is added to the task pane. Close the Comments task pane by clicking the Close button in the task pane or by clicking the Show Comments button.

Figure 6.10 Comments task pane

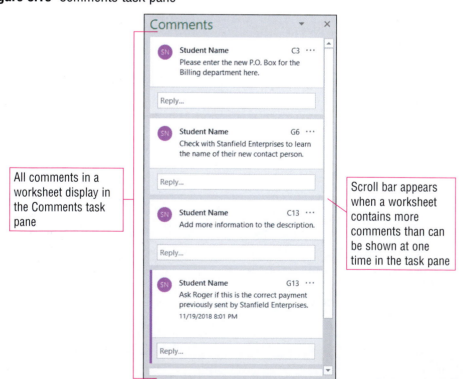

All comments in a worksheet display in the Comments task pane

Scroll bar appears when a worksheet contains more comments than can be shown at one time in the task pane

1. With 6-Billing open, edit the comment in cell G6 by completing the following steps:
   a. Click in cell G6.
   b. Position the mouse pointer anywhere in the Comment box.
   c. Click the Edit button.
   d. Move the insertion point to just before the period, press the spacebar, and then type in the Accounts department.
   e. Click the Save button.

2. Click the Show Comments button in the Comments group.
3. With the Comments task pane displayed, edit the comment in cell G13 by completing the following steps:
   a. Click the comment box with the cell reference G13 in the upper right corner.
   b. Click the Edit button.
   c. Change the text *Roger* to *Richard*.
   d. Click the Save button.

4. Click the first comment box in the Comments task pane and then click the Delete button in the Comments group.
5. Change the settings in the Page Setup dialog box in order to print the comments by completing the following steps:
   a. Click the Page Layout tab.
   b. Click the Page Setup group dialog box launcher.
   c. At the Page Setup dialog box, click the Sheet tab.
   d. Click the Comments option box arrow and then click *At end of sheet* at the drop-down list.

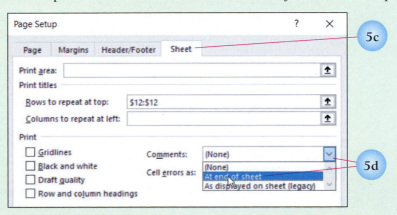

   e. Click OK.
6. Click the Close button in the Comments task pane.
7. Save, print, and then close **6-Billing**.

Activity 5 Calculate Payments and the Future Value of an Investment

2 Parts

You will use the PMT financial function to calculate payments and the FV financial function to find the future value of an investment.

Tutorial

Using Financial Functions

Writing Formulas with Financial Functions

Excel provides a number of financial functions that can be used in formulas. Use financial functions to determine different aspects of a financial loan or investment, such as the payment amount, present value, future value, interest rate, and number of payment periods. Each financial function requires some of the variables listed below to return a result. Two such financial functions are the PMT function and FV function. The PMT function calculates the payment for a loan based on constant payments and a constant interest rate. The FV function calculates the future value of an investment. Financial functions use some of the following arguments:

- **Rate:** The rate is the interest rate for a payment period. The rate may need to be modified for the function to produce the desired results. For example, most rate values are given as an APR (annual percentage rate), which is the percentage rate for one year, not a payment period. So a percentage rate may be given as 12% APR but if the payment period is a month, then the percentage rate for the function is 1%, not 12%. If a worksheet contains the annual percentage rate, enter the cell reference in the function argument and specify that it should be divided by 12 months. For example, if cell B6 contains the annual interest rate, enter *b6/12* as the Rate argument.

- **Nper:** The Nper is the number of payment periods in an investment. The Nper may also need to be modified depending on what information is provided. For example, if a loan duration is expressed in years but the payments are made monthly, the Nper value needs to be adjusted accordingly. A five-year loan has an Nper of 60 (five years times 12 months in each year).

- **Pmt:** The Pmt is the payment amount for each period. This argument describes the payment amount for a period and is commonly expressed as a negative value because it is an outflow of cash. However, the Pmt value can be entered as a positive value if the present value (Pv) or future value (Fv) is entered as a negative value. Whether the Pmt value is positive or negative depends on who created the workbook. For example, a home owner lists the variable as outflow, while the lending institution lists it as inflow.

- **Pv:** The Pv is the present value of an investment, expressed in a lump sum. The Pv argument is generally the initial loan amount. For example, if a person is purchasing a new home, the Pv is the amount of money he or she borrowed to buy the home. Pv can be expressed as a negative value, which denotes it as an investment instead of a loan. For example, if a bank issues a loan to a home buyer, it enters the Pv value as negative because it is an outflow of cash.

- **Fv:** The Fv is the future value of an investment, expressed in a lump sum amount. The Fv argument is generally the loan amount plus the amount of interest paid during the loan. In the example of a home buyer, the Fv is the sum of payments, which includes both the principle and interest paid on the loan. In the example of a bank, the Fv is the total amount received after a loan has been paid off. Fv can also be expressed as either a positive or negative value, depending on which side of the transaction is being reviewed.

Finding the Periodic Payments for a Loan

The PMT function finds the payment for a loan based on constant payments and a constant interest rate. In Activity 5a, the PMT function will be used to determine monthly payments for equipment and a used van as well as monthly income from selling equipment. The formulas created with the PMT function will include Rate, Nper, and Pv arguments. The Nper argument is the number of payments that will be made on the loan or investment, Pv is the current value of amounts to be received or paid in the future, and Fv is the value of the loan or investment at the end of all periods.

 Financial

To write the PMT function, click the Formulas tab, click the Financial button in the Function Library group, and then click the PMT function at the drop-down list. This displays the Function Arguments dialog box with options for inserting cell designations for Rate, Nper, and Pv. (These are the arguments displayed in bold formatting in the Function Arguments dialog box. The dialog box also contains the Fv and Type functions, which are dimmed.)

Activity 5a Calculating Payments   Part 1 of 2

1. Open **RPReports** and then save it with the name **6-RPReports**.
2. The owner of Real Photography is interested in purchasing a new developer and needs to determine monthly payments on three different models. Insert a formula that calculates monthly payments and then copy that formula by completing the following steps:
   a. Make cell E5 active.
   b. Click the Formulas tab.
   c. Click the Financial button in the Function Library group, scroll down the drop-down list, and then click *PMT*.

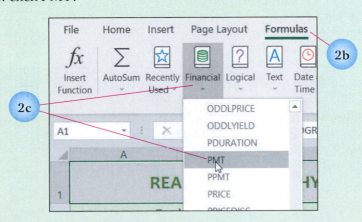

d. At the Function Arguments dialog box, type c5/12 in the *Rate* text box. (This tells Excel to divide the interest rate by 12 months.)

e. Press the Tab key. (This moves the insertion point to the *Nper* text box.)

f. Type d5. (This is the total number of months for the investment.)

g. Press the Tab key. (This moves the insertion point to the *Pv* text box.)

h. Type b5. (This is the purchase price of the developer.)

i. Click OK. (This closes the dialog box and inserts the monthly payment of *($316.98)* in cell E5. Excel shows the result of the PMT function as a negative number since the loan represents money going out of the company—a negative cash flow.)

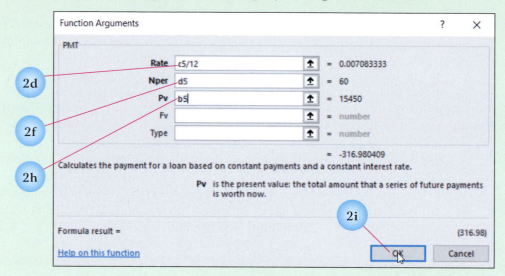

j. Copy the formula in cell E5 into cells E6 and E7.

3. The owner is interested in purchasing a used van for the company and wants an idea of what monthly payments would be at various terms and rates. Insert a formula that calculates monthly payments for a three-year loan at 5% interest by completing the following steps:

a. Make cell E12 active.

b. Make sure the Formulas tab is active.

c. Click the Financial button, scroll down the drop-down list, and then click *PMT*.

d. At the Function Arguments dialog box, type c12/12 in the *Rate* text box. (This tells Excel to divide the interest rate by 12 months.)

e. Press the Tab key.

f. Type d12 in the *Nper* text box. (This is the total number of months for the investment.)

g. Press the Tab key.

h. Type b12 in the *Pv* text box.

i. Click OK. (This closes the dialog box and inserts the monthly payment of *($299.71)* in cell E12.)

j. Copy the formula in cell E12 to the range E13:E15.

Term in Months	Monthly Payments
36	($299.71)
36	($449.56)
36	($599.42)
36	($749.27)

4. The owner has discovered that the interest rate for a used van will be 6.25% instead of 5%. Change the percentages in the range C12:C15 to 6.25%.

5. The owner is selling a camera and wants to determine the monthly payments for a two-year loan at 4.5% interest. Determine monthly payments on the camera (income to Real Photography) by completing the following steps:
   a. Make cell E20 active.
   b. Make sure the Formulas tab is active.
   c. Click the Financial button, scroll down the drop-down list, and then click *PMT*.
   d. At the Function Arguments dialog box, type c20/12 in the *Rate* text box.
   e. Press the Tab key.
   f. Type d20 in the *Nper* text box.
   g. Press the Tab key.
   h. Type -b20 in the *Pv* text box. (Enter the *Pv* cell reference preceded by a hyphen because the sale of the camera represents an outflow of an asset. Excel displays the result of the PMT function as a positive number since the camera payments represent a positive cash inflow.)
   i. Click OK. (This closes the dialog box and inserts the monthly income of *$185.92* in cell E20.)
6. Save, print, and then close **6-RPReports**.

Check Your Work

Tutorial

Using the FV Function to Find the Future Value of an Investment

Finding the Future Value of a Series of Payments

The FV function calculates the future value of a series of equal payments or an annuity. Use this function to determine information such as how much money can be earned in an investment account with a specific interest rate and over a specific period of time.

Activity 5b Finding the Future Value of an Investment   Part 2 of 2

1. Open **RPInvest** and then save it with the name **6-RPInvest**.
2. The owner of Real Photography has decided to save the money needed to purchase a new developer and wants to compute how much money can be earned by investing in an investment account that returns 7.5% annual interest. The owner determines that $1,200 per month can be invested in the account for three years. Complete the following steps to determine the future value of the investment account:
   a. Make cell B6 active.
   b. Click the Formulas tab.
   c. Click the Financial button in the Function Library group.
   d. At the drop-down list, scroll down the list and then click *FV*.
   e. At the Function Arguments dialog box, type b3/12 in the *Rate* text box.
   f. Press the Tab key.
   g. Type b4 in the *Nper* text box.
   h. Press the Tab key.
   i. Type b5 in the *Pmt* text box.
   j. Click OK. (This closes the dialog box and also inserts the future value of *$48,277.66* in cell B6.)
3. Save and then print **6-RPInvest**.
4. The owner decides to determine the future return after two years. To do this, change the amount in cell B4 from *36* to *24* and then press the Enter key. (This recalculates the future investment amount in cell B6.)
5. Save, print, and then close **6-RPInvest**.

Check Your Work

Chapter Summary

- Pin a frequently used workbook at the *Recent* options list at the Open backstage area or at the Home backstage area.

- Pinned workbooks will remain at the Open backstage area in the *Recent* options list or at the Home backstage area until unpinned.

- To move or copy a worksheet to another existing workbook, open both the source workbook and the destination workbook and then open the Move or Copy dialog box.

- Use options from the Cell Styles button drop-down gallery to apply predesigned styles to a cell or selected cells.

- Automate the formatting of cells in a workbook by defining and then applying cell styles. A style is a predefined set of formatting attributes.

- Define a cell style with formats already applied to a cell or display the Style dialog box, click the Format button, and then choose formatting options at the Format Cells dialog box.

- To apply a style, select the desired cell or cells, click the Cell Styles button in the Styles group on the Home tab, and then click the style at the drop-down gallery.

- Modify a style and all the cells to which it is applied update automatically. To modify a style, click the Cell Styles button in the Styles group on the Home tab, right-click the style, and then click *Modify* at the shortcut menu.

- Custom styles are saved in the workbook they are created in but can be copied to another workbook. Do this with options at the Merge Styles dialog box.

- Remove any new style formatting in a cell by applying the Normal style to the cell.

- Delete cell styles at the Cell Styles drop-down gallery by right-clicking a style and then clicking *Delete*.

- With options at the Insert Hyperlink dialog box, create a hyperlink to a web page, another workbook, a location within a workbook, a new workbook, or an email address. Or create a hyperlink using a graphic.

- Hyperlinks can be modified, edited, and removed.

- Excel provides templates for creating forms. Search for and download templates at the New backstage area.

- Templates contain unique areas called placeholders where information is entered at the keyboard. These areas vary depending on the template.

- Comments are a feature that allows users to provide commentary on a specific cell.

- A comment must be posted before another comment is created or before another user replies to the comment.

- Display all of the comments in a worksheet by opening the Comments task pane.

- Financial functions are available in Excel that calculate an aspect of a financial loan or investment.

- Financial functions generally use Nper, FV, PV, and Pmt as function arguments.

- Use the PMT function to determine the payments on a loan or investment.

- Use the FV function to determine the future value on a loan or investment.

Commands Review

FEATURE	RIBBON TAB, GROUP/OPTION	BUTTON, OPTION	KEYBOARD SHORTCUT
cell styles	Home, Styles		
delete comment	Review, *Comments*		
financial functions	Financial, Function Library		
Insert Hyperlink dialog box	Insert, Links		Ctrl + K
Merge Styles dialog box	Home, Styles	, *Merge Styles*	
New backstage area	File, *New*		
new comment	Review, *Comments*		
Open backstage area	File, *Open*		Ctrl + O
show comments	Review, *Comments*		
Style dialog box	Home, Styles	, *New Cell Style*	

Microsoft®

Excel®

Creating Charts and Inserting Formulas

Performance Objectives

Upon successful completion of Chapter 7, you will be able to:

1 Create a chart with data in an Excel worksheet

2 Size, move, edit, format, and delete charts

3 Print a selected chart and print a worksheet containing a chart

4 Change a chart design

5 Change a chart location

6 Insert, move, size, and delete chart elements and shapes

7 Use the Quick Analysis feature

8 Format a chart at a task pane

9 Write formulas with the IF logical function

In previous chapters, you learned how to create and format worksheets in Excel to display and organize data. While a worksheet does an adequate job of representing data, some data are better represented visually with a chart. A chart, which is sometimes referred to as a *graph*, is a picture of numeric data. In this chapter, you will learn to create and customize charts in Excel. You will also learn how to write formulas using logical functions.

Data Files

Before beginning chapter work, copy the **EL1C7** folder to your storage medium and then make **EL1C7** the active folder.

The online course includes additional training and assessment resources.

Activity 1 Create a Quarterly Sales Column Chart

3 Parts

You will open a workbook containing quarterly sales data and then use the data to create a column chart. You will decrease the size of the chart, move it to a different location in the worksheet, and then make changes to sales numbers. You will also use buttons to customize and filter chart elements and styles.

Tutorial

Creating Charts

Creating a Chart

To provide a visual representation of data, consider inserting data in a chart. Use buttons in the Charts group on the Insert tab to create a variety of charts, such as a column chart, line chart, pie chart, and much more. Excel provides 17 basic chart types, as described in Table 7.1.

Table 7.1 Types of Charts

Chart	Description
Column	Displays values in vertical bars; useful for comparing items or showing how values vary over time.
Line	Shows trends and overall change across time at even intervals. Emphasizes the rate of change across time rather than the magnitude of change.
Pie	Shows proportions and the relationship of the parts to the whole.
Bar	Shows individual figures at a specific time or shows variations between components but not in relationship to the whole.
Area	Similar to a line chart, but with the area below the line filled in. Emphasizes the magnitude of change over time.
X Y (Scatter)	Shows the relationships among numeric values in several data series or plots the interception points between x and y values. Shows uneven intervals of data and is commonly used for scientific data.
Map	Compares values and shows categories across geographical regions.
Stock	Shows four values for a stock: open, high, low, and close.
Surface	Shows trends in values across two dimensions in a continuous curve.
Radar	Emphasizes differences and amounts of change over time as well as variations and trends. Each category has a value axis radiating from the center point. Lines connect all values in the same series.
Treemap	Provides a hierarchical view of data and compares proportions within the hierarchy.
Sunburst	Displays hierarchical data. Each level is represented by one ring; the innermost ring is the top of the hierarchy.
Histogram	Condenses a data series into a visual representation by grouping data points into logical ranges called *bins*.

continues

Table 7.1 Types of Charts—*continued*

Chart	Description
Box & Whisker	Displays medians, quartiles, and extremes of a data set on a number line to show the distribution of data. Lines extending vertically are called *whiskers* and indicate variability outside the upper and lower quartiles.
Waterfall	Illustrates how an initial value is affected by a series of positive and negative values.
Funnel	Shows values over multiple stages in a process; typically, the values decrease, making the shape of the chart resemble a funnel.
Combo	Combines two or more chart types to make data easy to understand.

Ŏuick Steps

Create Chart
1. Select cells.
2. Click Insert tab.
3. Click chart button.
4. Click chart style.

Recommended Charts

To create a chart, select the cells in the worksheet to be charted, click the Insert tab, and then click a specific chart button in the Charts group. At the drop-down gallery, click a specific chart style. Excel will make a recommendation on the type of chart that will best illustrate the data. To let Excel recommend a chart, select the data, click the Insert tab, and then click the Recommended Charts button. This displays the data in a chart in the Insert Chart dialog box. Customize the recommended chart with options in the left panel of the dialog box. Click the OK button to insert the recommended chart in the worksheet. Another method for inserting a recommended chart is to use the keyboard shortcut Alt + F1.

Tutorial

Resizing, Positioning, and Moving Charts

Sizing and Moving a Chart

By default, a chart is inserted in the same worksheet as the selected cells. Figure 7.1 shows the worksheet and chart that will be created in Activity 1a. The chart is inserted in a box, which can be sized or moved within the worksheet.

Figure 7.1 Activity 1a Chart

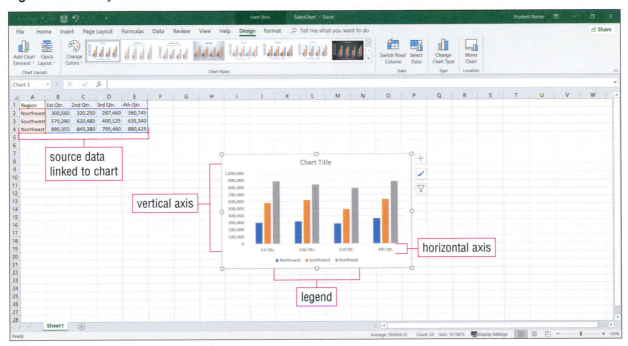

Change the size of the chart using the sizing handles (white circles) on the chart borders. Drag the top-middle and bottom-middle sizing handles to increase or decrease the height of the chart; use the left-middle and right-middle sizing handles to increase or decrease the width; and use the corner sizing handles to increase or decrease the height and width at the same time. To increase or decrease the size of the chart but maintain its proportions, press and hold down the Shift key while dragging one of the chart's corner borders.

To move the chart, make sure it is selected (a border with sizing handles appears around the chart), position the mouse pointer on a border until the pointer displays with a four-headed arrow attached, click and hold down the left mouse button, drag to the new position, and then release the mouse button.

Editing Chart Data

Editing Data and Adding a Data Series

The cells selected to create a chart are linked to it. To change the data for a chart, edit the data in the specific cells and the corresponding sections of the chart update automatically. If data is added to cells within the range of cells used for the chart, called the *source data*, the new data will be included in the chart. If a data series is added in cells next to or below the source data, click in the chart to display the source data with sizing handles and then drag with a sizing handle to include the new data.

Activity 1a Creating a Chart

Part 1 of 3

1. Open **SalesChart** and then save it with the name **7-SalesChart**.
2. Select the range A1:E4.
3. Let Excel recommend a chart type by completing the following steps:
   a. Click the Insert tab.
   b. Click the Recommended Charts button in the Charts group.

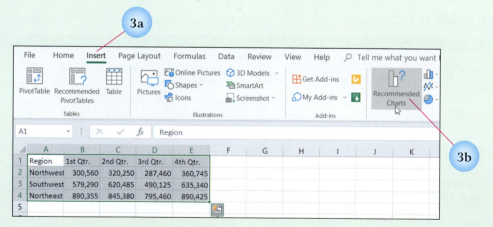

   c. At the Insert Chart dialog box, look at the options in the left panel and then click OK.
4. Slightly increase the size of the chart and maintain its proportions by completing the following steps:
   a. Position the mouse pointer on the sizing handle in the lower right corner of the chart border until the pointer turns into a two-headed arrow pointing diagonally.
   b. Press and hold down the Shift key and then click and hold down the left mouse button.

c. Drag out approximately 0.5 inch. Release the mouse button and then release the Shift key.

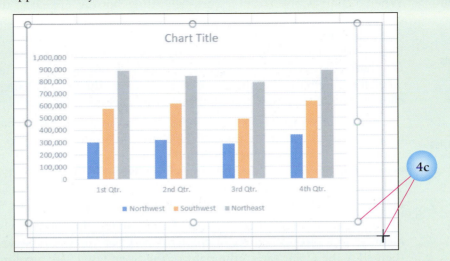

4c

5. Move the chart below the cells containing data by completing the following steps:
   a. Make sure the chart is selected. (When the chart is selected, the border surrounding it displays with sizing handles.)
   b. Position the mouse pointer on the chart border until the pointer displays with a four-headed arrow attached.
   c. Click and hold down the left mouse button, drag the chart to row 6 below the cells containing data, and then release the mouse button.

	A	B	C	D	E
1	Region	1st Qtr.	2nd Qtr.	3rd Qtr.	4th Qtr.
2	Northwest	300,560	320,250	287,460	360,745
3	Southwest	579,290	620,485	490,125	635,340
4	Northeast	890,355	845,380	795,460	890,425
5					
6				Chart Title	
7					
8	1,000,000				

5c

6. Make the following changes to the specified cells:
   a. Make cell B2 active and then change *300,560* to *421,720*.
   b. Make cell D2 active and then change *287,460* to *397,460*.

7. Add a new data series by typing data in the following cells:

   A5   Southeast
   B5   290,450
   C5   320,765
   D5   270,450
   E5   300,455

8. Add the new data series to the chart by completing the following steps:
   a. Click in a blank area of the chart. (This selects the data source, which is the range A1:E4.)
   b. Position the mouse pointer on the sizing handle in the lower right corner of cell E4 until the pointer displays as a two-headed diagonally pointing arrow.
   c. Click and hold down the left mouse button, drag down into cell E5, and then release the mouse button. (This incorporates data row 5 in the chart.)

9. Save **7-SalesChart**.

4	Northeast	890,355	845,380	795,460	890,425
5	Southeast	290,450	320,765	270,450	300,455
6					
7				Chart Title	
8	1,000,000				

8c

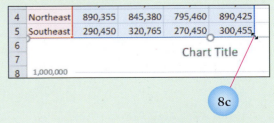

Check Your Work

Formatting with Chart Buttons

Chart
Elements

When a chart is inserted in a worksheet, three buttons appear at the right of the chart border. Click the top button, Chart Elements, and a side menu displays chart elements, as shown in Figure 7.2. The check boxes containing check marks indicate the elements that are currently part of the chart. Add a new element to the chart by inserting a check mark in the check box for that element and remove an element by removing the check mark. Remove the Chart Elements side menu by clicking one of the other chart buttons or by clicking the Chart Elements button.

Chart Styles

Excel offers a variety of chart styles that can be applied to a chart. Click the Chart Styles button at the right of the chart and a side menu gallery of styles displays, as shown in Figure 7.3. Scroll down the gallery, hover the mouse pointer over a style option, and the style formatting is applied to the chart. Click the chart style that applies the desired formatting. Remove the Chart Styles side menu gallery by clicking one of the other chart buttons or by clicking the Chart Styles button.

In addition to offering a variety of chart styles, the Chart Styles button side menu gallery offers a variety of chart colors. Click the Chart Styles button and then click the Color tab to the right of the Style tab. Click a color option at the color palette. Hover the mouse pointer over a color option to view how the color change affects the elements in the chart.

Chart Filters

Use the bottom button, Chart Filters, to isolate specific data in the chart. Click the button and a side menu displays, as shown in Figure 7.4. Specify the series or categories to display in the chart. To do this, remove the check marks from those elements that should not appear in the chart. After removing the specific check marks, click the Apply button at the bottom of the side menu. Click the Names tab at the Chart Filters button side menu and options display for turning on/off the display of column and row names.

Figure 7.2 Chart Elements Button Side Menu

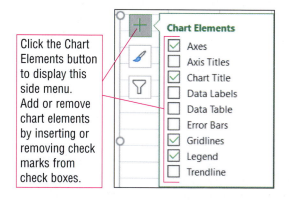

Click the Chart Elements button to display this side menu. Add or remove chart elements by inserting or removing check marks from check boxes.

Figure 7.3 Chart Styles Button Side Menu Gallery

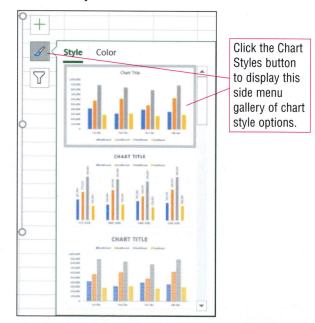

Click the Chart Styles button to display this side menu gallery of chart style options.

Figure 7.4 Chart Filters Button Side Menu

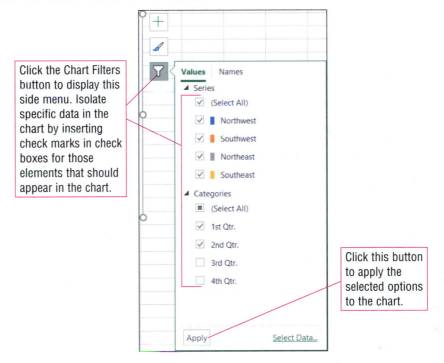

Click the Chart Filters button to display this side menu. Isolate specific data in the chart by inserting check marks in check boxes for those elements that should appear in the chart.

Click this button to apply the selected options to the chart.

Activity 1b Formatting with Chart Buttons

Part 2 of 3

1. With **7-SalesChart** open, make the chart active by clicking inside it but outside any elements.
2. Insert and remove chart elements by completing the following steps:
   a. Click the Chart Elements button outside the upper right corner of the chart.
   b. At the side menu, click the *Chart Title* check box to remove the check mark.
   c. Click the *Data Table* check box to insert a check mark.
   d. Hover the mouse pointer over *Gridlines* in the Chart Elements button side menu and then click the right-pointing triangle.
   e. At the side menu, click the *Primary Major Vertical* check box to insert a check mark.

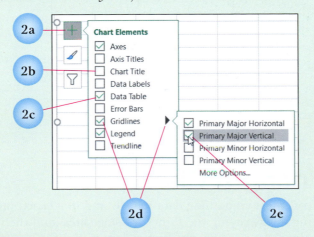

   f. Click the *Legend* check box to remove the check mark.

3. Apply a different chart style by completing the following steps:
   a. Click the Chart Styles button outside the upper right corner of the chart (immediately below the Chart Elements button). (Clicking the Chart Styles button removes the Chart Elements button side menu.)
   b. At the side menu gallery, click the *Style 3* option (third option in the gallery).
4. Display only the first-quarter and second-quarter sales by completing the following steps:
   a. Click the Chart Filters button outside the upper right corner of the chart (immediately below the Chart Styles button). (Clicking the Chart Filters button removes the Chart Styles button side menu gallery.)
   b. Click the *3rd Qtr.* check box in the *Categories* section to remove the check mark.
   c. Click the *4th Qtr.* check box in the *Categories* section to remove the check mark.
   d. Click the Apply button at the bottom of the side menu.
   e. Click the Chart Filters button to remove the side menu.

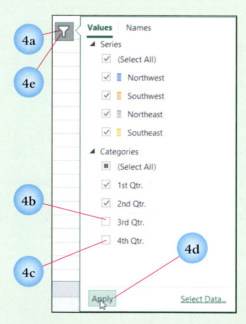

5. Save **7-SalesChart**.

Check Your Work

Tutorial

Printing a Chart

Printing a Chart

In a worksheet containing data in cells and in a chart, print only the chart by selecting it, displaying the Print backstage area, and then clicking the Print button. With the chart selected, the first gallery in the *Settings* category automatically changes to *Print Selected Chart*. A preview of the chart is shown at the right side of the Print backstage area.

1. With **7-SalesChart** open, make sure the chart is selected.
2. Click the File tab and then click the *Print* option.
3. At the Print backstage area, look at the preview of the chart in the preview area and notice that the first gallery in the *Settings* category is set to *Print Selected Chart*.
4. Click the Print button.
5. Save and then close **7-SalesChart**.

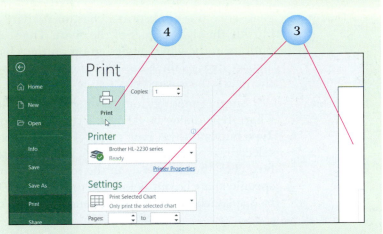

> Check Your Work

Activity 2 Create a Department Expenditures Bar Chart and Column Chart

2 Parts

You will open a workbook containing expenditure data by department and then create a bar chart with the data. You will then change the chart type, layout, and style; add chart elements; and move the chart to a new worksheet.

> Tutorial

Changing Chart Design

Changing the Chart Design

Along with the buttons at the upper right corner of the chart, buttons and options on the Chart Tools Design tab can be used to apply formatting to change the chart design. This tab, shown in Figure 7.5, appears when a chart is inserted in a worksheet or a chart is selected. Use buttons and options on the tab to add chart elements, change the chart type, specify a different layout or style for the chart, and change the location of the chart so it appears in a separate worksheet.

Figure 7.5 Chart Tools Design Tab

Changing the Chart Style

Quick Steps
Change Chart Type and Style
1. Make chart active.
2. Click Chart Tools Design tab.
3. Click Change Chart Type button.
4. Click chart type.
5. Click chart style.
6. Click OK.

Change Chart Type

Excel offers a variety of custom charts and varying styles for each chart type. A chart style was applied to a chart in Activity 1b using the Chart Styles button outside the right border of the chart. The style of a chart can also be changed with options in the Chart Styles group on the Chart Tools Design tab. To do this, click a chart style in the Chart Styles group or click the More Chart Styles button and then click the desired chart style.

Another method for applying a chart style is to use options at the Change Chart Type dialog box. Display this dialog box by clicking the Change Chart Type button in the Type group. The dialog box displays with the All Charts tab selected, as shown in Figure 7.6. Click a chart type in the left panel of the dialog box, click the chart style in the row of options at the top right, and then click a specific chart layout below the row of styles. Click the Recommended Charts tab to display chart styles recommended for the data by Excel.

Switching Rows and Columns

Switch Row/Column

Quick Steps
Switch Rows and Columns
1. Make chart active.
2. Click Chart Tools Design tab.
3. Click Switch Row/Column button.

When creating a chart, Excel uses row headings for grouping data along the bottom of the chart (the horizontal axis) and column headings for the legend (the area of a chart that identifies the data in the chart). Change this order by clicking the Switch Row/Column button in the Data group on the Chart Tools Design tab. Click this button and Excel uses the column headings to group data along the horizontal axis and the row headings for the legend.

Figure 7.6 Change Chart Type Dialog Box

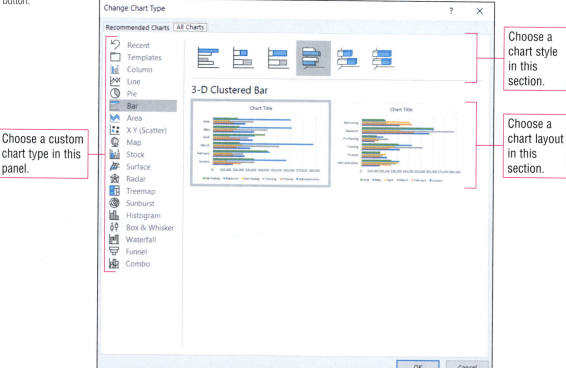

1. Open **DIDeptExp** and then save it with the name **7-DIDeptExp**.
2. Create a bar chart by completing the following steps:
   a. Select the range A3:G9.
   b. Click the Insert tab.
   c. Click the Insert Column or Bar Chart button in the Charts group.
   d. Click the *3-D Clustered Bar* option (first option in the *3-D Bar* section).
3. With the Chart Tools Design tab active, change the chart type by completing the following steps:
   a. Click the Change Chart Type button in the Type group.
   b. At the Change Chart Type dialog box, click the *Column* option in the left panel.
   c. Click the *3-D Clustered Column* option in the top row (fourth option from left).
   d. Click OK to close the Change Chart Type dialog box.
4. With the chart selected and the Chart Tools Design tab active, click the Switch Row/Column button in the Data group.

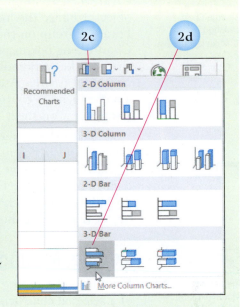

5. Save **7-DIDeptExp**.

Check Your Work

Changing Chart Layout and Colors

 Quick Layout

 Change Colors

The Chart Tools Design tab contains options for changing the chart layout and chart colors. Click the Quick Layout button in the Chart Layouts group and a drop-down gallery of layout options displays. Hover the mouse pointer over a layout option and the chart reflects the layout. Change the colors used in the chart by clicking the Change Colors button in the Chart Styles group and then clicking a color option at the drop-down gallery.

Changing the Chart Location

Quick Steps

Change Chart Location
1. Make chart active.
2. Click Chart Tools Design tab.
3. Click Move Chart button.
4. Click *New sheet* option.
5. Click OK.

Move Chart

Create a chart and it is inserted in the currently open worksheet as an embedded object. Change the location of a chart with the Move Chart button in the Location group on the Chart Tools Design tab. Click this button and the Move Chart dialog box displays, as shown in Figure 7.7. To move the chart to a new sheet in the workbook, click the *New sheet* option; Excel automatically names the new sheet *Chart1*. As explained earlier in the chapter, pressing Alt + F1 will insert a recommended chart in the active worksheet. To insert a recommended chart into a separate worksheet, press the F11 function key.

A chart that is moved to a separate sheet can be moved back to the original sheet or to a different sheet within the workbook. To move a chart to a different sheet, click the Move Chart button in the Location group. At the Move Chart dialog box, click the *Object in* option box arrow and then click the sheet at the drop-down list. Click OK and the chart is inserted in the specified sheet as an object that can be moved, sized, and formatted.

Adding, Moving, and Deleting Chart Elements

Removing, Modifying, and Adding Chart Elements

Add Chart Element

Quick Steps

Delete Chart Element
1. Click chart element.
2. Press Delete key.
OR
1. Right-click chart element.
2. Click *Delete*.

In addition to adding chart elements with the Chart Elements button at the right of a selected chart, chart elements can be added with the Add Chart Element button on the Chart Tools Design tab. Click this button and a drop-down list of elements displays. Point to a category of elements and then click the desired element at the side menu.

A chart element can be moved and/or sized. To move a chart element, click the element to select it and then move the mouse pointer over the border until the pointer turns into a four-headed arrow. Click and hold down the left mouse button, drag the element to the new location, and then release the mouse button. To size a chart element, click to select the element and then use the sizing handles to increase or decrease the size. To delete a chart element, click the element to select it and then press the Delete key. A chart element can also be deleted by right-clicking it and then clicking *Delete* at the shortcut menu.

Figure 7.7 Move Chart Dialog Box

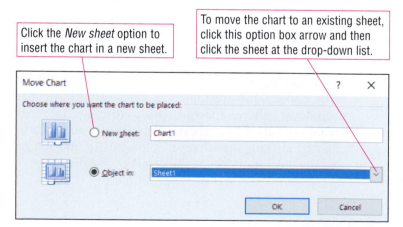

Click the *New sheet* option to insert the chart in a new sheet.

To move the chart to an existing sheet, click this option box arrow and then click the sheet at the drop-down list.

1. With **7-DIDeptExp** open, make sure the Chart Tools Design tab is active. (If it is not, make sure the chart is selected and then click the Chart Tools Design tab.)
2. Change the chart style by clicking the *Style 5* option in the Chart Styles group (fifth option from the left).

3. Change the chart colors by clicking the Change Colors button in the Chart Styles group and then clicking the *Colorful Palette 3* option (third option in the *Colorful* group).
4. Change the chart layout by clicking the Quick Layout button in the Chart Layouts group and then clicking the *Layout 1* option (first option in the drop-down gallery).

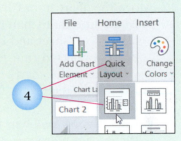

5. Add axis titles by completing the following steps:
   a. Click the Add Chart Element button in the Chart Layouts group on the Chart Tools Design tab.
   b. Point to *Axis Titles* and then click *Primary Horizontal* at the side menu.
   c. Type Department and then press the Enter key. (The word *Department* will appear in the Formula bar.)
   d. Click the Add Chart Element button, point to *Axis Titles*, and then click *Primary Vertical* at the side menu.
   e. Type Expenditure Amounts and then press the Enter key.
6. Click in the *Chart Title* placeholder text at the top of the chart, type Half-Yearly Expenditures, and then press the Enter key.
7. Delete the *Expenditure Amounts* axis title by clicking anywhere in it and then pressing the Delete key.
8. Move the legend by completing the following steps:
   a. Click in the legend to select it.
   b. Move the mouse pointer over the legend border until the pointer turns into a four-headed arrow.
   c. Click and hold down the left mouse button, drag up until the top border of the legend aligns with the top gridline in the chart, and then release the mouse button.

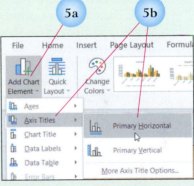

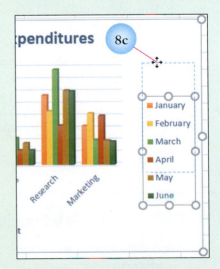

9. Move the chart to a new location by completing the following steps:

   a. Click the Move Chart button in the Location group.

   b. At the Move Chart dialog box, click the *New sheet* option and then click OK. (The chart is inserted in a worksheet named *Chart1*.)

10. Save **7-DIDeptExp**.

11. Print the Chart1 worksheet.

12. Move the chart from Chart1 to Sheet2 by completing the following steps:

   a. Make sure that Chart1 is the active worksheet and that the chart is selected (not just an element in the chart).

   b. Make sure the Chart Tools Design tab is active.

   c. Click the Move Chart button in the Location group.

   d. At the Move Chart dialog box, click the *Object in* option box arrow and then click *Sheet2* at the drop-down list.

   e. Click OK.

13. Change the amounts in Sheet1 by completing the following steps:

   a. Click the Sheet1 tab.

   b. Make cell B7 active and then change the amount from *10,540* to *19,750*.

   c. Make cell D8 active and then change the amount from *78,320* to *63,320*.

   d. Make cell G8 active and then change the amount from *60,570* to *75,570*.

   e. Make cell A2 active.

   f. Click the Sheet2 tab and notice that the chart displays the updated amounts.

14. Click outside the chart to deselect it.

15. Insert a header in the Sheet2 worksheet that prints your name at the left, the current date in the middle, and the workbook file name at the right.

16. Display the worksheet at the Print backstage area and make sure it will print on one page. If the chart does not fit on the page, return to the worksheet and then move and/or decrease the size of the chart until it fits on one page.

17. Print the active worksheet (Sheet2).

18. Save and then close **7-DIDeptExp**.

 Check Your Work

Activity 3   Create a Population Comparison Line Chart   2 Parts

You will open a workbook containing population comparison data for Seattle and Portland and then create a line chart with the data. You will move the chart to a new worksheet, format the chart elements, and insert a shape in the chart.

Tutorial

Changing Chart
Formatting

Changing Chart Formatting

Customize the formatting of a chart and its elements with options on the Chart Tools Format tab, as shown in Figure 7.8. Use buttons in the Current Selection group to identify specific elements in the chart and then apply formatting. Insert a shape in a chart with options in the Insert Shapes group and format shapes with options in the Shape Styles group. Apply WordArt formatting to data in a chart with options in the WordArt Styles group. Arrange, align, and size a chart with options in the Arrange and Size groups.

Formatting a Selection

Identify a specific element in a chart for formatting by clicking the *Chart Elements* option box arrow in the Current Selection group on the Chart Tools Format tab and then clicking the element at the drop-down list. This selects the specific element in the chart. Click the Reset to Match Style button to return the formatting of the element back to the original style. Use buttons in the Shape Styles group to apply formatting to a selected object and use buttons in the WordArt Styles group to apply formatting to selected data.

Figure 7.8 Chart Tools Format Tab

Activity 3a **Creating and Formatting a Line Chart**   Part 1 of 2

1. Open **PopComp** and then save it with the name **7-PopComp**.
2. Create a line chart and add a chart element by completing the following steps:
   a. Select the range A2:I4.
   b. Click the Insert tab.
   c. Click the Insert Line or Area Chart button in the Charts group.
   d. Click the *Line with Markers* option at the drop-down list (fourth column, first row in the *2-D Line* section).
   e. Click the Chart Elements button at the upper right corner of the chart.
   f. Hover the mouse pointer over the *Data Table* option at the side menu, click the right-pointing triangle, and then click *No Legend Keys* at the side menu.
   g. Click the Chart Elements button to remove the side menu.
3. Move the chart to a new sheet by completing the following steps:
   a. Click the Move Chart button in the Location group on the Chart Tools Design tab.
   b. At the Move Chart dialog box, click the *New sheet* option.
   c. Click OK.

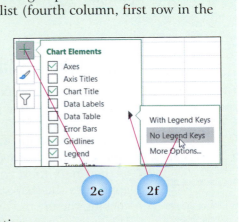

4. Format the *Portland* line by completing the following steps:
   a. Click the Chart Tools Format tab.
   b. Click the *Chart Elements* option box arrow in the Current Selection group and then click *Series "Portland"* at the drop-down list.
   c. Click the Shape Fill button arrow in the Shape Styles group and then click the *Green* color (sixth color in the *Standard Colors* section).

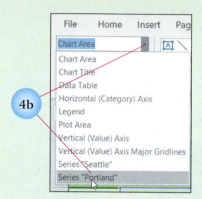 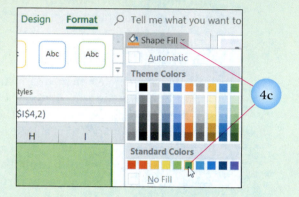

   d. Click the Shape Outline button arrow in the Shape Styles group and then click the *Green* color (sixth color in the *Standard Colors* section).
5. Type a title for the chart and format the title by completing the following steps:
   a. Click the *Chart Elements* option box arrow in the Current Selection group and then click *Chart Title* at the drop-down list.
   b. Type Population Comparison between Seattle and Portland and then press the Enter key.
   c. Click the *Fill: Black, Text color 1; Shadow* WordArt style in the WordArt Styles group (first style in the WordArt Styles gallery).

6. Format the legend by completing the following steps:
   a. Click the *Chart Elements* option box arrow and then click *Legend* at the drop-down list.
   b. Click the *Colored Outline - Blue, Accent 1* shape style in the Shape Styles group (second shape style).
7. Save **7-PopComp**.

Check Your Work ▸

Inserting a Shape

Quick Steps

Insert Shape
1. Make chart active.
2. Click Chart Tools Format tab.
3. Click More Shapes button.
4. Click shape at drop-down list.
5. Click or drag to create shape.

The Insert Shapes group on the Chart Tools Format tab contains options for inserting shapes in a chart. Click a shape option and the mouse pointer turns into crosshairs (thin black plus symbol [+]). Click in the chart or drag with the mouse to create the shape in the chart. The shape is inserted in the chart and the Drawing Tools Format tab is active. This tab contains many of the same options as the Chart Tools Format tab. For example, a shape style or WordArt style can be applied to the shape and the shape can be arranged and sized. Size a shape by clicking the up and down arrows at the right sides of the *Shape Height* and *Shape Width* measurement boxes in the Size group on the Drawing Tools Format tab. Or select the current measurement in the *Shape Height* or *Shape Width* measurement box and then type a specific measurement.

Creating Alternative Text for an Image

 Alt Text

Alternative text, also known as alt text, is a brief description of an object, such as a chart, that can be read by a screen reader to help a person with a visual impairment understand what objects are included in a worksheet. Create alternative text at the Alt Text task pane. Display this task pane by clicking the Alt Text button in the Accessibility group on the Chart Tools Format tab. Or, right-click a chart and then click *Edit Alt Text* at the shortcut menu. At the Alt Text task pane, type a description of the chart. If the chart is only decorative and not important for understanding the content of the worksheet, insert a check mark in the *Mark as decorative* check box. A chart marked as decorative will not include any description for screen readers.

Activity 3b Inserting and Customizing a Shape and Adding Alt Text to a Chart   Part 2 of 2

1. With **7-PopComp** open, create a shape similar to the one shown in Figure 7.9 by completing the following steps:

   a. Click the More Shapes button in the Insert Shapes group on the Chart Tools Format tab.

   b. Click the *Callout: Up Arrow* shape (last column, second row in the *Block Arrows* section).

   c. Click in the chart to insert the shape.

   d. Click in the *Shape Height* measurement box in the Size group on the Drawing Tools Format tab, type 1.5, and then press the Enter key.

   e. Click in the *Shape Width* measurement box, type 1.5, and then press the Enter key.

   f. Apply a shape style by clicking the More Shape Styles button in the Shape Styles group and then clicking the *Subtle Effect - Blue, Accent 1* option (second column, fourth row in the *Theme Styles* section).

   g. Type Largest disparity in the shape, press the Enter key, and then type (184,411).

   h. Select the text you just typed.

   i. Click the Home tab.

   j. Click the Bold button in the Font group.

   k. Click the *Font Size* option box arrow and then click *14*.

   l. Click the Center button in the Alignment group.

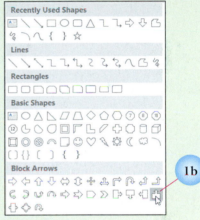

2. With the shape selected, drag the shape so it is positioned as shown in Figure 7.9.

3. Select the entire chart and then create alternative text for the chart by completing the following steps:

   a. Click the Drawing Tools Format tab.

   b. Click the Alt Text button in the Accessibility group.

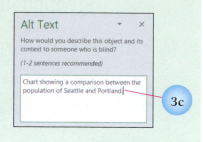

Check Your Work

Figure 7.9 Activity 3 Chart

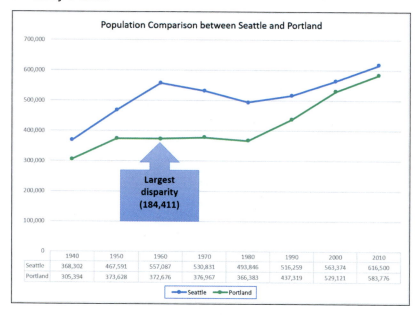

Activity 4 Create a Costs Pie Chart and Treemap Chart   **2 Parts**

You will create a pie chart and a treemap chart, add data labels, apply a style, format chart elements, and then size and move the treemap chart.

Using Quick Analysis to Create a Chart

Using the Quick Analysis Feature

A variety of methods are available for adding visual elements to a worksheet, including charts, sparklines, and conditional formatting. The Quick Analysis feature consists of a toolbar that has buttons and options for inserting all of these visual elements plus common formulas in one location. When a range is selected, Excel determines how the data in the range can be analyzed and then provides buttons and options for inserting relevant visual elements or formulas. When a range of data that is used to create a pie chart is selected, the Quick Analysis Toolbar provides buttons and options for inserting many different visual elements or formulas but also specifically including a pie chart.

Hint Ctrl + Q is the keyboard shortcut to display the Quick Analysis Toolbar for selected cells.

A Quick Analysis button appears at the bottom right corner of the selected range and when clicked, displays the Quick Analysis Toolbar, as shown in Figure 7.10. The Quick Analysis Toolbar includes the *Formatting*, *Charts*, *Totals*, *Tables*, and *Sparklines* options. Each option provides buttons that relate to how the data can be analyzed. Click a button to insert an element or formula into the worksheet.

Figure 7.10 Quick Analysis Toolbar

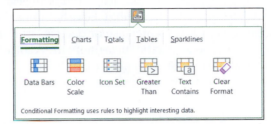

Applying Formatting at a Task Pane

Quick Steps

Display Task Pane
1. Select chart or specific element.
2. Click Chart Tools Format tab.
3. Click Format Selection button.

Format Selection

To view and apply more formatting options for charts, display the formatting task pane by clicking the Format Selection button in the Current Selection group on the Chart Tools Format tab. The task pane displays at the right side of the screen and the name of and contents in the task pane vary depending on what is selected. If the entire chart is selected, the Format Chart Area task pane displays, as shown in Figure 7.11. Format the chart by clicking formatting options in the task pane. Display additional formatting options by clicking the icons at the top of the task pane. For example, click the Effects icon in the Format Chart Area task pane and options display for applying shadow, glow, soft edges, and three-dimensional formatting.

Click a chart element and then click the Format Selection button and the task pane name and options change. Another method for displaying the task pane is to right-click a chart or chart element and then click the format option at the shortcut menu. The name of the format option varies depending on the selected element.

Figure 7.11 Format Chart Area Task Pane

Display additional formatting options by clicking icons in this section of the task pane.

Click the Format Selection button with the chart selected to display this task pane. Apply formatting to the chart with options in the task pane.

Click an option to expand it and display additional options.

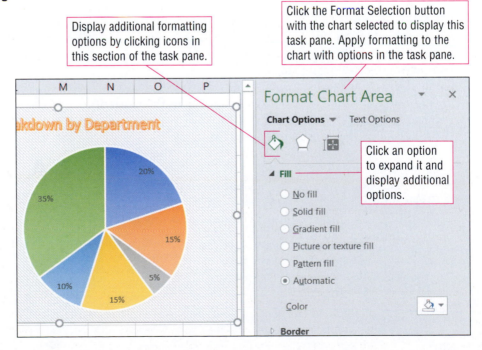

Changing Chart Height and Width Measurements

A chart that is inserted into the current worksheet (not a separate new worksheet) can be sized by selecting it and dragging a sizing handle. A chart can also be sized with the *Shape Height* and *Shape Width* measurement boxes in the Size group on the Chart Tools Format tab. Click the up or down arrow at the right side of the measurement box to increase or decrease the size or click in the measurement box and then type a specific measurement. Another method for changing a chart size is to use options at the Format Chart Area task pane. Display this task pane by clicking the Size group task pane launcher on the Chart Tools Format tab.

Activity 4a   Deleting a Chart and Creating and Formatting a Pie Chart   Part 1 of 2

1. Open **DIDeptCosts** and then save it with the name **7-DIDeptCosts**.
2. Create the pie chart shown in Figure 7.11 by completing the following steps:
   a. Select the range A3:B9.
   b. Click the Quick Analysis button at the bottom right corner of the selected range.
   c. Click the *Charts* option.
   d. Click the Pie button.
3. Insert data labels in the chart by completing the following steps:
   a. Click the Chart Elements button outside the upper right border of the chart.
   b. Hover the mouse pointer over the *Data Labels* option and then click the right-pointing triangle.
   c. Click *Inside End* at the side menu.
   d. Click the Chart Elements button to hide the side menu.
4. Click the *Style 6* option in the Chart Styles group on the Chart Tools Design tab.
5. Type a title and then apply a WordArt style to it by completing the following steps:
   a. Click the Chart Tools Format tab.
   b. Click the *Chart Elements* option box arrow in the Current Selection group.
   c. Click *Chart Title* at the drop-down list.
   d. Type Costs Breakdown by Department and then press the Enter key.
   e. Click the More WordArt Styles button in the WordArt Styles group.
   f. Click the option in the fourth column, third row (white fill with orange outline).

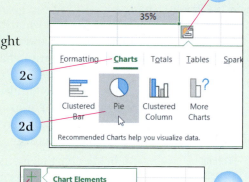

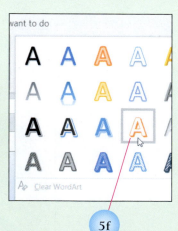

6. Use the Format Legend task pane to apply formatting to the legend by completing the following steps:

   a. Click the *Chart Elements* option box arrow and then click *Legend* at the drop-down list.

   b. Click the Format Selection button in the Current Selection group.

   c. At the Format Legend task pane, click the *Left* option in the *Legend Options* section to select it.

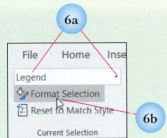

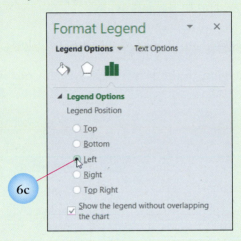

   d. Click the Effects icon in the task pane. (This changes the options in the task pane.)

   e. Click *Shadow* to expand the shadow options in the task pane.

   f. Click the Shadow button to the right of *Presets* and then click the *Offset: Bottom Right* option (first option in the *Outer* section).

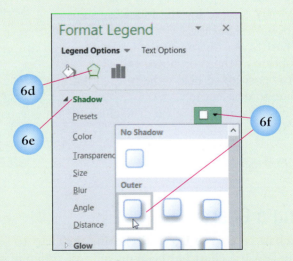

   g. Click the Fill & Line icon in the task pane.

   h. Click *Fill* to expand the fill options in the task pane.

   i. Click the *Gradient fill* option.

   j. Close the task pane by clicking the Close button in the upper right corner of the task pane.

7. Use the Format Chart Area task pane to apply formatting to the chart by completing the following steps:
   a. Click inside the chart but outside any chart elements.
   b. Click the Format Selection button in the Current Selection group.
   c. Make sure the Fill & Line icon in the Format Chart Area task pane is selected. (If not, click the icon.)
   d. Make sure the *Fill* option is expanded. (If not, click *Fill*.)
   e. Click the *Gradient fill* option.
   f. Click the Size & Properties icon in the task pane.
   g. Click *Size* to expand the size options in the task pane.
   h. Select the current measurement in the *Height* measurement box, type 3.5, and then press the Enter key.
   i. Select the current measurement in the *Width* measurement box, type 5.5, and then press the Enter key.
   j. Close the task pane.

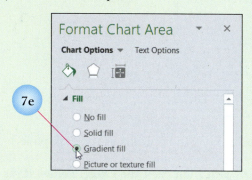
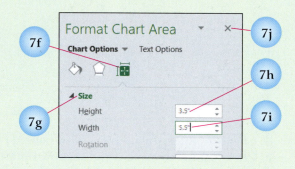

8. Save **7-DIDeptCosts** and then print only the chart.
9. Change the chart style by completing the following steps:
   a. Click the Chart Tools Design tab.
   b. Click the More Chart Styles button in the Chart Styles group.
   c. Click the *Style 9* option at the drop-down gallery.
10. Move the chart so it is positioned below the cells containing data.
11. Click outside the chart to deselect it.
12. Display the Print backstage area, make sure the chart fits on one page with the data, and then click the Print button.
13. Save **7-DIDeptCosts**.

> Check Your Work

Deleting a Chart

Delete a chart created in Excel by clicking the chart to select it and then pressing the Delete key. If a chart has been moved to a different worksheet in the workbook, deleting the chart will delete the chart but not the worksheet. To delete the worksheet and the chart, position the mouse pointer on the sheet tab, click the right mouse button, and then click *Delete* at the shortcut menu. At the message box indicating that the selected sheet will be permanently deleted, click the Delete button.

1. With **7-DIDeptCosts** open, click the Sheet2 tab.
2. Delete the column chart by completing the following steps:
   a. Click the column chart to select it. (Make sure the chart is selected, not a specific element in the chart.)
   b. Press the Delete key.
3. Create a treemap chart by completing the following steps:
   a. Select the range A2:C8.
   b. Click the Insert tab.
   c. Click the Insert Hierarchy Chart button in the Charts group.
   d. Click the *Treemap* option (first option).

4. Click the *Style 4* option in the Chart Styles group on the Chart Tools Design tab (fourth option from the left).
5. Click the Change Colors button in the Chart Styles group and then click the *Colorful Palette 3* option in the *Colorful* section of the drop-down gallery.
6. Click the Add Chart Element button, position the mouse pointer over the *Legend* option, click the right-pointing triangle, and then click the *None* option.
7. Click in the *Chart Title* placeholder text and then type Proportionate Departmental Expenses.

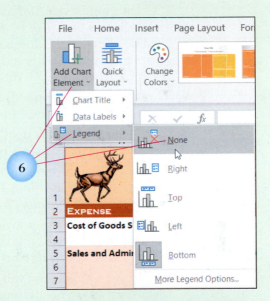

8. Change the chart height and width by completing the following steps:
   a. Make the entire chart active and then click the Chart Tools Format tab.
   b. Click in the *Shape Height* measurement box, type 5, and then press the Enter key.
   c. Click in the *Shape Width* measurement box, type 4, and then press the Enter key.
9. Move the chart so it is positioned below the cells containing data.
10. Click outside the chart to deselect it.
11. Center the worksheet horizontally and vertically.
12. Save, print, and then close **7-DIDeptCosts**.

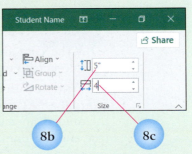

 Check Your Work

You will write formulas using the IF logical function to calculate sales bonuses, determine pass/fail grades based on averages, and identify discounts and discount amounts.

Tutorial

Using Logical IF
Functions

Writing Formulas with the Logical IF Function

A question that can be answered true or false is considered a *logical test*. The **IF function** can be used to create a logical test that performs a particular action if the answer is true (condition met) and another action if the answer is false (condition not met).

For example, an IF function can be used to write a formula that calculates a salesperson's bonus as 10% if he or she sells more than $99,999 worth of product and 0% if he or she does not sell more than $99,999 worth of product. When writing a formula with an IF function, think about the words *if* and *then*. For example, the formula written out for the bonus example would look like this:

If the salesperson sells more than $99,999 of product, *then* the salesperson receives a bonus of 10%.

If the salesperson does not sell more than $99,999 of product, *then* the salesperson receives a bonus of 0%.

When writing a formula with an IF function, use commas to separate the condition and the action. The formula for the bonus example would look like this: **=IF(sales>99999,sales*0.1,0)**. The formula contains three parts:

- the condition or logical test: **IF(sales>99999**
- the action taken if the condition or logical test is true: **sales*0.1**
- the action taken if the condition or logical test is false: **0**

In Activity 5a, you will write a formula with cell references rather than cell data. You will write a formula with an IF function that determines the following:

If the sales amount is greater than the quota amount, *then* the salesperson will receive a 15% bonus.

If the sales amount is not greater than the quota amount, *then* the salesperson will not receive a bonus.

Written with cell references in the activity, the formula looks like this: **=IF(C4>B4,C4*0.15,0)**. In this formula, the condition, or logical test, is whether the number in cell C4 is greater than the number in cell B4. If the condition is true and the number is greater, then the number in cell C4 is multiplied by 0.15 (providing a 15% bonus). If the condition is false and the number in cell C4 is less than the number in cell B4, then nothing happens (no bonus). Notice how commas are used to separate the logical test from the action.

1. Open **CMPReports** and then save it with the name **7-CMPReports**.
2. Write a formula with the IF function that determines if a sales quota has been met and if it has, inserts the bonus of 15% of actual sales. (If the quota has not been met, the formula will insert a 0.) Write the formula by completing the following steps:
   a. Make cell D4 active.
   b. Type =if(c4>b4,c4*0.15,0) and then press the Enter key.

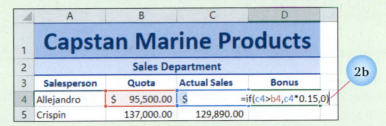

	A	B	C	D
1	**Capstan Marine Products**			
2		Sales Department		
3	**Salesperson**	**Quota**	**Actual Sales**	**Bonus**
4	Allejandro	$ 95,500.00	$	=if(c4>b4,c4*0.15,0)
5	Crispin	137,000.00	129,890.00	

2b

   c. Make cell D4 active and then use the fill handle to copy the formula to the range D5:D9.
3. Print the worksheet.
4. Revise the formula so it inserts a 20% bonus if the quota has been met by completing the following steps:
   a. Make cell D4 active.
   b. Click in the Formula bar, edit the formula so it displays as *=IF(C4>B4,C4*0.2,0)*, and then click the Enter button on the Formula bar.
   c. Copy the formula in cell D4 to the range D5:D9.
   d. Make cell D4 active and then apply the Accounting format with a dollar symbol ($) and two digits after the decimal point.
5. Save **7-CMPReports**.

Check Your Work

Writing Formulas with an IF Function Using the Function Arguments Dialog Box

Logical

A formula containing an IF function can be typed directly into a cell or the Function Arguments dialog box can be used to help write the formula. To use the Function Arguments dialog box to write a formula with the IF function, click the Formulas tab, click the Logical button in the Function Library group, and then click *IF* at the drop-down list. This displays the Function Arguments dialog box, shown in Figure 7.12. The Function Arguments dialog box displays the information you will type in the three argument text boxes for Activity 5b.

At the Function Arguments dialog box, click in the *Logical_test* text box and information about the *Logical_test* argument displays in the dialog box. In this text box, type the cell designation followed by what is evaluated. In the figure, the *Logical_test* text box contains *b14>599*, indicating that what is being evaluated is whether the amount in cell B14 is greater than $599. The *Value_if_true* text box contains *b14*0.95*, indicating that if the logical test is true, then the amount in cell B14 is multiplied by 0.95. (The discount for any product price greater than $599 is 5%, and multiplying the product price by 0.95 determines the price after the 5% discount is applied.) The *Value_if_false* text box contains *b14*, indicating that if the logical test is false (the product price is not greater than $599), then the amount from cell B14 is simply inserted.

Figure 7.12 Function Arguments Dialog Box

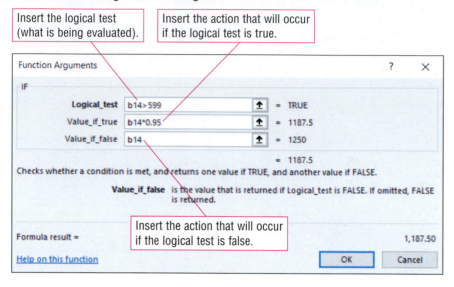

Insert the logical test (what is being evaluated).

Insert the action that will occur if the logical test is true.

Insert the action that will occur if the logical test is false.

Activity 5b Writing a Formula with an IF Function Using the Function Arguments Dialog Box

Part 2 of 3

1. With **7-CMPReports** open, insert a formula with an IF function using the Function Arguments dialog box by completing the following steps:
   a. Make cell C14 active.
   b. Click the Formulas tab.
   c. Click the Logical button in the Function Library group.
   d. Click *IF* at the drop-down list.
   e. At the Function Arguments dialog box, type b14>599 in the *Logical_test* text box and then press the Tab key.
   f. Type b14*0.95 in the *Value_if_true* text box and then press the Tab key.
   g. Type b14 in the *Value_if_ false* text box.

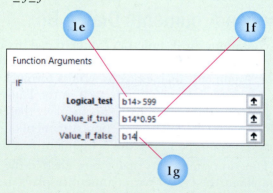

   h. Click OK to close the Function Arguments dialog box.
2. Copy the formula in cell C14 to the range C15:C26.
3. Apply the Accounting format with a dollar symbol and two digits after the decimal point to cell C14.
4. Save **7-CMPReports**.

Check Your Work

Writing IF Statements Containing Text

When writing a formula with an IF statement, if text is to be inserted in a cell rather than a value, put quotation marks around the text. For example, in Step 2 of Activity 5c, you will write a formula with an IF function that looks like this when written out:

> *If* the new employee averages more than 79 on the quizzes, ***then*** he or she passes.

> *If* the new employee does not average more than 79 on the quizzes, ***then*** he or she fails.

In Activity 5c, you will write the formula so the word *PASS* is inserted in a cell if the average of the new employee quizzes is greater than 79 and the word *FAIL* is inserted if the condition is not met. The formula would be ***=IF(E31>79, "PASS", "FAIL")***. The quotation marks before and after *PASS* and *FAIL* identify the data as text rather than values.

The Function Arguments dialog box can be used to write a formula with an IF function that contains text. For example, in Step 3 of Activity 5c, you will write a formula with an IF function using the Function Arguments dialog box that looks like this when written out:

> *If* the product price is greater than $599, ***then*** insert *YES*.

> *If* the product price is not greater than $599, ***then*** insert *NO*.

To create the formula in Step 3 using the Function Arguments dialog box, display the dialog box and then type *b14>599* in the *Logical_test* text box, *YES* in the *Value_if_true* text box and *NO* in the *Value_if_false* text box. When you press the Enter key after typing *YES* in the *Value_if_true* text box, Excel automatically inserts quotation marks around the text. Excel will do the same thing for *NO* in the *Value_if_false* text box.

Activity 5c Writing IF Statements Containing Text

Part 3 of 3

1. With **7-CMPReports** open, insert quiz averages by completing the following steps:
   a. Make cell E31 active and then insert a formula that calculates the average of the test scores in the range B31:D31.
   b. Copy the formula in cell E31 to the range E32:E35.
2. Write a formula with an IF function that inserts the word *PASS* if the new employee quiz average is greater than 79 and inserts the word *FAIL* if the quiz average is not greater than 79. Write the formula by completing the following steps:
   a. Make cell F31 active.
   b. Type =if(e31>79,"PASS","FAIL") and then press the Enter key.

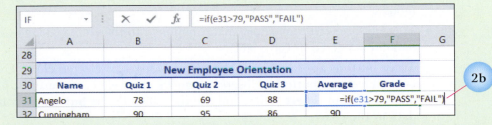

   c. Copy the formula in cell F31 to the range F32:F35.

3. Write a formula with an IF function using the Function Arguments dialog box that inserts the word *YES* in the cell if the product price is greater than $599 and inserts the word *NO* if the price is not greater than $599. Write the formula by completing the following steps:
   a. Make cell D14 active.
   b. Click the Formulas tab.
   c. Click the Logical button in the Function Library group.
   d. Click *IF* at the drop-down list.
   e. Type b14>599 in the *Logical_test* text box and then press the Tab key.
   f. Type YES in the *Value_if_true* text box and then press the Tab key.
   g. Type NO in the *Value_if_ false* text box.
   h. Click OK to close the Function Arguments dialog box.
   i. Copy the formula in cell D14 to the range D15:D26.

4. Save and then print **7-CMPReports**.
5. Press Ctrl + ` to turn on the display of formulas.
6. Print the worksheet again. (The worksheet will print on two pages.)
7. Press Ctrl + ` to turn off the display of formulas.
8. Save and then close **7-CMPReports**.

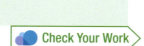

3e   **3f**

Function Arguments

IF

Logical_test	b14>599	⬆	= TRUE
Value_if_true	"YES"	⬆	= "YES"
Value_if_false	NO|	⬆	=

3g

Check Your Work

Chapter Summary

- A chart is a visual presentation of data. Excel provides 17 basic chart types: Column, Line, Pie, Bar, Area, X Y (Scatter), Map, Stock, Surface, Radar, Treemap, Sunburst, Histogram, Box & Whisker, Waterfall, Funnel, and Combo.

- To create a chart, select the cells, click the Insert tab, and then click a specific chart button in the Charts group. Click the Recommended Charts button in the Charts group and Excel will recommend a type of chart for the data.

- A chart is inserted in the same worksheet as the selected cells by default.

- Change the size of a chart using the mouse by dragging one of the sizing handles that display around the border of the chart. When changing the chart size, maintain the proportions of the chart by pressing and holding down the Shift key while dragging a sizing handle.

- Move a chart by positioning the mouse pointer on the chart border until the pointer displays with a four-headed arrow attached and then dragging with the mouse.

- The cells selected to create a chart are linked to the chart. Changes made to the data are reflected in the chart.

- Three buttons appear outside the right border of a selected chart. Use the Chart Elements button to insert or remove chart elements, use the Chart Styles button to apply chart styles, and use the Chart Filters button to isolate specific data in the chart.

- Print a chart by selecting it, displaying the Print backstage area, and then clicking the Print button.

- When a chart is inserted in a worksheet, the Chart Tools Design tab is active. Use buttons and options on this tab to add chart elements, change the chart type, specify a different layout or style for the chart, and change the location of the chart.

- Choose a chart style with options in the Chart Styles group on the Chart Tools Design tab or at the Change Chart Type dialog box.

- Click the Switch Row/Column button in the Data group on the Chart Tools Design tab to change what Excel uses to determine the grouping of data along the horizontal axis and legend.

- Use the Quick Layout button in the Chart Layouts group on the Chart Tools Design tab to change the chart layout.

- Use the Change Colors button in the Chart Styles group on the Chart Tools Design tab to apply different colors to a chart.

- Create a chart and it is inserted in the currently open worksheet. The chart can be moved to a new worksheet in the workbook with the *New sheet* option at the Move Chart dialog box.

- Add chart elements with the Add Chart Element button in the Chart Layouts group on the Chart Tools Design tab.

- Move a chart element by selecting it and then dragging it with the mouse. Use the sizing handles around a chart element to change its size. Delete a chart element by selecting it and then pressing the Delete key or by right-clicking the element and then clicking *Delete* at the shortcut menu.

- Customize the formatting of a chart and chart elements with options on the Chart Tools Format tab. Use these options to identify specific elements in the chart for formatting, insert a shape, apply formatting to a shape, apply WordArt formatting to data in a chart, insert alt text, and arrange, align, and size a chart.

- Insert a shape by clicking it in the Insert Shapes group on the Chart Tools Format tab and then clicking or dragging in the chart.

- Create alternate text for an object such as a chart and the text is read by a screen reader, helping people with a visual impairment understand what objects are included in the worksheet.

- Excel provides additional formatting options at a formatting task pane. A formatting task pane displays at the right side of the screen; the name and the contents in the task pane vary depending on whether the entire chart or an element in the chart is selected. Display a task pane by clicking the chart or element in the chart and then clicking the Format Selection button in the Current Selection group on the Chart Tools Format tab.

- Change the size of a chart with the *Shape Height* and *Shape Width* measurement boxes on the Chart Tools Format tab or at the Format Chart Area task pane.

- To delete a chart in a worksheet, click the chart to select it and then press the Delete key. To delete a chart created in a separate sheet, position the mouse pointer on the chart sheet tab, click the right mouse button, and then click *Delete*.

- A logical test is a question that can be answered with true or false. Use the IF function to create a logical test that performs one action if the answer is true (condition met) or another action if the answer is false (condition not met).

Commands Review

FEATURE	RIBBON TAB, GROUP	BUTTON	KEYBOARD SHORTCUT
add chart element	Chart Tools Design, Chart Layouts		
Change Chart Type dialog box	Chart Tools Design, Type		
change colors	Chart Tools Design, Chart Styles		
chart or chart element task pane	Chart Tools Format, Current Selection		
logical functions	Formulas, Function Library		
Move Chart dialog box	Chart Tools Design, Location		
quick layout	Chart Tools Design, Chart Layouts		
recommended chart	Insert, Charts		Alt + F1
recommended chart in separate sheet			F11
switch row/column	Chart Tools Design, Data		

Excel

Adding Visual Interest to Workbooks

Performance Objectives

Upon successful completion of Chapter 8, you will be able to:

1 Insert symbols and special characters

2 Insert, size, move, and format images

3 Create and insert screenshots

4 Draw, format, and copy shapes

5 Insert, format, and type text in text boxes

6 Insert, format, and modify icons and 3D models

7 Insert, format, size, move, and delete SmartArt graphics

8 Insert, format, size, and move WordArt

Microsoft Excel includes a variety of features that you can use to enhance the appearance of a workbook. Some of the methods for adding visual appeal that you will learn in this chapter include inserting and modifying images, screenshots, shapes, text boxes, icons, 3D models, SmartArt, and WordArt.

 **Data Files**

Before beginning the chapter work, copy the EL1C8 folder to your storage medium and then make EL1C8 the active folder.

 The online course includes additional training and assessment resources.

Activity 1 Insert Symbols, Images, and Shapes in a Financial Analysis Workbook

5 Parts

You will open a financial analysis workbook and then insert symbols and move, size, and format an image in the workbook. You will also insert an arrow shape, type and format text in the shape, and then copy the shape.

Tutorial

Inserting Symbols and Special Characters

 Symbol

Quick Steps

Insert Symbol
1. Click in cell.
2. Click Insert tab.
3. Click Symbol button.
4. Double-click symbol.
5. Click Close.

Insert Special Character
1. Click in cell.
2. Click Insert tab.
3. Click Symbol button.
4. Click Special Characters tab.
5. Double-click special character.
6. Click Close.

💡 **Hint** Increase or decrease the size of the Symbol dialog box by positioning the mouse pointer on the lower right corner until the pointer displays as a two-headed arrow and then dragging with the mouse.

Inserting Symbols and Special Characters

Use the Symbol button on the Insert tab to insert symbols in a worksheet. Click the button and the Symbol dialog box displays, as shown in Figure 8.1. At the dialog box, double-click a symbol to insert it, click the symbol and then click the Insert button, or type the code in the *Character code* text box. Click the Close button to exit the dialog box.

At the Symbol dialog box with the Symbols tab selected, additional symbols are available with different fonts. Change the font by clicking the *Font* option box arrow and then clicking a font at the drop-down list. Click the Special Characters tab at the Symbol dialog box and a list of special characters displays. Insert a special character by double-clicking a character and then clicking the Close button or by clicking the character, clicking the Insert button, and then clicking the Close button.

Figure 8.1 Symbol Dialog Box with the Symbols Tab Selected

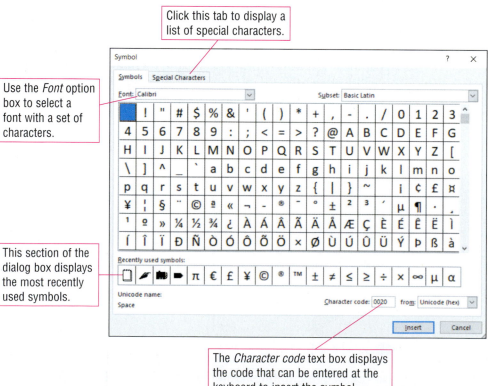

Click this tab to display a list of special characters.

Use the *Font* option box to select a font with a set of characters.

This section of the dialog box displays the most recently used symbols.

The *Character code* text box displays the code that can be entered at the keyboard to insert the symbol.

1. Open **SMFFinCon** and then save it with the name **8-SMFFinCon**.
2. Insert a symbol by completing the following steps:
   a. Double-click in cell A2.
   b. Delete the *e* at the end of *Qualite*.
   c. With the insertion point positioned immediately right of the *t* in *Qualit*, click the Insert tab.
   d. Click the Symbol button in the Symbols group.
   e. At the Symbol dialog box, scroll down the list box and then click the *é* symbol (located in approximately the ninth through eleventh rows). (You can also type *00E9* in the *Character code* text box to select the symbol.)
   f. Click the Insert button and then click the Close button.

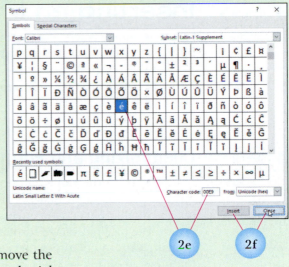

3. Insert a special character by completing the following steps:
   a. With cell A2 selected and in Edit mode, move the insertion point so it is positioned immediately right of *Group*.
   b. Click the Symbol button in the Symbols group.
   c. At the Symbol dialog box, click the Special Characters tab.
   d. Double-click the ® *Registered* symbol (tenth option from the top).
   e. Click the Close button.

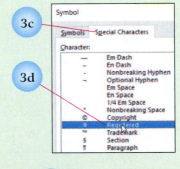

4. Insert a symbol by completing the following steps:
   a. With cell A2 selected and in Edit mode, move the insertion point so it is positioned immediately left of the *Q* in *Qualité*.
   b. Click the Symbol button in the Symbols group.
   c. At the Symbol dialog box, click the *Font* option box arrow and then click *Wingdings* at the drop-down list. (You will need to scroll down the list to see this option.)
   d. Click the ❖ symbol (located in approximately the fifth or sixth row). (You can also type *118* in the *Character code* text box to select the symbol.)
   e. Click the Insert button and then click the Close button.
5. Click in cell A3.
6. Save **8-SMFFinCon**.

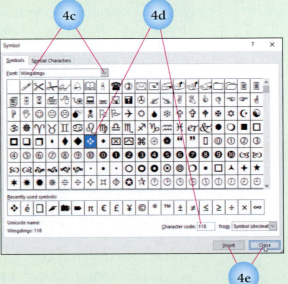

Check Your Work

Figure 8.2 Picture Tools Format Tab

Inserting an Image

Inserting an Image

  Pictures

Insert an image, such as a picture or clip art image, in an Excel workbook with buttons in the Illustrations group on the Insert tab. Click the Pictures button to display the Insert Picture dialog box with options for inserting an image from a folder on the computer or a removable drive. Or click the Online Pictures button and search for images online. When an image is inserted in a worksheet, the Picture Tools Format tab appears, as shown in Figure 8.2.

Modifying Images

  Compress Pictures

Quick Steps

Insert Image
1. Click Insert tab.
2. Click Pictures button.
3. Navigate to folder.
4. Double-click image.

Customizing and Formatting an Image

Use buttons in the Adjust group on the Picture Tools Format tab to remove unwanted parts of an image, correct the image brightness and contrast, change the image color, apply artistic effects to the image, change to a different image, and restore the original image formatting. Use the Compress Pictures button in the Adjust group to compress the size of an image file and reduce the amount of space the image requires on the storage medium. Use buttons in the Picture Styles group to apply a predesigned style to the image, change the image border, or apply other effects to the image. Use the Alt Text button in the Accessibility group to add alternate text for the image. With options in the Arrange group, position the image on the page, specify how text will wrap around the image, align the image with other elements in the worksheet, and rotate the image. Use the Crop button in the Size group to remove any unwanted parts of the image and use the *Shape Height* and *Shape Width* measurement boxes to specify the image size.

In addition to options at the Picture Tools Format tab, options at the shortcut menu can be used to format an image. Display this menu by right-clicking the image. Use options at the shortcut menu to change the image, choose text wrapping around the image, insert alt text, size and position the image, and display the Format Picture task pane.

Sizing and Moving an Image

Change the size of an image with the *Shape Height* and *Shape Width* measurement boxes in the Size group on the Picture Tools Format tab or with the sizing handles around the selected image. To change size with a sizing handle, position the mouse pointer on a sizing handle until the pointer turns into a double-headed arrow and then drag in or out to decrease or increase the size of the image. Use the middle sizing handles at the left and right sides of the image to make the image wider or thinner. Use the middle sizing handles at the top and bottom of the image to make the image taller or shorter. Use the sizing handles at the corners of the image to change both the width and height at the same time. Press and hold down the Shift key while dragging a sizing handle to maintain the proportions of the image.

Move an image by positioning the mouse pointer on the image border until the pointer displays with a four-headed arrow attached and then dragging the image to the new location. Rotate the image by positioning the mouse pointer on the white round rotation handle until the pointer displays as a circular arrow. Click and hold down the left mouse button, drag in the desired direction, and then release the mouse button.

1. With **8-SMFFinCon** open, insert an image by completing the following steps:
   a. Click the Insert tab and then click the Pictures button in the Illustrations group.
   b. At the Insert Picture dialog box, navigate to your EL1C8 folder and then double-click *WallStreet*.
2. Change the size of the image by clicking in the *Shape Height* measurement box in the Size group on the Picture Tools Format tab, typing 1.8, and then pressing the Enter key.
3. Remove the yellow background from the image by completing the following steps:
   a. Click the Remove Background button in the Adjust group.
   b. Click the Keep Changes button in the Close group on the Background Removal tab.
4. Change the color by clicking the Color button in the Adjust group and then clicking the *Blue, Accent color 1 Light* option (second column, third row in the *Recolor* section).
5. Apply a correction by clicking the Corrections button in the Adjust group and then clicking the *Brightness: +20% Contrast: +20%* option (fourth column, fourth row in the *Brightness/Contrast* section).
6. Apply an artistic effect by clicking the Artistic Effects button in the Adjust group and then clicking the *Glow Edges* option (last option in the drop-down gallery).

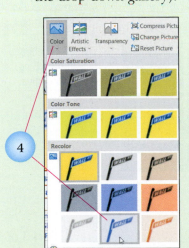
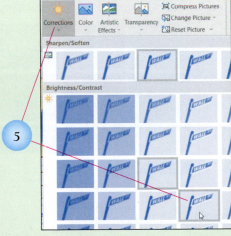
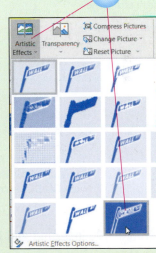

7. Move the image by completing the following steps:
   a. Position the mouse pointer on the image (displays with a four-headed arrow attached).
   b. Click and hold down the left mouse button, drag the image to the upper left corner of the worksheet, and then release the mouse button.
8. Save and then print **8-SMFFinCon**.

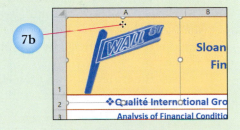

> **Check Your Work**

Formatting an Image at the Format Picture Task Pane

In addition to the Picture Tools Format tab, the Format Picture task pane provides options for formatting an image. Click the Picture Styles group task pane launcher or the Size group task pane launcher and the Format Picture task pane displays at the right side of the screen. Click the Picture Styles group task pane launcher and the task pane displays with the Effects icon selected; click the Size group task pane launcher and the Size & Properties icon is selected. Two other icons are also available in this task pane: the Fill & Line icon and the Picture icon. The formatting options may need to be expanded. For example, click *Size* with the Size & Properties icon selected and options for changing the size of the image display. Close the task pane by clicking the Close button in the upper right corner.

Tutorial

Inserting an Online Image

 Online Pictures

Quick Steps

Insert Online Image
1. Click Insert tab.
2. Click Online Pictures button.
3. Type search word or topic.
4. Press Enter key.
5. Double-click image.

Inserting an Online Image

Use the Bing Image Search feature to search for images online. To use this feature, click the Insert tab and then click the Online Pictures button in the Illustrations group. This displays the Online Pictures window, shown in Figure 8.3. Click in the search text box, type the search term or topic, and then press the Enter key. Images that match the search term or topic display in the window. To insert an image, click the image and then click the Insert button or double-click the image. This downloads the image to the document. Customize the image with options and buttons on the Picture Tools Format tab.

Figure 8.3 Online Pictures Window

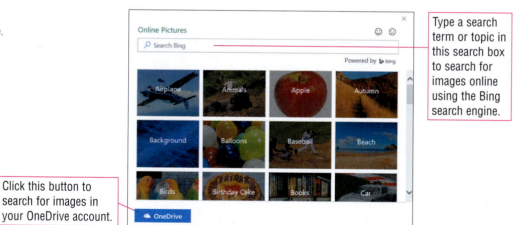

Type a search term or topic in this search box to search for images online using the Bing search engine.

Click this button to search for images in your OneDrive account.

Activity 1c Inserting and Formatting an Image

Part 3 of 5

1. With **8-SMFFinCon** open, delete the Wall Street sign image by clicking the image and then pressing the Delete key.
2. Insert a different image by completing the following steps:
   a. Make cell A1 active.
   b. Click the Insert tab and then click the Online Pictures button in the Illustrations group.

c. At the Online Pictures window, type stock market clip art in the search box and then press the Enter key.

d. Double-click the graph image shown below and to the right. (If this image is not available online, click the Pictures button on the Insert tab. At the Insert Picture dialog box, navigate to your EL1C8 folder and then double-click *StockMarket*.)

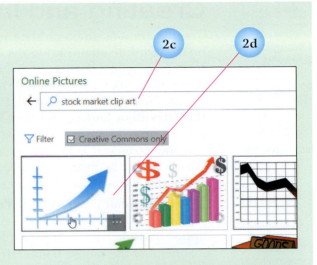

3. Display the Format Picture task pane with the Size & Properties icon selected by clicking the Size group task pane launcher on the Picture Tools Format tab.

4. If necessary, click *Size* in the task pane to display the sizing options.

5. Change the height of the image by selecting the current measurement in the *Height* measurement box, typing 1.65, and then pressing the Enter key. (The width automatically changes to maintain the proportions of the image.)

6. Change the properties of the image by clicking *Properties* in the Format Picture task pane to expand the options and then clicking the *Move and size with cells* option. (With this option selected, changing the size of the row also changes the size of the image.)

7. Make a correction to the image by completing the following steps:
   a. Click the Picture icon at the top of the task pane.
   b. Click *Picture Corrections* to expand the options.
   c. Select the current percentage in the *Brightness* text box and then type -25.
   d. Select the current percentage in the *Contrast* text box, type 40, and then press the Enter key.

8. Close the Format Picture task pane by clicking the Close button in the upper right corner.

9. Create alternative text for the image by completing the following steps:
   a. Click the Alt Text button in the Accessibility group on the Picture Tools Format tab.
   b. At the Alt Text task pane, click in the description text box and then type Chart containing an up-pointing arrow.
   c. Close the Alt Text task pane.

10. Click outside the image to deselect it.

11. Increase the height of row 1 to 126.00 points and notice that the image size increases with the row height.

12. Save 8-SMFFinCon.

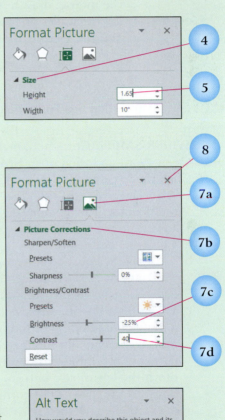

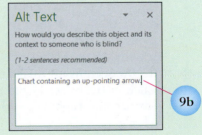

Check Your Work

Tutorial

Creating and
Inserting a
Screenshot

 Screenshot

Quick Steps

Insert Screenshot
1. Open window to be captured.
2. Make Excel active.
3. Open workbook.
4. Click Insert tab.
5. Click Screenshot button.
6. Click window at drop-down list.
OR
1. Click Screenshot button and then *Screen Clipping*.
2. Drag to specify capture area.

Creating and Inserting a Screenshot

The Illustrations group on the Insert tab contains a Screenshot button that can be used to capture all or part of the contents of a screen as an image. This is useful for capturing information from a web page or a file in another program. To create a screenshot, open the web page or file to be captured so that it is visible on the screen. Next, make Excel active and open a workbook. Click the Insert tab, click the Screenshot button, and then look in the drop-down list to see thumbnails of windows open in other programs. Click the thumbnail of the screen to be captured and the screenshot is inserted as an image in the open workbook, the image is selected, and the Picture Tools Format tab is active. Use buttons on this tab to customize the screenshot image.

A screenshot can also be made of a specific portion of the screen by clicking the *Screen Clipping* option at the Screenshot button drop-down list. Click this option and the open web page, file, or Windows desktop displays in a dimmed manner and the mouse pointer displays as crosshairs (a plus symbol [+]). Using the mouse, draw a border around the specific area of the screen to be captured. The area identified is inserted in the workbook as an image, the image is selected, and the Picture Tools Format tab is active.

Activity 1d Inserting and Formatting a Screenshot

Part 4 of 5

1. With **8-SMFFinCon** open, make sure that no other programs are open.
2. Open Word and then open **SMFProfile** from your EL1C8 folder.
3. Click the Excel button on the taskbar.
4. Insert a screenshot of the table in the Word document by completing the following steps:
   a. Click the Insert tab.
   b. Click the Screenshot button in the Illustrations group and then click *Screen Clipping* at the drop-down list.
   c. When **SMFProfile** displays in a dimmed manner, position the mouse crosshairs in the upper left corner of the table, click and hold down the left mouse button, drag down to the lower right corner of the table, and then release the mouse button. (This creates a screenshot of the entire table.)

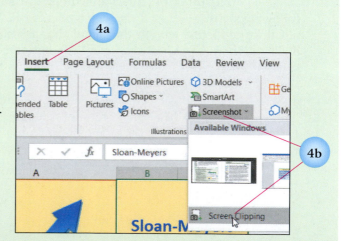

5. With the screenshot image inserted in **8-SMFFinCon**, make the following changes:
   a. Click in the *Shape Width* measurement box in the Size group on the Picture Tools Format tab, type 3.7, and then press the Enter key.

b. Click the Corrections button and then click the *Sharpen: 25%* option (fourth option in the *Sharpen/Soften* section).

c. Click the Corrections button and then click the *Brightness: 0% (Normal) Contrast: -40%* (third column, first row in the *Brightness/Contrast* section).

d. Using the mouse, drag the screenshot image one row below the data in row 10.

6. Make cell A4 active.

7. Save **8-SMFFinCon**.

8. Click the Word button on the taskbar, close **SMFProfile**, and then close Word.

Check Your Work

 Tutorial

Inserting a Shape

 Tutorial

Formatting a Shape

 Shapes

Inserting and Formatting a Shape

Chapter 7 covered how to insert shapes in a chart with options on the Chart Tools Format tab. Shapes can also be inserted in a worksheet with the Shapes button in the Illustrations group on the Insert tab. Use the Shapes button to draw shapes in a worksheet, including lines, basic shapes, block arrows, flow chart symbols, callouts, stars, and banners. Click a shape and the mouse pointer displays as crosshairs. Click in the worksheet or position the crosshairs where the shape is to begin, click and hold down the left mouse button, drag to create the shape, and then release the mouse button. Click or drag in the worksheet and the shape is inserted and the Drawing Tools Format tab, shown in Figure 8.4, becomes active. Use options and buttons on this tab to choose a shape, apply a style to a shape, arrange a shape, and change the size of a shape.

Choose a shape in the *Lines* section of the Shapes button drop-down list and the shape that is drawn is considered a line drawing. Choose an option in another section of the drop-down list and the shape drawn is considered an enclosed object. When drawing an enclosed object, maintain the proportions of the shape by pressing and holding down the Shift key while dragging with the mouse. Text can be typed in an enclosed object and then formatted using buttons in the WordArt Styles group (or options on the Home tab).

Copy a shape in a worksheet by selecting the shape and then clicking the Copy button in the Clipboard group on the Home tab. Make active the cell where the shape is to be copied and then click the Paste button. A shape can also be copied by pressing and holding down the Ctrl key while dragging the shape to the new location.

Quick Steps

Insert Shape
1. Click Insert tab.
2. Click Shapes button.
3. Click shape option at drop-down list.
4. Click or drag in worksheet.

Copy Shape
1. Select shape.
2. Click Copy button.
3. Position insertion point in new location.
4. Click Paste button.
OR
1. Select shape.
2. Press and hold down Ctrl key.
3. Drag shape to new location.

Figure 8.4 Drawing Tools Format Tab

1. With **8-SMFFinCon** open, create the larger arrow shown in Figure 8.5 by completing the following steps:

   a. Click the Insert tab.

   b. Click the Shapes button in the Illustrations group and then click the *Arrow: Up* shape (third column, first row in the *Block Arrows* section).

   c. Position the mouse pointer (appears as crosshairs) near the upper left corner of cell D1 and then click the left mouse button. (This inserts the arrow in the worksheet.)

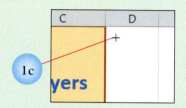

   d. Click in the *Shape Height* measurement box and then type 3.7.

   e. Click in the *Shape Width* measurement box, type 2.1, and then press the Enter key.

   f. If necessary, drag the arrow so it is positioned as shown in Figure 8.5. (To drag the arrow, position the mouse pointer on the border of the selected arrow until the pointer displays with a four-headed arrow attached, click and hold down the left mouse button, drag the arrow to the new position, and then release the mouse button.)

   g. Click the More Shape Styles button in the Shape Styles group on the Drawing Tools Format tab and then click the *Intense Effect - Blue, Accent 1* option (second column, last row in the *Theme Styles* section).

   h. Click the Shape Effects button in the Shape Styles group, point to *Glow*, and then click the *Glow: 11 point; Orange, Accent color 2* option (second column, third row in the *Glow Variations* section).

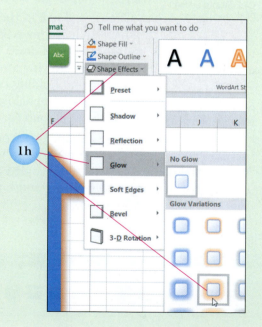

2. Insert text in the arrow by completing the following steps:
   a. With the arrow selected, type McGuire Mutual Shares 5.33%.
   b. Select the text you just typed (*McGuire Mutual Shares 5.33%*).
   c. Click the More WordArt Styles button in the WordArt Styles group and then click the option in the fourth column, third row (orange outline with white fill).
   d. Press Ctrl + E to center the text.
3. With the arrow selected, copy it by completing the following steps:
   a. Press and hold down the Ctrl key.
   b. Position the mouse pointer on the arrow border until the pointer displays with a square box and plus symbol attached.
   c. Click and hold down the left mouse button and drag to the right so the outline of the arrow is positioned at the right of the existing arrow.
   d. Release the mouse button and then release the Ctrl key.
4. Format the second arrow by completing the following steps:
   a. With the second arrow selected, click in the *Shape Height* measurement box on the Drawing Tools Format tab and then type 2.
   b. Click in the *Shape Width* measurement box, type 1.6, and then press the Enter key.
   c. Select the text *McGuire Mutual Shares 5.33%* and then type SR Linus Fund 0.22%.
   d. Drag the arrow so it is positioned as shown in Figure 8.5.
5. Change to landscape orientation. (Make sure the cells containing the data, screenshot image, and arrows will print on the same page.)
6. Save, print, and then close **8-SMFFinCon**.

Check Your Work

Figure 8.5 Activity 1e

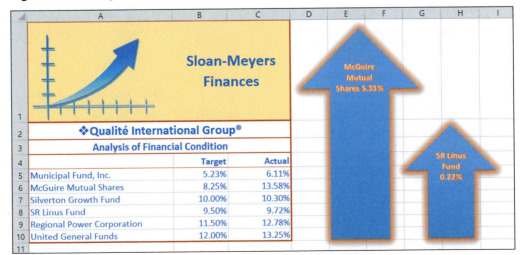

Activity 2 Insert an Icon, 3D Model, and Text Box in a Division Sales Workbook 2 Parts

You will open a division sales workbook and then insert, move, and size an image, an icon, and a 3D model. You will also insert a text box and then format the text.

Tutorial

Inserting and Modifying Text Boxes

 Text Box

Inserting and Modifying Text Boxes

To draw a text box in a worksheet, click the Insert tab and then click the Text Box button in the Text group. This causes the mouse pointer to display as a long, thin, upside-down cross (↧). Position the pointer in the worksheet and then drag to create the text box. When a text box is selected, the Drawing Tools Format tab displays with options for customizing it.

Click a text box to select it and a dashed border and sizing handles display around it. To delete the text box, click the border again to change the dashed lines to solid lines and then press the Delete key.

Tutorial

Inserting and Modifying an Icon

Quick Steps

Draw Text Box
1. Click Insert tab.
2. Click Text Box button.
3. Click or drag in worksheet to create text box.

Insert Icons
1. Click Insert tab.
2. Click Icons button.
3. Click icon.
4. Click Insert button.

 Icons

Inserting and Customizing Icons

Use the Icons button in the Illustrations group on the Insert tab to insert an icon in a Word document. An icon is a simple graphic used to represent a concept or idea, such as emotions, weather, nature, the arts, and so on. Icons can be used to highlight or label data in a worksheet. These simple graphics draw the eye to important information and can be understood at a glance. Click the Icons button on the Insert tab and the Insert Icons window opens, as shown in Figure 8.6. At this window, scroll down the list box to view the various icons or click a category in the left panel to display a specific category of icons. To insert an icon in a document, double-click the icon in the list box or click the icon and then click the Insert button.

Figure 8.6 Insert Icons Window

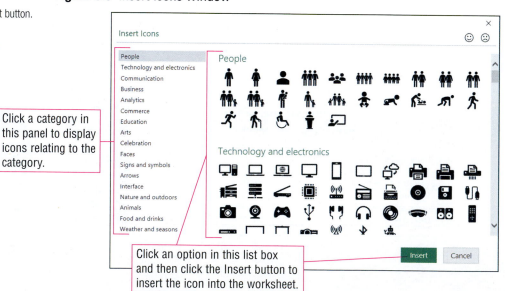

Click a category in this panel to display icons relating to the category.

Click an option in this list box and then click the Insert button to insert the icon into the worksheet.

When an icon is inserted and selected in a worksheet, the Graphics Tools Format tab is active, as shown in Figure 8.7. Use options on this tab to apply a graphic style, fill, outline, and effect; type alternate text for the icon; position, align, group, rotate, and size the icon; and apply text wrapping.

Icons, like other images, can be formatted with options at the Format Graphic task pane. Display this task pane by clicking the Graphics Styles group or Size group task pane launcher. The task pane contains four icons: Fill & Line, Effects, Size & Properties, and Picture. Use options at the Format Graphic task pane to format an icon in a manner similar to formatting an image, shape, and text box.

Figure 8.7 Graphics Tools Format Tab

Activity 2a Inserting and Customizing an Icon and a Text Box

Part 1 of 2

1. Open **HPDivSales** and then save it with the name **8-HPDivSales**.
2. Insert and format an icon by completing the following steps:
   a. Click in cell A2.
   b. Click the Insert tab.
   c. Click the Icons button in the Illustrations group.

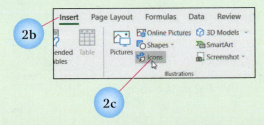

   d. At the Insert Icons window, click *Arts* at the left side of the window.
   e. Click the video camera icon shown below and then click the Insert button.

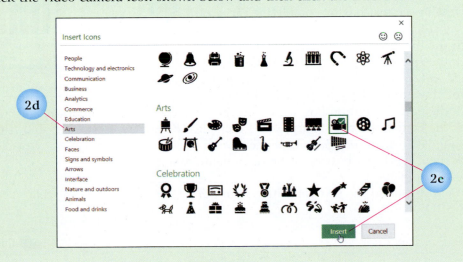

f. With the Icon selected, click the Rotate button in the Arrange group and then click the *Flip Horizontal* option at the drop-down list.

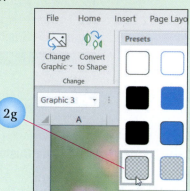

g. Click the More Graphic Styles button in the Graphics Styles group and then click the *Transparent, Colored Outline - Dark 1* option at the drop-down gallery (first column, last row).

h. Move the icon it so it is positioned as shown in Figure 8.8.

3. Draw a text box by completing the following steps:
   a. Click the Insert tab.
   b. Click the Text Box button in the Text group.
   c. Drag to cell A1 to draw a text box the approximate size and shape shown below.

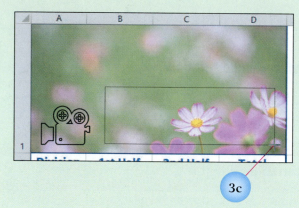

4. Format the text box by completing the following steps:
   a. Click the Drawing Tools Format tab.
   b. Click the Shape Fill button arrow in the Shape Styles group and then click *No Fill* at the drop-down gallery.
   c. Click the Shape Outline button arrow in the Shape Styles group and then click *No Outline* at the drop-down gallery.

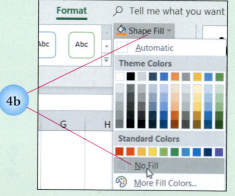

5. Insert text in the text box by completing the following steps:
   a. With the text box selected, click the Home tab.
   b. Click the *Font* option box arrow and then click *Lucida Calligraphy* at the drop-down gallery. (Scroll down the gallery to display this font.)
   c. Click the *Font Size* option box arrow and then click *24* at the drop-down gallery.
   d. Click the Font Color button arrow and then click *Blue, Accent 1, Darker 50%* (fifth column, last row in the *Theme Colors* section).
   e. Click the Align Right button in the Alignment group.
   f. Type Hummingbird Productions.

6. Move the text box so the text is positioned in cell A1, as shown in Figure 8.8.
7. Save **8-SPDivSales**.

Check Your Work

Figure 8.8 Activity 2a

Tutorial ›

Inserting and
Modifying 3D
Models

Quick Steps

Insert 3D Model
1. Click Insert tab.
2. Click 3D Models
   button.
3. Click category.
4. Click model.
5. Click Insert button.

3D Model

Inserting and Customizing 3D Models

A 3D model is a graphic file of an image shown in three dimensions. The model can be rotated or tilted to allow viewing from various angles or to display a specific portion or feature. Microsoft's Remix 3D library includes a collection of free 3D models that can be inserted into a Word document, PowerPoint presentation, or Excel worksheet. Access these images by clicking the 3D Models button in the Illustrations group on the Insert tab. At the Online 3D Models window, shown in Figure 8.9, click a category to view all 3D models within the category or type a keyword(s) in the search text box and then press the Enter key. Insert a 3D model in a worksheet by double-clicking the model or clicking the model and then clicking the Insert button.

Figure 8.9 Online 3D Models Window

Click a category to
display 3D model
in the category.

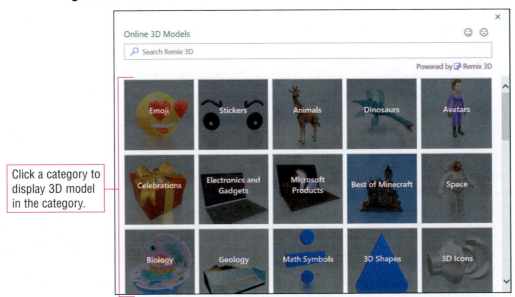

When a 3D model is inserted in a document, the 3D Model Tools Format tab is active. Use buttons in the Adjust group to insert a different 3D model or reset the selected model to its original size and position. The 3D Model Views group includes a gallery of preset views for the model. Click the Alt Text button in the Accessibility group and the Alt Text task pane displays, where a description of the model can be added. Use options in the Arrange group to position the model, apply text wrapping, send the model forward or backward, and align the model. Change the height and width of the model with options in the Size group.

 Pan & Zoom

The Size group also contains the Pan & Zoom button. Click this button to lock the position of the 3D model and a button (a magnifying glass with a plus symbol inside) will display at the right of the selected model. Position the mouse pointer on this button, hold down the left mouse button, and then drag up to increase the size of the model (zoom in) or drag down to decrease the size (zoom out). Use the 3D control in the middle of the model to freely rotate the model. Pan the model by clicking and dragging within the frame to change the model's position within the frame. Turn off the pan and zoom feature by clicking the Pan & Zoom button to deactivate it.

Use the 3D control that displays in the middle of a selected 3D model to rotate or tilt the model. To use the 3D control, position the mouse pointer on the control, click and hold down the left mouse button, and then drag with the mouse to rotate or tilt the model.

Options for formatting and customizing a 3D model are available at the Format 3D Model task pane. Display the task pane by clicking the 3D Model Views group or Size group task pane launcher. The task pane displays with four icons: Fill & Line, Effects, Size & Properties, and 3D Model.

Click the Fill & Line icon to display options for formatting the border line and fill of the 3D model. Use options at the task pane with the Effects icon selected to apply formatting effects, such as shadow, reflection, glow, and soft edges, and to format and rotate the model. Click the Size & Properties icon to display options for adjusting the size of the 3D model, or click the 3D Model icon to specify the rotation and camera view.

Activity 2b Inserting and Customizing a 3D Model

Part 2 of 2

1. With **8-HPDivSales** open, click in cell E1.
2. Insert a 3D model from the Remix 3D library by completing the following steps:
   a. Click the Insert tab.
   b. Click the 3D Models button in the Illustrations group.
   c. At the Online 3D Models window, click the *Animals* category.
   d. Scroll down and click the hummingbird model.
   e. Click the Insert button.
   Note: If you do not have access to the Online 3D Models window, open Bird3D from your EL1C8 folder. This workbook contains the 3D hummingbird model. Copy the model and then paste it into 8-DivSales.

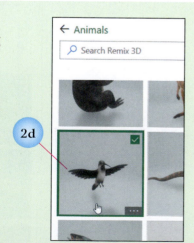

3. Change the size of the model at the Format 3D Model task pane by completing the following steps:
   a. Click the Size group task pane launcher.
   b. Select the value in the *Width* measurement box.
   c. Type 3 and then press the Enter key.
4. Change the view of the model by clicking the *Right* view (fifth option) in the 3D Model Views gallery.

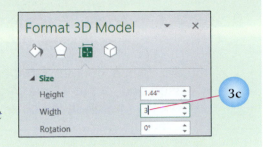

5. Reset the bird model by clicking the Reset 3D Model button in the Adjust group.

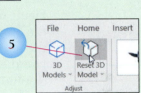

6. Use the 3D control that displays in the middle of the bird model by positioning the mouse pointer on the 3D control, pressing and holding down the left mouse button, and then dragging with the mouse to rotate the model. Rotate the model so it displays as shown in Figure 8.10.
7. Zoom in and pan the model by completing the following steps:
   a. Click the Pan & Zoom button in the Size group on the 3D Model Tools Format tab.
   b. Position the mouse pointer on the button that displays as a magnifying glass with a plus symbol inside (at the right of the model), press and hold down the left mouse button, and then drag down to decrease the size of the model so it displays as shown in Figure 8.10.
   c. Position the mouse inside the model and then pan the hummingbird within the frame by click-dragging it to the position as shown in Figure 8.10.
   d. Click the Pan & Zoom button to deactivate it.
   e. Move the model to the upper left corner of cell A1.
8. Close the Format 3D Model task pane.
9. Save, print, and then close **8-HPDivSales**.

Figure 8.10 Activity 2b

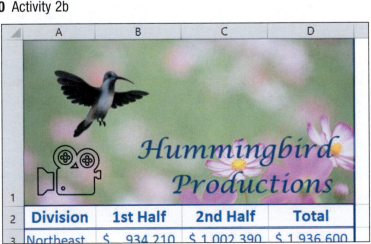

You will open a workbook that contains two company sales worksheets. You will insert and format a SmartArt cycle graphic in one worksheet and a SmartArt relationship graphic in the other. You will also create and format WordArt text.

Tutorial

Inserting a SmartArt Graphic

SmartArt

Quick Steps

Insert SmartArt Graphic
1. Click Insert tab.
2. Click SmartArt button.
3. Double-click graphic.

Text Pane

Hint Generally, you would use a SmartArt graphic to represent text and a chart to represent numbers.

Inserting a SmartArt Graphic

Use the SmartArt feature included in Excel to insert graphics, such as diagrams and organizational charts, in a worksheet. SmartArt offers a variety of predesigned graphics that are available at the Choose a SmartArt Graphic dialog box, shown in Figure 8.11. Display this dialog box by clicking the Insert tab and then clicking the SmartArt button in the Illustrations group. At the dialog box, *All* is selected in the left panel and all the predesigned graphics are available in the middle panel. Use the scroll bar at the right side of the middle panel to scroll down the list of graphic choices. Click a graphic in the middle panel and the name of the graphic displays in the right panel along with a description of the graphic type. SmartArt includes graphics for presenting lists of data; showing data processes, cycles, and relationships; and presenting data in a matrix or pyramid. Double-click a graphic in the middle panel of the dialog box and the graphic is inserted in the worksheet.

Entering Data in a SmartArt Graphic

Some SmartArt graphics are designed to include text. Type text in a graphic by selecting a shape in the graphic and then typing text in the shape, or display a text pane and then type text in the pane. Display the text pane by clicking the Text Pane button in the Create Graphic group on the SmartArt Tools Design tab. Turn off the display of the pane by clicking the Text Pane button or clicking the Close button in the upper right corner of the pane.

Figure 8.11 Choose a SmartArt Graphic Dialog Box

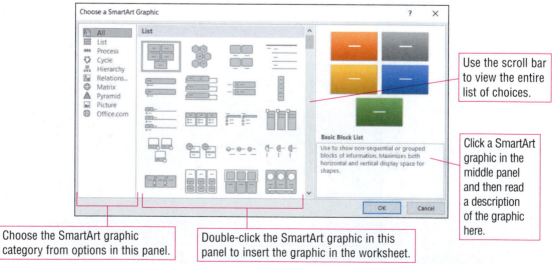

Use the scroll bar to view the entire list of choices.

Click a SmartArt graphic in the middle panel and then read a description of the graphic here.

Choose the SmartArt graphic category from options in this panel.

Double-click the SmartArt graphic in this panel to insert the graphic in the worksheet.

Tutorial

Modifying a
SmartArt Graphic

Sizing, Moving, and Deleting a SmartArt Graphic

Increase or decrease the size of a SmartArt graphic by dragging one of the sizing handles that display around the selected graphic. Use the corner sizing handles to increase or decrease the height and width at the same time. Use the middle sizing handles to increase or decrease the height or width of the SmartArt graphic.

To move a SmartArt graphic, select it and then position the mouse pointer on the graphic border until the pointer displays with a four-headed arrow attached. Click and hold down the left mouse button, drag the graphic to the new position, and then release the mouse button. Delete a graphic by selecting it and then pressing the Delete key.

Activity 3a Inserting, Moving, and Sizing a SmartArt Graphic in a Worksheet   Part 1 of 4

1. Open **EPCoSales** and then save it with the name **8-EPCoSales**.
2. Create the SmartArt graphic shown in Figure 8.12. To begin, click the Insert tab.
3. Click the SmartArt button in the Illustrations group.
4. At the Choose a SmartArt Graphic dialog box, click *Cycle* in the left panel.
5. Double-click *Radial Cycle* in the middle panel (as shown in the image at the right).
6. If the text pane is not open, click the Text Pane button in the Create Graphic group. (The text pane will display at the left of the SmartArt graphic.)
7. With the insertion point positioned after the top bullet in the text pane, type Evergreen Products.
8. Click in the *[Text]* placeholder below *Evergreen Products* and then type Seattle.
9. Click in the next *[Text]* placeholder and then type Olympia.
10. Click in the next *[Text]* placeholder and then type Portland.
11. Click in the next *[Text]* placeholder and then type Spokane.
12. Click the Text Pane button to close the text pane.
13. Drag the SmartArt graphic so it is positioned as shown in Figure 8.12. To drag the graphic, position the mouse pointer on the graphic border until the pointer displays with a four-headed arrow attached. Click and hold down the left mouse button, drag the graphic to the new position, and then release the mouse button.
14. Use the sizing handles around the SmartArt graphic to increase or decrease the size so it displays as shown in Figure 8.12.
15. Save **8-EPCoSales**.

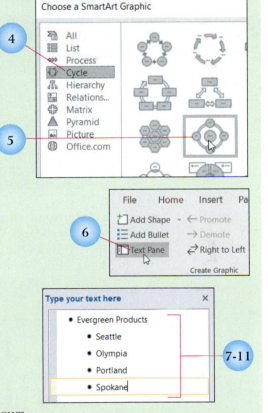

Check Your Work

Figure 8.12 Activity 3a

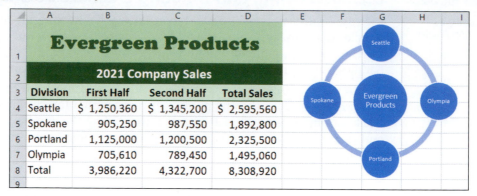

Changing the SmartArt Graphic Design

💡 **Hint** To restore the SmartArt default layout and color, click the Reset Graphic button in the Reset group on the SmartArt Tools Design tab.

Double-click a SmartArt graphic at the Choose a SmartArt Graphic dialog box and the graphic is inserted in the worksheet and the SmartArt Tools Design tab is active. Use options and buttons on this tab to add objects, change the graphic layout, apply a style to the graphic, and reset the original formatting of the graphic.

Activity 3b Changing the SmartArt Graphic Design

Part 2 of 4

1. With **8-EPCoSales** open, make sure the SmartArt Tools Design tab is active and then click the *Spokane* circle shape in the graphic to select it.
2. Click the Right to Left button in the Create Graphic group. (This switches *Olympia* and *Spokane*.)
3. Click the More SmartArt Styles button in the SmartArt Styles group and then click the *Polished* option at the drop-down list (first column, first row in the *3-D* section).

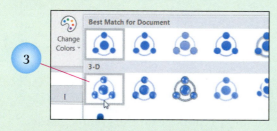

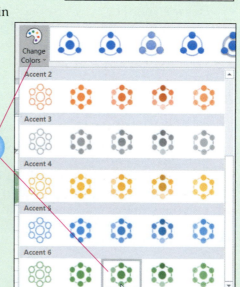

4. Click the Change Colors button in the SmartArt Styles group, scroll down the drop-down gallery, and then click the *Gradient Range - Accent 6* option (third option in the *Accent 6* section).
5. Click outside the SmartArt graphic to deselect it.
6. Change to landscape orientation. (Make sure the graphic fits on the first page.)
7. Save **8-EPCoSales** and then print the Total Sales worksheet.

Check Your Work

Changing the SmartArt Graphic Formatting

Click the SmartArt Tools Format tab and options display for formatting a SmartArt graphic. Use buttons on this tab to insert and customize shapes; apply a shape style; apply WordArt styles; and specify the position, alignment, rotation, wrapping style, height, and width of a graphic.

Activity 3c Changing the SmartArt Graphic Formatting   Part 3 of 4

1. With **8-EPCoSales** open, click the Seattle Sales sheet tab.
2. Create the SmartArt graphic shown in Figure 8.13. To begin, click the Insert tab and then click the SmartArt button in the Illustrations group.
3. At the Choose a SmartArt Graphic dialog box, click *Relationship* in the left panel and then double-click *Gear* in the middle panel.

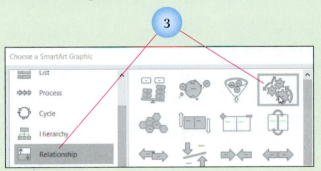

4. Click in the *[Text]* placeholder in the bottom gear and then type Quality Products.
5. Click in the *[Text]* placeholder in the left gear and then type Customized Plans.
6. Click in the *[Text]* placeholder in the top gear and then type Exemplary Service.
7. Click inside the SmartArt graphic border but outside any specific shape.
8. Click the More SmartArt Styles button in the SmartArt Styles group and then click the *Inset* option (second column, first row in the *3-D* section).
9. Click the Change Colors button and then click the *Gradient Loop - Accent 6* option (fourth option in the *Accent 6* section).
10. Click the SmartArt Tools Format tab.
11. Click in the *Height* measurement box in the Size group and then type 4.
12. Click in the *Width* measurement box, type 4.5, and then press the Enter key.

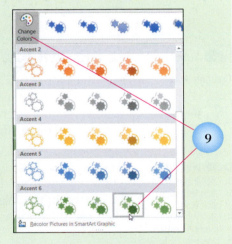

13. Click the bottom gear to select it.

14. Click the Shape Fill button arrow in the Shape Styles group and then click the *Green, Accent 6, Darker 50%* option (last column, last row in the *Theme Colors* section).

15. Click the top gear to select it.

16. Click the Shape Fill button arrow and then click the *Green, Accent 6, Darker 25%* option (last column, fifth row in the *Theme Colors* section).

17. Change to landscape orientation.

18. Move the SmartArt graphic so it fits on the first page and displays as shown in Figure 8.13.

19. Click outside the SmartArt graphic to deselect it.

20. Save **8-EPCoSales** and then print the Seattle Sales worksheet.

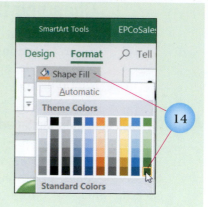

Check Your Work

Figure 8.13 Activity 3c

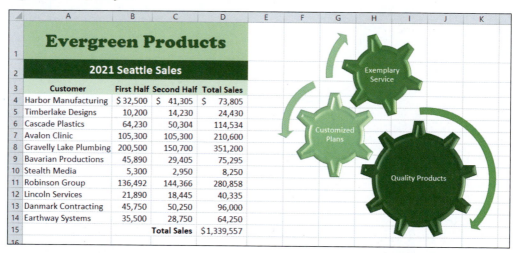

 Tutorial

Creating WordArt

 WordArt

Quick Steps

Create WordArt
1. Click Insert tab.
2. Click Text button.
3. Click WordArt button.
4. Click WordArt style at drop-down list.
5. Type text.

Creating, Sizing, and Moving WordArt

Use the WordArt feature to distort or modify text so it conforms to a variety of shapes. This is useful for creating company logos and headings. Change the font, style, and alignment of text with WordArt and use fill patterns and colors, customize border lines, and add shadow and three-dimensional effects.

To insert WordArt in an Excel worksheet, click the Insert tab, click the Text button, click the WordArt button at the drop-down list, and then click an option at the drop-down list. This inserts the text *Your text here* in the worksheet, formatted in the WordArt option selected at the drop-down list. Type text and then use the options and buttons on the Drawing Tools Format tab to format the WordArt.

WordArt text inserted in a worksheet is surrounded by white sizing handles. Use these sizing handles to change the height and width of the WordArt text. To move WordArt text, position the mouse pointer on the border of the WordArt text box until the pointer displays with a four-headed arrow attached and then drag the outline of the text box to the new location.

Make WordArt text conform to a variety of shapes using the *Transform* option from the Text Effects button drop-down list. Apply a transform shape and a small yellow circle displays below the WordArt text. Use this circle to change the slant of the WordArt text.

Activity 3d Inserting and Formatting WordArt

Part 4 of 4

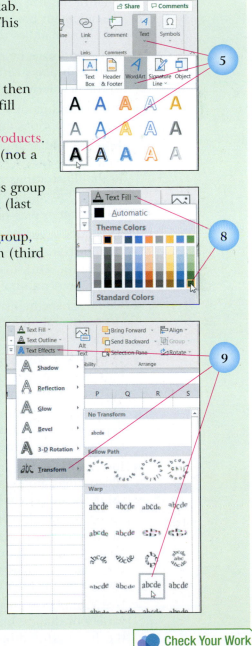

1. With **8-EPCoSales** open, click the Total Sales sheet tab.
2. Make cell A1 active and then press the Delete key. (This removes the text from the cell.)
3. Increase the height of row 1 to 138 points.
4. Click the Insert tab.
5. Click the Text button, click the WordArt button, and then click the option in the first column, third row (black fill with white outline).
6. Type Evergreen, press the Enter key, and then type Products.
7. Click the WordArt border to change it to a solid line (not a dashed line).
8. Click the Text Fill button arrow in the WordArt Styles group and then click the *Green, Accent 6, Darker 50%* option (last column, last row in the Theme Colors section).
9. Click the Text Effects button in the WordArt Styles group, point to *Transform*, and then click the *Warp Up* option (third column, fourth row in the *Warp* section).
10. Position the mouse pointer (turns into a white arrow) on the small yellow circle immediately below the *d* in *Products*, click and hold down the left mouse button, drag up approximately 0.25 inch, and then release the mouse button. (This changes the slant of the text.)
11. Drag the WordArt text so it is positioned in cell A1.
12. If necessary, size the SmartArt graphic and position it so it prints on one page with the data.
13. Click the Seattle Sales sheet tab and then complete steps similar to those in Steps 2 through 11 to insert *Evergreen Products* as WordArt in cell A1.
14. Make sure the SmartArt graphic fits on one page with the data. If necessary, decrease the size of the graphic.
15. Save **8-EPCoSales** and then print both worksheets.
16. Close **8-EPCoSales**.

Check Your Work ▸

Chapter Summary

- Insert symbols with options at the Symbol dialog box with the Symbols tab or Special Characters tab selected.

- Use buttons in the Illustrations group on the Insert tab to insert an image such as a picture, clip art image, screenshot, shape, or SmartArt graphic.

- Insert an image by clicking the Insert tab, clicking the Pictures button in the Illustrations group, and then double-clicking an image at the Insert Picture dialog box.

- Insert an image in a worksheet and the Picture Tools Format tab is active. It provides options for adjusting the image, applying preformatted styles to the image, and arranging and sizing the image.

- Change the size of an image with the *Shape Height* and *Shape Width* measurement boxes in the Size group on the Picture Tools Format tab or with the sizing handles that display around a selected image.

- Move an image by positioning the mouse pointer on the image border until the pointer displays with a four-headed arrow attached and then dragging the image to the new location.

- Format and modify an image by displaying the Format Picture task pane and using the options and buttons to alter the image.

- Insert an online image with options at the Online Pictures window. Display this window by clicking the Insert tab and then clicking the Online Pictures button in the Illustrations group.

- Use the Screenshot button in the Illustrations group on the Insert tab to capture all or part of the contents of a screen as an image.

- To draw a shape in a workbook, click the Insert tab, click the Shapes button in the Illustrations group, and then click a shape at the drop-down list. Click or drag in the worksheet to insert the shape. To maintain the proportions of the shape, press and hold down the Shift key while dragging in the worksheet.

- Copy a shape by using the Copy and Paste buttons in the Clipboard group on the Home tab or by pressing and holding down the Ctrl key while dragging the shape.

- Draw a text box in a worksheet by clicking the Insert tab, clicking the Text Box button in the Text group, and then clicking or dragging in the worksheet. Use options on the Drawing Tools Format tab to format and customize the text box.

- Use the Icons button to insert simple images into a worksheet. Customize the appearance of an icon using buttons and options on the Graphics Tools Format tab and at the Format Graphic task pane.

- Insert a 3D model into a worksheet by clicking the 3D Model button in the Illustrations group on the Insert tab. Customize the appearance of a 3D model using the object control inside the model and also by using buttons and options on the 3D Models Tool Format tab and at the Format 3D Model task pane.

- Insert a SmartArt graphic in a worksheet by clicking the Insert tab, clicking the SmartArt button in the Illustrations group, and then double-clicking a graphic at the Choose a SmartArt Graphic dialog box. Customize a SmartArt graphic with options on the SmartArt Tools Design tab and SmartArt Tools Format tab.

- Use WordArt to create, distort, and modify text and to make it conform to a variety of shapes. Insert WordArt in a worksheet with the WordArt button in the Text button drop-down list on the Insert tab. Customize WordArt text with options on the Drawing Tools Format tab.

Commands Review

FEATURE	RIBBON TAB, GROUP	BUTTON
alternative text	Picture Tools Format, Accessibility	
Choose a SmartArt Graphic dialog box	Insert, Illustrations	
Insert Icons window	Insert, Illustrations	
Insert Picture dialog box	Insert, Illustrations	
Insert WordArt button drop-down list	Insert, Text	
Online 3D Models window	Insert, Illustrations	
Online Pictures window	Insert, Illustrations	
screenshot	Insert, Illustrations	
Shapes button drop-down list	Insert, Illustrations	
Symbol dialog box	Insert, Symbols	
text box	Insert, Text	

Index

fill handle to copy formula, 18

with functions, 38–44

mixed cell references in, 47–48

ranges in, 130–131

Trace Error button, 36

writing

    with AVERAGE, MIN, MAX, COUNT functions, 40–43

    with financial functions, 170–173

    with IF logical function, 200–204

    with mathematical operators, 32–37

    with NOW and TODAY function, 44

    by pointing, 34–35

    with statistical functions, 40–43

Formula tab, 38

Fraction, as category in Format Cells dialog box, 66

Freeze Panes button, 128–129

Function Arguments dialog box, 39, 201–202

Function Library group, 38

functions

    argument, 38

    AVERAGE, 18, 40–41

    constants, 38

    COUNT, 43

    COUNTA, 43

    defined, 38

    FV, 170

    identifying common errors, 36

    inserting formulas with, 38–44

    MAX, 41–43

    MIN, 41–43

    NOW, 44

    PMT, 170

    SUM, 17

    TODAY, 44

    writing formulas

        with financial functions, 170–173

        finding future value of investment, 173

        finding periodic payments for loan, 171–173

        with IF logical function, 200–204

with statistical functions, 40–43

funnel chart, 179

future value, 171

    finding, 173

Fv, in financial functions, 171

FV function, 170

G

Go To feature, 6

graphic, linking using, 161–162

Graphics Tools Format Tab, 219

gridlines, 6

    printing, 89

H

Header & Footer button, 91

Header & Footer Tools Design tab, 91–92

headers, inserting, 91–96

headings, printing row and column headings, 89

Help feature

    in dialog box or backstage area, 28

    Help Task Pane, 26

    ScreenTips, 27

Hide button, 134

hiding

    columns and rows, 75–76

    worksheet, 125–126

histogram chart, 178

horizontal scroll bar, 4, 5, 7

hyperlinks

    automatic formatting of, 158–159

    editing, 162–163

    inserting, 158–163

    linking

        to existing web page or file, 158–160

        to new workbook, 160–162

        to place in workbook, 160–162

        using email address, 161

        using graphic, 161–162

    modifying, 162–163

    navigating using, 159

    purposes of, 148

    removing, 162–163

I

icons, inserting and customizing, 218–221

Icons button, 218

IF function, writing formulas with, 200–204

IF statements

    writing, containing text, 203–204

images

    compress and crop, 210

    creating alternative text for, 193–194

    customizing and formatting, 210–211

    formatting with Format Picture task pane, 212

    inserting, 210–213

    inserting and formatting clip art images, 212–213

    sizing and moving, 210

Increase Decimal button, 22, 64

Increase Font Size button, 59

indenting, data, 67–68

Info backstage area, 10

Insert button, 55

Insert dialog box, 55

Insert Function button, 38

Insert Function dialog box, 38–39

Insert Hyperlink dialog box, 158

inserting

    background picture, 88

    clip art, 212–213

    columns, 56–57

    comments, 166–167

    data in cells with fill handle, 14, 15–16

    footers, 91–96

    formulas

        AutoSum, 17–18

        fill handle to copy, 18

        with functions, 38–44

    headers, 91–96

    hyperlinks, 158–163

    icons, 218–221

    images, 210–213

    new worksheet, 116–118

    page breaks, 83–86

    rows, 55–56

    screenshots, 214–215

    shapes, 192–194, 215–217

    SmartArt graphic, 224–228

symbols and special characters, 208–209
text boxes, 218–221
3D Models, 221–223
WordArt, 228–229
integration, 138–139
interest, simple, formula with mixed cell references, 48
Italic button, 59

K

keyboard shortcuts
    to activate cells, 6
    closing Excel, 12
    closing workbook, 11
    displaying Open backstage area, 15
    display Print backstage area, 10
    insert SUM function, 17
    Open dialog box, 15
    repeat last action, 73
    selecting cell with, 19, 20
    selecting data within cell, 19–20

L

landscape orientation, 82
line chart, 178
    creating and formatting, 191–192
Link button, 158
linking
    cells between worksheets, 137–138
    data, 137–138
live preview feature, 62
loan, finding periodic payments for, 171–173
logical test, 200

M

map chart, 178
margins
    changing in worksheet, 80–82
    default settings, 80
Margins button, 80
marquee, 117

mathematical operations, writing formulas with, 32–37
MAX function, 40
    writing formulas with, 41–43
Maximize button, 135
Merge & Center button, 21, 59–60
Merge Styles dialog box, 157
merging, cells, 21
MIN function, 40
    writing formulas with, 41–43
Minimize button, 135
Mini toolbar, formatting with, 59
mixed cell reference, 45
mouse
    to activate cells, 7
    moving split lines, 128
    selecting cell with, 19
    selecting data within cell, 20
Move Chart button, 188
Move Chart dialog box, 188
Move or Copy dialog box, 146
moving
    chart, 179–180
    chart element, 188
    chart location, 188–190
    data, 136
    images, 210
    SmartArt graphic, 225
    split lines, 128
    WordArt, 229
    workbook, 135
    worksheet, 123–124
        to another workbook, 148–149
multiple cell reference, using in formula, 46
multiplication, 32
    order of operations, 35

N

N/A error code, 36
Name box, 4, 5, 6
NAME? error code, 36
navigating, using hyperlinks, 159
nested parentheses, 35
New Comment button, 166
New sheet button, 4, 5, 116
New Window button, 132
Normal button, 84

NOW function, writing formulas with, 44
Nper, in financial functions, 170
Number, as category in Format Cells dialog box, 66
Number Format option box, 64
numbers
    AutoSum
        to add, 17–18
        to average numbers, 18
    formatting, 22–23
        with Format Cells dialog box, 65–67
        with Number group buttons, 63–65
    number symbol (###) for exceeding space in cell, 7
NUM! error code, 36

O

100% button, 127
OneDrive, 7
Online Pictures button, 212
Open Backstage Area, elements of, 144
Open dialog box, 15
opening, workbook
    multiple, 132, 134
    from Open dialog box, 15
    from Recent option list, 15
order of operations, 35
Orientation button, 60, 82

P

page break, inserting and removing, 83–86
Page Break Preview button, 84–85
page orientation
    changing, 82–83
    default, 80
Page Setup dialog box
    centering horizontally/vertically, 81–82
    changing margins, 80
    inserting headers and footers, 93–96
    printing column and row titles on multiple pages, 86–87

Interior Photo Credits

Page GS-1, © lowball-jack/GettyImages, Courtesy of Paradigm Education Solutions; *page GS-2*, © irbis picture/Shutterstock.com; *page GS-3*, © th3fisa/Shutterstock.com; *page GS-4*, © goldyg/Shutterstock.com; *page GS-5*, © Pressmaster/Shutterstock.com.